Redrawing the Map to Promote Peace

Innovations in the Study of World Politics

Series Editor
Zeev Maoz, University of California, Davis

Advisory Board

Michael Barnett, University of Wisconsin, Madison
Deborah Larson, UCLA
Brett Ashley Leeds, Rice University
Jack Levy, Rutgers University

This series provides a forum for the publication of original theoretical, empirical, and conceptual studies that seek to chart new frontiers in the field of international relations. The key emphasis is on innovation and change. Books in the series will offer insights on and approaches to a broad range of issues facing the modern world, in an effort to revolutionize how contemporary world politics are studied, taught, and practiced.

Redrawing the Map to Promote Peace

Territorial Dispute Management Via Territorial Changes

Jaroslav Tir

LEXINGTON BOOKS

A Division of
ROWMAN & LITTLEFIELD PUBLISHERS, INC.
Lanham • Boulder • New York • Toronto • Oxford

LEXINGTON BOOKS

A division of Rowman & Littlefield Publishers, Inc.
A wholly owned subsidary of The Rowman & Littlefield Publishing Group, Inc.
4501 Forbes Boulevard, Suite 200
Lanham, MD 20706

PO Box 317
Oxford
OX2 9RU, UK

British Library Cataloguing in Publication Information Available

Library of Congress Cataloging-in-Publication Data

Tir, Jaroslav, 1972-
  Redrawing the map to promote peace : territorial dispute management via territorial
changes / Jaroslav Tir.
      p. cm.
  Includes bibliographical references and index.
  ISBN-13: 978-0-7391-1285-4 (cloth : alk. paper)
  ISBN-13: 978-0-7391-1286-1 (pbk. : alk. paper)
  ISBN-10: 0-7391-1285-6 (cloth : alk. paper)
  ISBN-10: 0-7391-1286-4 (pbk. : alk. paper)
  1. Territory, National. 2. Jurisdiction, Territorial. 3. Pacific settlement of international
disputes. I. Title.
JZ3675.T57 206
327.1'72—dc22   2006011533

Printed in the United States of America

♾™ The paper used in this publication meets the minimum requirements of American
National Standard for Information Sciences—Permanence of Paper for Printed Library
Materials, ANSI/NISO Z39.48–1992.

To all those who have suffered as a result of war . . .

Contents

Acknowledgments

I owe a considerable debt of gratitude to the many people who have helped me in the completion of this project. I am most indebted to my advisers, Paul Diehl, Dina Zinnes, and John Vasquez. The following individuals have provided many helpful comments at various stages of this project: Bear Braumoeller, Doug Lemke, Doug Gibler, Paul Hensel, Zeev Maoz, Chad Atkinson, Doug Stinnett, Michael Greig, Bob Muncaster, Paul Huth, and numerous anonymous reviewers. I also wish to thank Paul Huth and Todd Allee for sharing their territorial dispute data with me. The University of Illinois, the Department of Political Science, and the Merriam Lab provided me with funding and other research support, including the Dissertation Completion Fellowship, which enabled me to complete the early phases of this project. Moreover, I thank Julie Elliott, Pam Hall, Julie Maynard, Candra Grant, Leila Denmark, and the staff at Lexington Books for their editorial assistance. Finally, no undertaking of this magnitude is accomplished without a great deal of moral support and encouragement. In this respect, I am grateful to my family on both sides of the Atlantic and especially to my Princess Carolyn.

Chapter 1

Territorial Changes as Consequences and Causes of Territorial Disputes

> The history of war and peace is largely identical with the
> history of territorial changes as results of war and causes of
> the next war (Weede 1973, 87).

At the end of the First World War, the Treaty of Versailles stipulated that some of the lands Germany controlled up to that point be taken away and given to its neighbors. Yet, with Adolph Hitler's rise to power, these territorial changes were challenged. In a particularly well-known event, Hitler asked that the Sudetenland be given to Germany at the 1938 Munich Conference; he claimed that this would be the last territory he would ask for. British Prime Minister Neville Chamberlain and his French counterpart Edouard Daladier acceded to Hitler's demand with the hope that Hitler's territorial ambitions would be appeased. "I believe it is peace for our time," declared Chamberlain upon return from Munich (Gilbert et al. 1971). Yet, Hitler's territorial ambitions against Czechoslovakia and other German neighbors were not satisfied; shortly thereafter, he initiated territorial conquests that eventually resulted in the onset of World War II.

This short story illustrates the link between *territorial changes* and *militarized international conflict*. Hitler used Germany's territorial losses to promote his even broader agenda of land conquest, known as *Lebensraum*. The initial and relatively peaceful acquisitions of Austria, Sudetenland, and Bohemia only made his ambitions bolder and he eventually used military force to conquer Poland and then other European countries. Yet, territorial changes do not always result in militarized international conflict and have in fact been used successfully as means of conflict management. For example, the American cession of the Panama Canal to Panama has not been—and is not expected to be—followed by militarized conflict. Under the Camp David Treaty, Israel returned the Sinai peninsula to Egypt in 1979 and—even though there have been some minor skirmishes—there have been no wars between these two countries since then. This outcome is even more impressive given the violent character of their prior relationship.

Besides dealing with interstate territorial disputes,[1] territorial changes have been offered as conflict management tools for domestic-level territorial disputes where sub-state groups disagree with the central government over who should have sovereign control over portions of the state's territory. The demands for (ethnic) self-determination have sometimes been addressed by breaking countries apart, that is by allowing secessions or partitions. The applications of this policy have also produced varied outcomes, with the consequences ranging from the peaceful interstate relations following the break-up of Czechoslovakia, to the interventions of Serbia-Montenegro and Croatia in Bosnia after the dissolution of the former Yugoslavia, to the apparent ability of the division to end hostilities between Serbia-Montenegro and Slovenia in the same case. Finally, the decades-long antagonism between the South and North Yemen—over the distribution of land, regime types, etc.—has been dealt with by unifying the two countries; a similar solution has been proposed for the Korean peninsula.

In this study, I am primarily concerned with territorial changes as an aspect of territorial disputes. Territorial disputes are disagreements over territorial control and both Vasquez (1993) and Holsti (1991) find that in the last several centuries territorial disputes are the most common cause of interstate war (see also Vasquez and Henehan 2001; Anderson 1999). Given the finding, territorial dispute resolution is an important subject matter and this project investigates the extent to and circumstances under which territorial changes are useful tools for dealing with territorial disputes.[2] In a typical territorial dispute, the dissatisfied party wants to gain control over land that it does not govern at the time;[3] that is, the dissatisfied party is seeking a favorable territorial change. Territorial change is, in turn, defined as a change of sovereignty over any piece of territory that alters internationally recognized borders. I investigate the impact of the change on the subsequent relations—peaceful or conflictual—between the countries that participated in the territorial change, that is between the gaining and losing states—or gainer and loser for short.

More formally, I pursue answers to two main questions. The *first question* is an empirical one, and it examines the track record of territorial changes: *to what extent do territorial changes resolve the underlying territorial dispute and thus promote peaceful outcomes between territorial gainers and losers?* Answering this question helps determine territorial changes' conflict management potential. The changes could make subsequent militarized conflicts over land rare or, perhaps, they may even prevent them completely in a notable number of gainer-loser pairs or, technically-speaking, gainer-loser dyads.

Additionally, one is also puzzled by a more theoretical query that speaks to the differing outcomes territorial changes produce. As discussed in the opening examples, some territorial changes lead to future militarized conflict and others do not. Accordingly, the *second question* focuses on the circumstances of the territorial change that could impact the future gainer-loser relations: *what factors influence the prospects for future militarized conflict (or peace) between territorial gainers and losers?* Answering this question requires both theoretical and empirical efforts. The theoretical part of the answer is developed in Chapter 2 and it considers two change-related factors that are thought to influence the gainer-loser relations after the change. The first factor deals with whether the territorial change has successfully resolved the underlying territorial dispute all the while avoiding creation of a new territorial dispute between the participants. As discussed below in greater detail, countries dispute possession of certain lands because they may contain important raw materials, represent important religious sites, house ethnic kin, or be strategically located. The second factor involves the process by which the territorial change was performed. The change can be a result of a conference (such as in Munich or Camp David), unilateral annexation (e.g. Bosnia by Austria-Hungary), conquest (e.g. the West Bank by Israel), or of still other means (e.g. court ruling, third party military intervention, mediation effort, arbitration decision, etc.). These different processes potentially affect the ability of the change to resolve the original territorial dispute and the degree to which the territorial losers and gainers are constrained against using military force to alter the changes' outcomes. The two factors are used as the primary building blocks of a model linking territorial changes and subsequent militarized territorial conflict, which is developed in the following chapter.

The empirical portions of the answers to both questions are derived by systematic examination of the aftermaths of all twentieth century territorial change cases. This comprehensive evaluation will reveal trends and patterns, all the while assuring that the findings are not unduly influenced by anecdotal evidence or familiar but not necessarily representative cases. In this sense, the systematic analysis will help build upon—and in some instances amend—the knowledge of the subject that has already been derived from historically-based case study works. The conclusions reached will therefore be applicable to a broad range of situations and unbiased by questionable case selection.

Even though the focus of this work is on whether and under what circumstances territorial changes can mitigate or perhaps even resolve territorial disputes, the reader should note that territorial changes are not the only means for dealing with territorial disputes. There are other ways through which countries attempt to deal with their inability to control desirable pieces of territory. For instance, although in the past centuries Western European countries set out to conquer much of the Southern hemisphere to gain access to raw materials, in the present day raw materials can be bought on the international markets; therefore, countries do not have to physically control certain pieces of land to benefit from them. Moreover, to fulfill the desires for self-governance, a dissatisfied ethnic group within a multi-ethnic country may not necessarily secede from that country. In some cases, autonomy or redesign of domestic institutions—and not the establishment of new of international borders—may be sufficient to satisfy the group's desires. Hence, the contentious issue of who controls what land may be dealt with through various policies. Territorial change is one—but certainly not the only—alternative. Nevertheless, in this work, I focus specifically on the territorial change alternative because it is not only important but also unique. Territorial change is the only alternative that would grant the dissatisfied side the full, sovereign access to the land in question. In contrast, other policies provide no or at best only a partial control over the valuable land, and thus the territorially dissatisfied party has to take into consideration preferences of actors who physically control the land. The autonomous ethnic group still has to answer to the central government, while the country needing raw materials is exposed to the whims of the domestic politics in the exporting country. Therefore, even though territorial change is but one way for dealing with the question of territorial control, it possesses characteristics that set it apart from the alternatives. For these reasons, it is worthy of its own, separate investigation.

The layout of the introductory chapter is as follows. The next section provides a brief overview of the scholarly efforts aiming to understand the territory-conflict link, that is it highlights the extent of the extant knowledge and explains how this project expands on what is already known. The subsequent segment deals with issues relating to how the project answers the main questions of interest. The definitions of the three different types of territorial change (state-to-state territorial transfer, partition/secession, and unification), theoretical and policy reasons for studying the links between each of the three types and future militarized conflict, and a discussion of the unified logic by which territorial changes are connected to future militarized conflict are offered. The final portion of this chapter lays out the plan of the book.

What Is Already Known about the Territory-Conflict Link?

Much of what is known about territorial disputes and how they relate to militarized conflict concerns the issue of what makes territory a valuable commodity. Chapter 2 offers a more detailed answer to this question, so only a brief preview is given here. Countries seek control of territory because the land in question has some value to them. Newman (1999) divides the value of territory into tangible and intangible dimensions, which are comparable to Goertz and Diehl's (1992) intrinsic and relational aspects. Tangibly-valued land has utilitarian value, in the sense that it can make a country controlling it more powerful or wealthier because such territory has on it industry, infrastructure, economically important areas, ports, natural resources, or places that give the country that controls it strategic military advantages. In contrast, intangibly-valued territory has value in terms of meaning. A group of people may value a certain piece of land not because it can directly enhance its military power, but because the land may be where the group's ancestors once lived, where important religious sites are located, or where ethnic kin currently lives. Overlapping claims toward the same land—however valued—are the sources of territorial disputes and sometimes of militarized territorial conflicts. From the standpoint of a state opposing the territorial status quo, arguably the most natural way to resolve the territorial dispute is to acquire the territory in question, that is to prompt a favorable territorial change. The process of acquisition itself can vary from peaceful (e.g. land sale) to violent (e.g. military conquest). Regardless of the process, the point is that a territorial change can be thought of as one—but certainly not the only one—of the potential means for dealing with territorial disputes.

There has been quite a bit of recent scholarly effort aiming to understand territorial disputes. For instance, Huth (1996) and Vanzo (1999) study the origins of territorial disputes. Escalation from territorial disputes to militarized territorial conflicts is considered by Huth (1996), Goertz and Diehl (1992), Hensel (2001), Vasquez and Henehan (2001), Senese and Vasquez (2003), and Senese (2005). Given international-level militarized conflict, works such as Mandel (1980), Vasquez (1993, 1995), Hensel (1996, 1999), Senese and Vasquez (2003) and Senese (1999, 2005) compare territorial disputes versus non-territorial issues to assess their impacts on conflict severity and escalation. Finally, the problem of settling territorial dispute is investigated by Gibler (1996)—by the method of alliances—Brams and Togman (1996)—by the method of fairness in the Camp David territorial settlement agreement—and Hensel (2001)—by the methods of bilateral negotiation, militarized conflict, mediation, and binding arbitration/adjudication. In contrast, comparatively little effort has been devoted to understanding territorial changes as an aspect of territorial disputes. Exceptions include Weede (1973), who notes the broad connection between territorial changes and war, Kacowicz (1994), who studies the factors promoting peaceful territorial changes, and Goertz and Diehl (1992), whose work on the relationship between territorial changes and militarized international conflict lays the groundwork for this study.

Often times, territorial changes are thought of as the endpoints of territorial disputes. For example, Huth's (1996) research investigates how territorial disputes arise and why they are likely to become militarized. The author, however, supposes that one of the ways territorial dispute ends (see Figure 1 in Huth 1996, 30) is by a territorial change where the challenger acquires some or all of the disputed territory; a similar approach is taken by Huth and Allee's (2002) investigation of democracies' approaches to territorial disputes. Kacowicz (1994) focuses more directly on how (peaceful) territorial changes take place but also assumes that the underlying territorial dispute has been resolved by a peaceful change. None of these works therefore examine what happens *after* the change. In the authors' defense, this omission is more of a matter of analytic convenience rather than a reflection of strongly held belief that no militarized territorial conflict can occur after the change.

Whether territorial changes bring peace—or whether they actually invite future militarized conflict—is an open and rarely explored question (Diehl 1999a). By considering frequency and causes of militarized territorial conflict after the change, this work expands in particular on Huth's (1996), Vasquez's (1993), and Kacowicz's (1994) works. The project also advances on Goertz and Diehl's (1992) research. Their work offers an important foundation by linking territorial changes with subsequent militarized territorial conflicts via (1) unresolved territorial disputes and—somewhat less successfully—(2) via the process by which the boundary was altered. This study incorporates these two vital building blocks, while also advancing this research vein in the following respects. First, Goertz and Diehl (1992) assume that only the loser's attempts to re-gain lost territory will be the reasons for future problems. I postulate that the gainer's additional territorial ambitions can be a source of future militarized conflict too. Often times, the gainer did not acquire all the land it wanted (e.g. Hitler's initial acquisition of Sudetenland was followed by the occupation of Bohemia), so leaving its perspective out of the analysis represents a potentially critical omission. Second, the post-change militarized conflict behavior could be driven in part by factors other than the ones Goertz and Diehl consider (e.g. additional aspects of territory's value, the broader gainer-loser relationship) and which may matter according to the international conflict literature; hence, they should be incorporated both on the theoretical and empirical levels. Third, the variables are brought together into a coherent theoretical model, which postulates multiple paths to militarized territorial conflict. Fourth, the above-discussed works almost exclusively focus only on territorial changes where a segment of territory changes ownership between two sovereign states, while other types of territorial changes are seldom incorporated. To remedy the omission, the concept of territorial change is broadened to include situations where two or more countries emerge from a single country (i.e. secession or partition) and where two or more countries merge into a single country (i.e. unification). Finally, the current project benefits from improvements in the quality and coverage of the available data. Due to the then-data limitations, Goertz and Diehl had to include all—not just territorial—militarized conflicts. The link between territorial changes and subsequent militarized conflict over territory is not entirely clear in their empirical evaluation, because gaining and losing countries could be fighting over other, non-territorial and unrelated issues. Similarly, the end point of their analysis was 1980, which prevented the authors from taking into account the consequences of the many territorial changes taking place at the end of the Cold War. With the new data, I am able to investigate specifically the militarized conflicts over territory and cover the entire twentieth century.[4]

Territorial Changes: The Three Types

The answers to the two main questions of interest—dealing with the extent and causes of post-change peaceful and militarized interactions—are provided in three parts. Territorial changes are not all alike and they can be divided into three major categories based on the type of border alteration and the associated effect on the membership of the interstate system. First, state-to-state territorial transfers are produced by the movement or relocation of an existing international boundary between two sovereign states. Both states exist both prior to and after the transfer, so the membership of the interstate system is unaffected. Via the boundary movement, these states transfer the ownership of a piece of territory between them (e.g. Sinai after the Camp David Accords), with the consequence that the gaining state increases its territory (Egypt) while the losing state decreases the territory it controls (Israel). Second, secessions (or partitions) entail the creation of new international boundaries and add new members to the interstate system. That is, an existing state's territory is divided by the new boundary into a now territorially smaller rump successor state (e.g. Russia in the case of the USSR) and one or more new secessionist states (e.g. Ukraine, Kazakhstan). Finally, unification is the process through which two or more existing states remove their common boundary. By doing so, the unification decreases the number of members of the interstate system. One of the pre-unified states can usually be identified as the initiator of the unification—and this state's political institutions become models for the entire unified state (e.g. West Germany in case of the recent German unification)—while the other state becomes subsumed through the unification (e.g. East Germany).

For all three processes, I limit my analysis to the boundary alterations that affect territories that are considered homeland (i.e. non-colonial) by all the participant countries. As Goertz and Diehl (1992) argue, losses and gains of homeland territories produce much stronger reactions among the affected populations than do losses and gains of colonial territories because homeland regions are seen as integral to the state.[5] Accordingly, the inability to control homeland territory after the change is expected to be a much more salient political issue than the inability to control a far-away colonial region. Finally, much of the territorial conflict literature centers its analytic interest on the homeland-based territorial disputes. This is especially true in the context of the (ethnic) secession literature, which focuses on the breakup of states and not on the breakup of colonial empires (i.e. decolonization).

The following three subsections discuss each type of territorial change and some of the key reasons for why it is important to study the links between each type and future militarized conflict. That is, I identify analytic gaps in the extant literature and consider the real-world importance of the three types of territorial change. The final subsection discusses the idea of developing a single theoretical model to study the aftermath of all the types of change.

State-to-State Territorial Transfers

Different types of territorial changes are induced by the disputants as responses to different types of territorial problems. In the first scenario, two sovereign countries are engaged in a typical international-level territorial dispute:

country A wants a portion of country B's territory. To fulfill its territorial ambitions, country A hopes to obtain, through a state-to-state territorial transfer, some or all of the desired land (e.g. Alsace-Lorraine, Kashmir, Golan Heights, Spratly Islands). These attempts are often associated with threats and actual uses of military force. In fact, Vasquez (1993; Vasquez and Henehan 2001) finds that over the past two centuries territorial disputes have been more likely to escalate to full-fledged international wars than disputes over other issues (e.g. trade, regime type) and that territorial disputes have accounted for a majority of war outbreaks (see also Kocs 1995). Furthermore, territorial disputes are not a thing of the past: Huth and Allee's (2002) dataset identifies sixty-seven *active* territorial disputes unsettled as of 1995. Another scholar claims that about one quarter of land and two thirds of maritime borders are currently unstable (Anderson 1999). The number of *dormant* territorial disputes is arguably even greater.

From this study's perspective, the important point is that whenever there is a territorial dispute, at least one of the states seeks a transfer that would increase its land area. This means that the dissatisfied state may attempt to resolve the dispute by inducing a territorial change at the expense of the status quo side through a variety of means, including violent and non-violent techniques.[6] Yet, regardless of the means used, the transfer does not necessarily indicate the end of the dispute as the gainer and/or loser may be dissatisfied with the new territorial distribution; the aforementioned examples of Sudetenland and Sinai illustrate this point. Therefore, the transfer may only indicate a point in the life of the dispute.

Preliminary answers to the question of how often transfers succeed in preventing future rounds of militarized confrontations can be found in Goertz and Diehl (1992). Their research indicates that transfers are followed by militarized interstate conflict between the participants about 40 percent of the time. Nevertheless, the available data, at the time of Goertz and Diehl's writing, did not allow the authors to note whether the confrontations were over territory or a different issue. Such information is now available from Ghosn, Palmer, and Bremer (2004), allowing for a more precise empirical test.

The answer to the questions of interest is unfortunately not as simple as postulating that peaceful transfers of territory are followed by peaceful relations. Aggregate-level results from Goertz and Diehl (1992) suggest that the relationship does not hold. While almost three-quarters of transfers are accomplished peacefully, about 40 percent of the transfers are linked to future militarized conflicts. This means that *at least* 20 percent of the peaceful transfers are linked to future militarized conflict. Since some of the violent transfers do not incite future militarized conflict, this figure is likely to be even higher than 20 percent.[7] Thus, the original questions stand and suggest that answers have significant theoretical and policy implications.

Theoretically, the answer would speak both to the territorial conflict and broader causes of militarized international conflict literatures. Although we know that states fight for control of territory from previous research, we know little about how achieving that control influences the future prospects of militarized conflict or which factors play significant roles in increasing its likelihood. This study seeks to find out the extent to which territorial changes are useful in severing the well-known territory-militarized conflict link and what factors influence the chances for breaking this connection. Do factors such as the nature of the underlying territorial dispute play important roles, in the sense that post-transfer territorial disputes over, say, intangibly-valued lands are more likely to lead to future militarized confrontations than disputes over tangibly-valued lands? Or does the process by which the land is transferred curtail the prospects of future confrontations? In short, does it matter how, and if so to what extent, the borders are relocated and what valuable lands this leaves in the foe's possession? Or perhaps the obsession with territory-based factors is misguided and non-territorial factors actually determine what happens after a state gains control over disputed land. For instance, are the "usual" sources of militarized conflict to blame, such as relative power and alliances? Or, are certain regime types more likely to attempt a violent territorial revision? In any case, the answers will contribute to the theoretical development of the international conflict research.

From a policymaking standpoint, transfers have been offered as solutions for conflict for decades. Using an above example, policy makers hoped that the transfer of Sudetenland from Czechoslovakia to Germany was going to appease Hitler. Moreover, the on-again, off-again proposed transfer of Golan Heights from Israel to Syria is expected to decrease tensions and head off future armed conflict between these two countries. Hence, greater understanding of which factors affect the prospects for future militarized conflict is necessary. The manipulable factors can then be purposefully influenced in order to minimize the possibility of future problems. For example, what if the disputants are engaged in a dispute over land valued for both its economic and ethnic characteristics and re-drawing the border can resolve one but not both of the aspects of the dispute? Would it be better to resolve the ethnically-based dispute at the expense of the economically-based dispute or vice versa? Or, would the effort be futile regardless of what is done? Should the more powerful side be favored in the ensuing territorial re-distribution or are such considerations disastrous? In terms of the process by which the land is transferred, if a formal agreement substantially reduces the possibility of future conflict (as Vasquez 1993; Huth 1996; Kocs 1995 argue), parties to a territorial dispute may be offered to work out territorial disputes via mediation. The current conventional wisdom seems to imply this, as some states have sought international help for their territorial disputes (Simmons 1999). Yet, whether this practice really works for prevention of future militarized conflict is not that clear. Contrary to expectations, Hensel (2001) finds that successful attempts to settle peacefully territorial disputes via negotiations and non-binding and binding third party assistance actually increase the chances of future militarized confrontations. Similarly, Goertz and Diehl (1992) find that land transfer formal agreements are actually associated with a higher likelihood of future militarized conflict than are transfers not accompanied by agreements[8]—a finding that has not been confirmed nor conclusively refuted in later research. Moreover, many states do not want third-party influences to determine their borders, so it would be useful to know if anything can be done in those cases as well.

Secessions

In the second scenario, a group of people—defined by their religious, ethnic, economic, regional, ideological, or other characteristics and residing within the boundaries of the same state wants to form its own country by establishing exclusive, sovereign control over some portion of the original country's territory. If the desire is fulfilled, secession from (or partition of) the original state took place. Similarly to transfers, secessions may or may not produce lasting peace. The rump and secessionist states may fight in the future over the secession itself—that is, the rump state tries to re-integrate the secessionist country—or over the location of the new border. To what extent do secessions lead to peace or future militarized international conflict over territory, and why or why not, are some of the questions explored in this study.

Keeping with the spirit of territorial disputes as motivators of territorial changes, note the above focus on the *internally-motivated* division of countries.[9] In these cases, secessionists—in their drive for self-determination—disagree with the central government over who should have sovereign control over not only which people but also over what land. Hence, the disagreement is territorial in nature and what commences as a territorial dispute with domestic origins leads—if the country is divided—to the creation of new international boundaries. I investigate one of the consequences of the border creation, that is the circumstances under which the secession attenuates the underlying territorial dispute to the extent that subsequent armed confrontations over the new boundaries are avoided. The internal motivation for the breakup focus therefore eliminates cases of externally-imposed divisions (i.e. Vietnam, Germany, Korea) that had little to do with territorial dispute management.

Secession has received the most attention from scholars who study its relationship to inter-ethnic conflict. Events surrounding the end of the Cold War— and which are still unfolding today in areas such as the Balkans, Caucasus, Central Asia, Indonesia, the Middle East, and the Horn of Africa—indicate that struggles for secession create much bloodshed. In other instances, however, ethnically-based secessions are relatively unproblematic (e.g. Czech Republic-Slovakia, Norway-Sweden) and even credited with the capacity to prevent ethnic tensions from escalating into full-blown conflicts. Moreover, secessions at times appear able to bring ethnic hostilities to a halt, as in the cases of Slovenia-Yugoslavia and Bangladesh-Pakistan.

Puzzled by secessionist problems and motivated by the differing outcomes ethnic secessions produce, recent scholarly literature debates whether secessions are able to prevent or end ethnic conflicts or if they are just exacerbating extant conflicts by creating new issues—such as border location and cross-border ethnic ties—to fight over. See, for instance, Mearsheimer (1993, 1998), Mearsheimer and Van Evera (1995, 1996, 1999), Kaufmann (1996, 1998), and Tullberg and Tullberg (1997) for the pro-secession side and Horowitz (1985), Rothchild (1997), and Brown (1993) for the opposing perspective. Much of the debate on whether secessions result in future armed conflict hinges on factors that deal with territorial issues. Proponents—especially Kaufmann (1996, 1998), and Tullberg and Tullberg (1997)—argue that, for secession to prevent future conflict, population transfers have to be performed. The transfers would eliminate cross-border ethnic ties and hence decrease the value the associated land holds. In contrast, the opponents argue that the transfers are hard to conduct and they also invite the controversy over whether third parties and international organizations should be working toward the goal of ethnic separation (UNHCR 1992). Thus, cross-border ethnic ties are likely to be present, giving the disputed territory value and the dissatisfied side(s) a reason to seek violent border revisions.

Even though the secession debate is informative in terms of identifying issues important for future militarized conflict and peace, it is at the same time too narrow. It ignores other potentially relevant factors and depicts the post-secession situation in black-and-white terms. To push the theoretical investigation of the secession-future militarized conflict link further, I both incorporate the factors on which the debate hinges (i.e. the ethnic, that is intangible, aspect of disputed territory's value) and consider the roles of other potentially-relevant variables overlooked by the debate. I expand on the debate by including the tangible dimension of territory's value: rump and secessionist countries may seek border revisions not only because there exist cross-border ethnic ties, but also to gain control of, for instance, valuable strategic lands. Another improvement is made by considering roles of factors such as the secession process, power distribution, alliance ties, and democracy. These factors may be responsible for whether future relations are peaceful, so there is a need to incorporate them both theoretically and empirically. Besides the theoretical improvements, an additional improvement over these works is made empirically. While arguments on both sides of the issue are presented in the aforementioned works, they are rarely discussed beyond a small sample of cases that tend to be selected for their alleged support of the argument. While the arguments may sound compelling, it is important to examine systematically the track record of such solutions and from it infer how effective these solutions really have been. Finally, although most attention has been paid to the post-Cold War ethnic secessions, they are neither recent nor exclusively ethnic phenomena. For instance, Sweden and Norway ended their union in 1905 and countries have broken apart over ideological (e.g. China-Taiwan) as well as economic (e.g. Singapore-Malaysia) reasons. I strive for a parsimonious approach that applies to ethnic and non-ethnic cases alike as well as to a time period significantly longer than the post-Cold War era. These improvements can help move the debate beyond the simplistic characterization of secession as all good or all bad to a more nuanced view where the secession's consequences depend on its circumstances.

Additionally, this project seeks to make a policymaking contribution. Even though the application of this work to secessions is broader than the problem of inter-ethnic conflict, this problem is given special attention because of the growing scholarly and real world importance of these types of conflicts. The extant scholarly advice to policymakers has been either to encourage secession in cases of civil war (e.g. Mearsheimer 1993, 1998; Mearsheimer and Van Evera 1995, 1996, 1999) or never to allow it (e.g. Etzioni 1992; Kaldor 1996; Kumar 1997). Perhaps reflective of such contradictory advice, policy-makers have been inconsistent in the manner they have dealt with ethnic secessionist conflicts. The case of the former Yugoslavia illustrates the apparent confusion well: after initial signals to the contrary, Bosnia, Croatia, Macedonia, and Slovenia were allowed to secede while the secessions of Kosovo, Montenegro, or Republika Srpska were not permitted by the international community. Knowing when to divide countries and when not to do so is important because there exist many potential decision points in the future where the division or preservation of a (multi-ethnic) state will have to be addressed (e.g. Indonesia, Russia, Rwanda, Israel, Sudan, Iraq, Afghanistan, Sri Lanka, Nigeria, Congo, Cyprus, Spain, Canada). The international community is inevitably involved in such decisions because it ultimately determines—by extending or denying recognition—whether a secessionist region becomes a new country. The international community also decides within what borders to recognize the new countries. The commonly accepted rule in recent recognitions has been to make the former internal, administrative borders the new international borders. Are the policy-makers making a mistake by not tackling potential post-secession territorial disputes? Is there a particular aspect of the dispute (e.g. ethnically-based territorial dispute) that should be resolved at the expense—if necessary—of other aspects of the dispute (e.g. economically-based territorial dispute)? Should the more powerful country be favored in the ensuing distribution of the land? If possible, would it be better if the international community recognized new states before the secessionists take up arms against the central government (or before the latter tries to suppress the movement violently) and force a violent secession or is the secession process irrelevant? These are all important policymaking questions that are in need of systematically-derived answers.

Unifications

The third type of territorial change is unification. At times, two or more countries merge with one another, voluntarily or not. In some cases, a unification may have a "theme" such as bringing together territories inhabited by people of similar ethnic origin (e.g. the nineteenth and twentieth century German unifications). Otherwise, the unification may simply reflect a country's greed more land (e.g. the Soviet acquisition of Latvia, Lithuania, and Estonia during World War II). Similarly to transfers and secessions, unifications may or may not produce lasting peace. The unified country may be encouraged by the gains made through the unification to acquire even more land. Russian expansion in the last few centuries exemplifies unifications that have led to further territorial conquests.

The examination of the consequences of this type of territorial change forces me to depart from the exclusive focus on the gainer-loser relationship. Unlike in the transfer and secession scenarios, in a unification the territorial loser country ceases to exist and therefore by definition the gainer-loser international-level armed conflict cannot take place. Instead, I investigate the impact of unification on the relationship between the unified country and neighboring states, which are likely to be affected if the unified state harbors unfulfilled territorial ambitions.

This topic is seriously understudied even though the world is currently facing several possible unifications (e.g. China-Taiwan, North-South Korea, Belarus-Russia). The 1990 German unification caused a temporary surge of journalistic interest due to Germany's violent past (e.g. "Germany's . . . " 1990; Nelan 1994). In contrast, the Yemeni unification was hardly noticed by journalists and the on-again, off-again Belarus-Russia integration is proceeding without much attention either. The move toward the far-fetched Belarus-Russia-Yugoslavia unification was noted (CNN 1999), but perhaps only because of the recent conflict between NATO and Yugoslavia over Kosovo. Even though the recent German unification has been unproblematic in terms of militarized conflict so far, the Yemeni unification has already produced serious internal conflict (Halliday 1995). In all cases, implications for future militarized conflict remain relatively unknown.

Unlike transfers and secessions, which are sometimes conducted with the hopes of conflict management, unifications are usually not pursued with this goal in mind even though peaceful outcomes may result. Nevertheless, unifications represent a type of territorial change and leaving them out of analyses considering the impact of territorial changes on militarized conflict patterns would represent an omission. Moreover, including unifications is important for theoretical development, because there is almost no existing scholarly research on the subject. Historical works dealing with unifications do exist but they are primarily concerned, as can be expected, with particular events (e.g. Gilbert et al. 1971) or developments (such as evolution of nationalism, e.g. Hayes 1968; Kohn 1955) rather than advancement of international relations theory.

Unifications present another possible source of armed international conflict, but how often this is the case and why is simply not well understood. Numerous scenarios linking unifications and conflict are possible, and one example is noted here for the purpose of illustration. Unifications may pose problems internationally because they can affect the existing balances of power. Classical realism in the geopolitical school of thought (e.g. Mackinder 1919; Spykman 1944) is concerned with territorial control as one of the critical determinants of power. As states unify, they gain more population, strategic territory, technology, greater area for defense, and resources hence upsetting the existing balances of power. If these gains are substantial, the unified state's role in international politics that was based on its old characteristics may become too limiting for the amount of power it now possesses. The unified state may attempt to increase its role either regionally or globally and encounter resistance from status quo powers.[10] A process akin to a power transition (Kugler and Organski 1989), with associated militarized conflicts, can take place. Hypothetically, unification between China and Taiwan would place the sizable Taiwanese military and economy at Chinese disposal, leading to a marked expansion in Chinese power. For decades, China has been trying to increase its sway in the eastern part of Asia and new sources of power may give a unified China both opportunity and added willingness to pursue the path of greater influence. Such expansionism would place China at odds with other states in the region, most notably with its long-standing rivals such as Japan, India, Russia, and Vietnam. Moreover, China may even seek influence beyond its region and then its interests would clash more directly with those of the United States.

Besides the aforementioned historical works, extant scholarly research provides little guidance in how unifications affect prospects of future violence. We do not know to what extent unifications produce future militarized conflict nor, with a degree of confidence, what factors make some unifications problematic and other less so. Hence, an examination of possible influences is crucial for understanding the impact of unifications and for building a more complete theory that links territorial concerns and militarized international conflict. Insights from other types of territorial changes are used to develop a connection between unifications and future militarized conflict and peace; details are given in the following chapter.

Regarding policy making, it is not clear whether future unifications should be feared or encouraged. In the events data sets such as COPDAB (Azar 1980), unification is coded as the friendliest of actions. Yet, unifications can create instabilities and wars (e.g. the nineteenth century German and Italian unifications), so in some cases they should be avoided and alternatives found. For instance, Chinese desire to take over Taiwan could be resisted by offering Taiwan greater international recognition, improving its defense capabilities, and linking policy issues such as trade with China to continued Taiwanese independence. In contrast, if unifications have positive effects, the pursuit of unification policies ought to be encouraged. Following this logic, perhaps the West should help Belarus and Russia forge stronger ties. Let us now turn to the discussion of how the theoretical connections between the three types of change and militarized conflict will be tested.

Theoretical and Empirical Approaches to the Three Types

The above discussion shows that each type of territorial change occurs under a different scenario. Moreover, as can be seen from the thematic lack of overlap among the above-referenced works, the extant literature tends to treat the types separately. On the one hand, works dealing with territorial disputes (e.g. Huth 1996; Huth and Allee 2002; Kacowicz 1994; Hensel 1996, 2001; Senese and Vasquez 2003; Senese 2005) and the Goertz and Diehl (1992) examination of territorial changes are cast predominantly in the context of relationship between two sovereign countries and their future, usually conflictual, interactions. On the other hand, writings on secession (e.g. Kaufmann 1996, 1998; Rothchild 1997) deal with ethnic conflicts that occur within a state and as a result can produce one or more new states—which may fight one another in the future. In contrast to both of these types, there are no works dealing directly with the impact of unifications on future militarized conflict over land. (This oversight is probably driven by the fact that the cases of unification are relatively rare.) In short, the extant literature does not tend to treat the types jointly.

Despite the separate treatment of the three types in the literature, the position taken here is that there is a similar, though not necessarily the same, logic that produces and prevents militarized conflict after the territorial change takes place. A common theoretical model linking territorial changes with future militarized conflict over land is hence developed. I provide a brief preview of the model, which is developed further in Chapter 2. The key variables constituting the model are first motivated by consulting works that provide clues about whether territorial changes can be expected to help mitigate the underlying territorial disputes. Multiple perspectives relying on the concepts of territory's value and the process of territorial change (e.g. peaceful vs. armed conquest) are offered. The model then integrates and expands these perspectives. In the model, both losing and gaining countries and, more specifically, their leaders are motivated and constrained by the same factors in their decision to engage in militarized conflict to revisit the change (i.e. to challenge militarily the ensuing territorial distribution). Regardless of the type of change, the country's leader is motivated to pursue a piece of land because control of the land can bring the leader international and domestic benefits (e.g. improved international stature and influence, greater domestic popularity and support of key constituents, etc.). There are multiple paths to future militarized territorial conflict, as the leaders can be motivated by tangible (i.e. strategic and economic) and/or intangible (i.e. religious sites, ancestral homeland, and cross-border kinship linkages) aspects of the land's value. How the change was performed (i.e. the process) may constrain the leader against following the path of militarized conflict.

Regardless of the territorial change type, the participant countries are facing similar circumstances. The leader of a country that has lost land through transfer or secession has an incentive to re-claim the lost land that is deemed valuable and hence derive the above benefits. The difference between secession and transfer may be only in the extent of the land to be re-acquired. In the case of secession, the entire secessionist country can constitute the disputed territory (i.e. the rump state may want to undo the secession) while in the case of transfer only the location of the common border may be disputed. The difference then is not in the reason why countries would fight to re-take the lost land but only in the extent of the land to be re-taken. Bringing the two types even closer together, the rump state may contest only the secessionist state-held border region in some cases. Note, however, that this logic does not apply to the leader of the country that has been subsumed through unification as that country ceases to exist. Furthermore, the leader of the country that has gained land through transfer, secession, or unification may have an incentive to push for further territorial gains in order to derive additional international and domestic benefits. Again, the extent of the desired territorial gains may differ somewhat across the three types, but the motivation—in terms of the land's value—remains the same.

In short, regardless of the type of territorial change, the leaders are motivated by the disputed land's value. The opportunity as well as constraint against taking the desired land by militarized conflict is presented by other factors, such as the process of territorial change, relative power, security interests similarity, domestic institutions, etc. Much like the potential territorial disputes, these factors are expected to influence the prospects for future peace regardless of the type of territorial change. In part to test the crucial premise of the theory regarding the similarity of the militarized conflict-producing logic across the three types, the empirical tests are divided according to the type of territorial change. Furthermore, the separate tests allow for dealing with the differences that do exist across the types. For instance, unifications do not leave behind a territorial loser country, so the interaction observed is between the unified and neighboring states, rather than between the territorial gainer and loser. Given these differences in the theorizing, it is necessary to conduct the empirical analyses separately to gauge the model's applicability to all three types of territorial change.

The Layout of the Book

The remainder of the book is organized as follows. Chapter 2 starts by considering diverging viewpoints on the issue of whether territorial changes can preclude future armed conflict over land; the viewpoints deal with territory's value and the process of change. The perspectives' arguments hinge on several important variables, which are then used as the building blocks of a unified model linking territorial changes and future militarized international conflict. The model integrates and expands on the original perspectives to produce testable hypotheses. Chapter 3 deals with research design issues. It operationalizes the three types of territorial change and the relevant outcome and explanatory variables in order to facilitate the testing of the hypotheses; methods of analysis are explained as well. Chapters 4, 5, and 6 present the results of empirical tests concerning the aftermaths of transfers, secessions, and unifications, respectively. Each starts out with examinations of the extent to which territorial changes leave unresolved territorial disputes behind and the degree to which the still unresolved disputes pose threats to peace. The following segment tests the relevant hypotheses from Chapter 2, to assess empirically the roles different variables play in the onset of future militarized territorial conflict. The chapters close with discussions of findings' implications and applications to currently relevant territorial dispute cases. The final chapter, Chapter 7, first reviews the aims of the project and the approach taken. It then pools the findings together and assesses the validity of the proposition that the conflict producing-logic is similar across the three territorial change types. The findings' implications for theoretical development of the territorial change-future militarized conflict relationship are addressed, as are policy implications and suggestions for future research.

Notes

1. Following much of the related scholarship (e.g. Huth 1996; Huth and Allee 2002; Vasquez and Henehan 2001) the term territorial dispute is used to indicate a disagreement over which country should be governing a certain piece of territory. Some researchers (e.g. Hensel 2001; Senese 2005) prefer the label territorial claim to refer to the same phenomenon.

2. An important simplifying assumption made in this study is that territorial changes are preceded by territorial disputes. Yet, one could argue that some territorial changes may take place without being preceded by a territorial dispute—such as in situations where two countries exchange small parcels of land for mutual benefit without ever having declared officially that they disputed the old boundary. Nevertheless, I maintain that countries rarely fail to vocalize their dissatisfaction with extant boundaries, especially when homeland territories are in question. The scenario is, arguably, more applicable to changes in colonial territory, where—according to Goertz and Diehl (1992)—many of the boundary alterations occurred as a result of simple sales of colonial lands. As discussed below, this study focuses precisely on changes in the sovereignty over homeland, non-colonial territory.

3. The dissatisfied party is either a state or, in case of partition/secession, a sub-state group that seeks to establish itself as an independent state by gaining control over a portion of the original state's land. See below.

4. One could also argue that Goertz and Diehl's (1992) use of factor analysis may not be entirely appropriate for assessing consequences of territorial changes that unfold over a period of time.

5. Evidence of the lack of attachment to colonial territories can be seen in Goertz and Diehl's finding than many of the territorial changes involving colonial lands were simple sales and purchases of the land.

6. The choice of methods the state may employ are investigated by, for example, Huth (1996), Huth and Allee (2002), Kacowicz (1994), Hensel (2001), and Goertz and Diehl (1992).

7. To make this inference clearer, suppose that there are one hundred transfers. Out

of this number, seventy-five of them have been performed peacefully. After a period of time, forty out of the one hundred transfers will lead to militarized conflict. Even if one were to assume (favorably to the idea that peaceful transfers promote peace) that all violent transfers lead to future violence, this leaves fifteen (i.e. 75 – 60) peaceful transfers that result in militarized conflict. This most optimistic assumption is likely wrong, meaning that more than fifteen out of seventy-five (that is, more than 20 percent of) peaceful transfers are linked to future conflict (see Chapter 4 for actual statistics). In short, peaceful transfers do not by any means guarantee that there will be no future militarized conflict.

8. This finding has largely been disowned by the authors.

9. This view of secessions is consistent with much of the literature (e.g. Heraclides 1997; Horowitz 1985; Sambanis 2000), which deems internal secessionist drives a key component of partitions and thus uses the terms partition and secession interchangeably. Even though Maoz (1989) consider decolonization partitioning, I maintain that decolonization is substantively different because people hold only weak emotional attachments to far-away colonial territories (Goertz and Diehl 1992). In contrast, homeland territory is thought of as an integral part of the state (e.g. Siberia to Russia but not New Caledonia to France), so its loss is more contentious and distressful.

10. See the status- or rank-discrepancy theory (Cashman 1993).

Chapter 2

Theoretical Linkages Between Territorial Changes and Subsequent Militarized Conflict over Land

This chapter develops a series of hypotheses connecting territorial changes and future militarized territorial conflicts, which are operationalized and tested in subsequent chapters. The investigation starts by considering theoretical answers to the question about whether a territorial change can decrease the prospects of future militarized conflict over land and bring about peace. Four different responses are derived from the literature. Although these responses are useful for identifying the relevant variables on which the answer depends, each is also narrow and incomplete in its explanation of the territorial change-future militarized conflict link. To remedy these shortcomings, the second section of this chapter uses the relevant variables as the building blocks to develop a model that integrates and extends upon the four perspectives. Testable hypotheses are derived from the model and discussed in the context of each type of territorial change—transfer, secession, and unification.

Can Territorial Changes Prevent Future Militarized Territorial Conflict?

Vasquez (1993; see also Holsti 1991; Vasquez and Henehan 2001) argues that there is a strong connection between territory and international war. In this project, I consider whether this link can be successfully severed by employing a territorial procedure—that is, territorial change—to deal with a territorial problem most responsible for the outbreak of war—that is, territorial dispute. Four different responses are developed in this section. The first two deal with the two different aspects of land's value—value as power and value as meaning—while the latter two are concerned with the process of territorial change—agreed-upon territorial change and a change resulting from an overwhelming victory.

Land Value

Tangible Value of the Territory

One reason a state may want certain land is because it has tangible (Newman 1999) or intrinsic (Goertz and Diehl 1992) value. Tangible value means that the land can be used for some utilitarian purpose, which would increase the state's power. Among others, two dimensions of tangible value stand out in particular: strategic and economic. Land's strategic value commonly arises from its characteristics and/or location. Capturing an industrial heartland of a country (e.g. Germany's Ruhr) can help the attacker seriously undermine the defender's ability to fight. By the same token, the industrial heartland also has strategic value to the defender, because it is key to its defensive ability. Alternatively, a high ground or impenetrable swamps or deserts separating potential attackers and defenders can be used to keep enemy troops from invading: the defender wants to control these lands to keep the attacker out, while the attacker wants to control such lands to invade the defender more easily. For instance, Golan Heights have strategic value to both Israel and Syria. To Israel, control of Golan means early warning against amassment of Syrian troops and high ground that is critical as a first line of defense to protect the flatlands of northern Israel. Israeli control also exposes the Syrian capital to potential shelling. Syria would like Golan back for similar strategic reasons: better protection of the capital, concealed troop movement, and easier defense of southern Syria. In addition, the control would give Syrian troops a plain view of northern Israel, which would make Israel more vulnerable.

Another aspect of tangible value includes economic resources, which encompass trade routes, key ports, infrastructure, factories, raw materials, and of course people (e.g. Rhineland, whose ownership Germany and France have disputed). All of these features can be used for military purposes if not directly then indirectly. For example, industry and raw materials (oil, uranium, hydroelectric potential, etc.) can be converted from the civilian use to produce or help produce weapons, ammunition, and other military equipment. The population can be used as soldiers or as labor to produce goods important to the military. Whatever the exact economic characteristics of the territory, they can be used with the end of bolstering a state's power vis-à-vis its foe.

The desire of countries to pursue power is one of the cornerstones of the realist school of thought. More precisely, relative gains in power are important: countries vie for each other's sources of power, hoping to increase their own and decrease their foes' power. Although not all realists emphasize the role of territorial control as crucial to a state's power (e.g. Waltz 1979; Walt 1987), others note that it is one of its primary ingredients (e.g. Spykman 1944; Mackinder 1919; Morgenthau 1948; Gulick 1955; Thucydides 1993).[1] Regardless of the differences among realists, the point is that states pursue power and that, arguably, control of important strategic and economic lands can be seen as contributing to a country's power base. Therefore, the possession of such lands will be contested.

In the context of a territorial change, the gainer can use the newly acquired land—provided that it contains strategically or economically important resources—to bolster its relative power at the loser's expense.[2] Yet, the losing country will want the land back in order to undo the associated drop in its relative power. Accordingly, the land is treated in zero-sum terms: one country's territorial gain inevitably produces a territorial loss for another, and by extension the gainer's increase in power will be the loser's loss. Because of their ability to affect the relative balance of power, territorial changes are only a part of the interplay between the gaining and losing countries and they do not represent solutions to territorial disputes. As noted more broadly by Erich Weede (1973, 87): "the history of war and peace is largely identical with the history of territorial changes as results of war and causes of the next war." In this view, a war introduces territorial changes, which become contested and therefore represent causes of another war. The losing state may try to reverse the change, while the gainer may want to push further for additional territories.

Note that the above argument about the continuing struggle over the same piece of land hinges on the idea that the territory that changed hands between countries A and B is valued by both sides. One could disagree with such a premise. Suppose that country A is an industrial nation that took the land from country B, an agrarian nation. The territory in question possesses raw materials important to industry, but is insignificant in terms of agricultural use. Country B does not have much economic use for the land because it lacks the technology and skill to exploit it. Thus, if A controls the land, it can increase its power by exploiting it; if B controls the land, it seemingly cannot make any gains in power. Yet even in this scenario, country B still has an incentive to re-claim the land, because it is relative and not absolute power that matters. If B were to reclaim the land, A's power would decrease and the relative power situation would become more favorable to B. That is, denying the control of the land to the foe can be as important as controlling the land itself. The case of decades-long Austro-Hungarian (an industrial state) dispute over and eventual acquisition of Bosnia (an almost exclusively mountainous entity rich in ore) from the Ottoman Empire (an agricultural state) in 1878/1908 fits this pattern.

In sum, given the proposition that interactions between countries are but a ceaseless struggle for power and the extension that the control of economically- and strategically-valuable territories in part determines power, one can expect that territorial disputes between any two countries could not be solved permanently. Territory is a zero-sum good and acquiring more of it means more power for that state and less power for the other. Hence, the desire for territory is constant, even though some territories will be desired more than others depending on their utility in terms of power.

The above story has apparent shortcomings, two of which are noted here. First, if the territory-as-power view is correct, countries should not fight over lands that have little strategic or economic value. Yet, conflicts such as the Armenia-Azerbaijan war over Nagorno Karabakh do take place. In the region that is otherwise endowed with oil, this particular land has little to offer in terms of economic—or even strategic—value. Thus, there must be another reason for why countries expend resources to capture certain pieces of land. Second, policy-makers and scholars alike have been arguing for some time now that territorial control is becoming less important to states (e.g. Keohane and Nye 1977; Rosecrance 1986; Cooper 1997; Brooks 1999). Strategic aspects of territory's value are becoming overshadowed by technological improvements in weaponry. Creating, for example, buffer zones—such as Afghanistan's "panhandle" that used to separate British and Russian empires—is no longer a useful policy. Buffers used to keep apart soldiers that moved by land, but today airplanes and helicopters can readily transport troops across such zones. Furthermore, widespread trade has made deriving benefits from a particular piece of land possible without direct territorial control. For instance, a country can now buy raw materials on the international market instead of having to conquer lands where the materials are located. An extension of this argument explains the decline of colonialism: it simply became economically unnecessary as the inexpensive trade replaced the relatively more costly colonialism to access raw materials. These examples indicate that international relations are becoming less of a struggle for territorial control.

As a response to the second criticism, Liberman (1996) notes that territorial conquest can still be useful if the victor is willing to be ruthless, that is exploit the conquered region beyond what trading could accomplish. Moreover, Brooks (1999) admits that territorial conquest can produce strategic and economic benefits in the lesser developed regions of the world where technology and trade have so far not produced as many benefits as in the developed world. Furthermore, as a response to both criticisms, the concept of territory's value is unpacked to include its intangible (Newman 1999) or relational (Goertz and Diehl 1992) aspects. Accordingly, it is argued that territorial conflict can take place not only over tangibly- but also over intangibly-valued lands; that is, there are multiple paths to territorial conflict. I now turn to this idea.

Intangible Value of the Territory

Territory can have intangible (Newman 1999) or relational (Goertz and Diehl 1992) value. Intangibly-valued land has some meaning—rather than utilitarian value—to a group of people. Value as meaning can take on several different forms, and these forms represent additional paths to territorial conflict. People may want a specific territory because it constitutes what is perceived to be the ancestral homeland; this is the primary reason for why Serbs value Kosovo, the most under-developed region of the former Yugoslavia. In addition, a group of people may want control of land because it holds religious significance to them. A good example of a contested area with religious significance is Jerusalem. Finally, and perhaps most importantly, land may be valued because it contains ethnic brethren. To achieve national unity, it is necessary, in this view, to bring the lands occupied by ethnic brethren but controlled by another country under the dissatisfied country's control.[3] Hungarian nationalists, for instance, advocate annexing parts of northern Serbia (i.e. Vojvodina) and Romania because they contain sizable Hungarian populations.

Thus, countries pursue lands they find valuable for intangible reasons. Yet, a crucial difference between the tangible and intangible aspects of territory's value is that the latter form of value does not necessitate—at least theoretically speaking—that both sides in a territorial change will find the same piece of land valuable. The loser may have lost the land that it does not value in terms of meaning and, therefore, it will not have an incentive to retake the lost land. This means that a territorial change that divides intangibly-valued lands in the way that lets each country control the land it values can resolve the territorial dispute between these two countries. Put differently, altering the borders with these aspects of value in mind can help prevent future militarized territorial conflict between the countries formerly engaged in a territorial dispute.

Unfortunately, this is not the whole story. Although in theory boundaries can be drawn that separate intangibly-valued lands, this is often not the case in practice. A group bound together by an identity characteristic (e.g. kinship, race, religion, origin, etc.) is almost certain to live next to another identity-based group. The territories these two neighboring groups have controlled throughout history overlap to some extent—because of reasons such as population migrations, shifts in demographics, economic conditions, wars, and the like. When controlling the lands, the groups leave their traces (e.g. ancestral graves, ethnic brethren, and religious sites) and the possession of a particular piece of land becomes the stuff of national myths and legends. Hence, overlapping territorial claims are left behind, as each group sees itself as having the exclusive right to the land in question. The motive to seek further territorial revisions after a territorial change takes place is thus not removed.

Importantly, the inability to control intangibly-valued territory may affect the likelihood of subsequent militarized conflict to a greater degree than the inability to control tangibly-valued territory.[4] Intangibly-valued land is integral to the national identity, and is therefore perceived as (1) personal, (2) indivisible, and (3) un-substitutable (Gottman 1973; Sack 1986). (1) The people feel as if they have a personal stake in the land. Acquisition of, say, a holy site brings to the people a greater sense of reward than does, say, a coal mine, because the reward from tangibly-valuable land is, somewhat ironically, seen as more abstract. Thus, the people will be more likely to support the conquest of intangibly- than tangibly-valued land. (2) Having another party in control of a portion of the holy site can lead to the feelings of the contamination of the site; the disputant will not want to allow another group either access or partial control over it. In contrast, the coal mine could be divided or its proceeds shared. (3) Another site cannot substitute for the original site because the emotional attachments cannot be replicated elsewhere; for example, think how ridiculous a proposal to build a replica of Jerusalem—so that Israelis and Palestinians can each have their own holy city—would be. In contrast, a different source of coal could be found. Furthermore, the attachments tend to persist, meaning that old disputes can be revisited even after prolonged periods of peace. Due in particular to the reasons (2) and (3), the control of intangibly-valued lands tends to be an all-or-nothing venture, so peaceful compromise, division, or land-sharing are difficult if not impossible. Militarized action is therefore more likely to be seen as the only alternative offering access to the land.

Consistently with this argument, mounting evidence suggests (e.g. Goertz and Diehl 1992; Diehl 1999b; Huth 1996; Vasquez 1993; Touval 1972) that states are more willing to fight for territory with intangible value. Recent surges in ethnic conflicts buttressed by claims for control over ancestral homelands (e.g. in the areas of the Caucasus Mountains, Central Asia, former Yugoslavia) add further credibility to this suspicion. What makes the intangible association to the land particularly problematic is the issue of land's non-substitutability: no other territory can offer the same intangible value. People are in essence socialized to the territory they inhabit and it becomes a part of their national identity (Duchacek 1970; Gottman 1973; Sack 1986). This territory cannot be substituted with another piece of land, unlike territory that is useful for agricultural, industrial, trade access, and similar purposes. To illustrate further, consider the Serbian perspective in the (attempted) secessions of Slovenia and Kosovo in the 1990s. The Serbs claim that Kosovo is the cradle of their national identity. Even though relatively few Serbs live there now, the area includes monasteries and historic battle sites to which Serbs trace their roots. Loss of Kosovo is thus a great loss because these connections cannot be replicated on other land. In contrast, no such attachment exists to Slovenia. The Serbs certainly have material reasons to want to keep or retake Slovenia as it has been and still is the richest and most developed area of the former Yugoslavia. Yet, arguably, material development can be replicated on other land so the need for this specific piece of land is consequently smaller than for retaining Kosovo.

In sum, when intangibly-valued territory changes owners through a territorial change, future militarized conflict between the gainer and loser may or may not result. If it is possible to draw borders in ways that would give each party control over land it finds valuable for intangible reasons—and the territorial change implements such a division—then future territorial conflict should be precluded. In practice, however, such divisions are rarely feasible. In these cases, the change does not decrease the foes' motive for seeking further territorial revisions and future rounds of militarized conflict can be expected.

The Process of Territorial Change

Shifting away from the concept of territory's value, the remaining two perspectives focus on the process of territorial change. The argument presented here is that the circumstances of the change may be able to reduce the participants' willingness or motivation to use military force to seek further territorial revisions. Specifically, territorial changes reached through agreements and through overwhelming victories are thought to be capable of bringing about future peace.

Agreed-upon Territorial Change

In his book on the causes of war, Vasquez (1993) argues that territorial disputes between neighboring countries are the primary culprits. To this analysis he adds the idea that it is possible for territorial disputants to come to a mutually-satisfactory agreement that either resolves the dispute or decreases its saliency to the point where it is not worth fighting over (Vasquez 1993, esp. 293-297). What matters the most in terms of preventing future militarized conflict is how the territorial dispute was settled. Territorial change that is agreed upon through a formal accord is thought to have potential to prevent future armed confrontations over the land in question. To achieve lasting peace, the settlement has to be acceptable to both of the concerned parties and especially to the loser. At the core of this proposition lie the ideas that countries can cooperate with one another to deal with difficult issues and that a treaty indicates mutual consent.

Post-territorial change armed conflicts result, Vasquez contends, from (often intentional) failure to accommodate the preference of the losing side. In a unilateral territorial change, the dispute is settled in the eyes of one party, but not in the eyes of the other. Yet, I add that in some of the unilateral cases it is possible that even the gainer is not completely satisfied. If the gainer was not able to conquer all the lands it sought, it still has an incentive to revisit the change even though it imposed it. Israeli enlargement is an example of such unilateral "settlement," where Israel expanded its holdings in a sequential process—thus showing that initial territorial gains were insufficient—and the Arab side acted on the incentive to re-claim the lost lands. Following Fearon (1995), one could add a less skeptical view: the participants' preferences fail to be satisfied because of lack of information and not because there was necessarily an intent to leave the opponent shortchanged. At the time of the territorial change, the disputants are not fully aware of each other's true preferences—or do not trust each other's statements of preferences over land division. The resulting agreements therefore fail to be as efficient as possible. The incentive to re-visit the change exists and, arguably, even the issue of intent may be manipulated to rally support for future revisions.

Chances to accommodate both parties are the best, Vasquez argues, when they can negotiate a land redistribution agreement. The problem of incomplete information still remains, but in a bilateral settlement there is at least a possibility to find out what each party is willing to give up. The resulting agreement is not likely to be contested because each party receives some benefits and suffers only acceptable losses in the settlement. If the agreement is not acceptable to one of the countries, it will not sign it. According to this reasoning, the militarized re-visitation of the settlement is less likely in this case than if the solution was unilaterally imposed—such as in a war followed by an imposed peace treaty. At most, in a unilateral solution, one of the parties gets what it wants and the loser retains the motive for wanting revisions.

As an additional guideline, Vasquez states that in reaching the agreements, countries should avoid trying to obtain territory that has intangible value to the other party. Links to intangible territory are hard to sever, and incentives to revisit the dispute years later exist. Yet, as noted above, cases where this can be accomplished are rather rare. For example, despite repeated negotiations over the status of Jerusalem, Israelis and Palestinians fail to resolve their overlapping claims to intangible land; and it was in particular the status of Jerusalem that made one of the most promising Israeli-Palestinian agreements (i.e. the one reached in 2000) to unravel. Therefore, this advice has only limited use.

Still, Vasquez's logic of agreement's benefits can be expanded further. In a mutual settlement, both parties receive some benefits, which may include land, security guarantees, or even just a decrease in uncertainty over future interactions in the region. These benefits decrease the utility of future militarized conflict because some of them may disappear if it ensues and there are costs to breaking the agreement in terms of damaged reputation as well. That is, the country reneging on the agreement may suffer costs that go beyond the material cost of the confrontation itself. The improvement made by the agreement decreases the utility of future fighting for both sides, as both countries face the loss of agreement's benefits. For these reasons, the dispute is not likely to transform into a future war. Yet, as noted below, this is not always the case.

To differentiate between mutually acceptable and other, non-consensual territorial solutions, Vasquez (1993) proposes the use of power politics as the test. If territorial disputes are dealt with by the means of power politics, recurring militarized territorial conflict can be expected. Yet, what he means by power politics is not entirely clear. Waging war to deal with the dispute clearly belongs to the realm of power politics. Territorial "settlements" reached through violence are likely to be disputed violently in the future because such "solutions" tend not to accommodate the interests of the losing side. The other aspect of power politics is more vague, and it involves manipulation of settlement outcomes where aspects of power other than militarized force are used to shortchange the loser. Since this is not a subject central to Vasquez's book, exactly what is included in and excluded from such manipulation is not clear. For example, in the context of mediation or negotiation, various aspects of power are often used to persuade (or pressure) a party to accept a proposal. The edges between an imposed and willingly accepted agreement are blurry and themselves subject to manipulation, so distinguishing between the two in practice is often difficult.

In addition, while a mutually-accepted agreement may indicate a temporary end of the dispute, this does not necessarily mean that it is resolved in the long run. For instance, as domestic political preferences change, so too may the perceptions of what is acceptable and unacceptable in terms of the past agreement. Both disputants can fall victim to this problem. The person or elites who accepted the agreement may not have represented the interests of other political elites who can come to power at a future time. For instance, the Serb/Yugoslav king gave up parts of Slovenia and Croatia to Italy under the Treaty of Rapallo. During and after World War II, this move was contested militarily by Tito and his Partisan movement.

In sum, even though the idea of a mutually acceptable solution to the territorial dispute is important, it is also problematic at the same time. First, the issue of what is acceptable is itself problematic because preferences about acceptability may change over time. For instance, a leader signing an agreement may represent one set of constituents and when another leader—representing a different constituency—comes to power, he/she may call for the nullification of the agreement. Second, one cannot reliably determine if agreements were imposed or agreed upon, in part because the distinction between the two is not clear. Many forms of pressure tactics—if not outright threats—can be applied at the negotiating table, unbeknownst to scholarly observers. Finally, the notion that borders can be drawn in ways that separate countries' intangibly valued territory is applicable to few cases. While I utilize parts of Vasquez's logic, these difficulties prompt me to introduce some modifications to his reasoning in the development of the model below.

Peace by Empire/Overwhelming Victory

A different view suggests that some territorial changes with highly coercive origins can bring lasting peace between the territorial gainer and loser. This view arises from the literature maintaining that outcomes of prior militarized conflicts and wars influence the prospects of future peace (e.g. Maoz 1984; Hensel 1994; Werner 1999). Although the literature as a whole does not produce clearly consistent findings with respect to which kinds of militarized conflict outcomes (e.g. victory or stalemate) and post-conflict settlements (e.g. imposed, negotiated, or none) are the most likely to produce peaceful relations, a theoretical answer applicable to territorial changes can nevertheless be offered.

Aron's (1966; see also Maoz 1984) "peace by empire" argument advances the idea that the most stable peace is the peace where the war's victor subdues its opponent and dictates the terms of their future relations. Peaceful relations are supposed to result because the winner can take all it wants and hence does not posses the willingness to fight for further concessions. The loser, in contrast, may maintain the willingness to challenge this outcome; however, it is unable to pursue this course of action. Part of the reason for the inability is that the military defeat leaves the loser even weaker.[5] In addition, the weakness may translate into a reduced willingness, a "feeling of impotence" as Maoz (1984, 229) puts it. The loser's military might and spirit have been broken, so it simply accepts the winner's terms. Maoz finds clear empirical support for this argument and discredits an alternative view where the winner negotiates a post-conflict settlement with the loser. In such a settlement, neither the winner or the loser fully satisfies its goals, so both parties retain willingness and, to some extent, opportunity to fight further.

Vasquez (1993) advances the similar "overwhelming victory" argument and brings us closer to the context of territorial change. After a decisive victory, the winner can impose on the loser terms of the peace that include a territorial change in the winner's favor. According to the logic similar to Aron's (1966), the winner is in the position to obtain all the land that it wants while the loser is unable and unwilling to challenge the outcome of the territorial change. Vasquez emphasizes the process by which the loser suffers a decrease in the willingness to revisit the change. After the overwhelming defeat, a process of internal political change—which may be helped along by the winner's meddling in loser's affairs—takes place. The hard-line leaders who advocate taking the land back are replaced by more moderate politicians who are willing to work within the new status quo. Moderates' influence rises because the citizens have grown tired of fighting and want peace instead of yet another costly militarized confrontation over lost lands. An example of peaceful relations following an overwhelming victory that included territorial concessions by the loser is the transfer of northern Mexican lands to the United States following the Mexican War of the mid-nineteenth century.

The expectations advanced by the peace by empire and overwhelming victory arguments are challenged by at least two schools of thought. First, the phoenix factor hypothesis (Organski and Kugler 1977) maintains that even countries defeated badly in wars "rise again from their ashes." After some time, the economy is rebuilt and with it the military power increases as well. The feeling of growing power and accomplishment in face of the defeat can also boost the loser's willingness to pursue the conflictual course of action. Second, the reciprocity argument (e.g. Goldstein and Freeman 1990; Goldstein and Pevehouse 1997; Rajmaira and Ward 1990; Rajmaira 1997; Pevehouse and Goldstein 1999) maintains that the loser will resort to military force—as opposed to peaceful means—in trying to reacquire the land. The use of non-violent techniques by the loser may be seen as a sign of weakness or lack of commitment to the territory in question and thus should be avoided if the loser is sincere about wanting the territory back. In short, future militarized confrontations can be expected in both cases.

In part in response to the problems identified in the post-conflict settlement logic above and to the idea that settlements may actually make future confrontations more likely (Maoz 1984; Aron 1966), I take a somewhat different approach to the issue of process below. In the development of the model, I agree that the process of change is important, but argue that an earlier phase of the process is determinative. I contend that that the basic means of the territorial change—did the land change hands peacefully, through militarized conflict short of an overwhelming victory, or through an overwhelming victory—set the stage for future relations more so than post-conflict settlement agreements. This argument is explained in the second part of the model. Integration as well as extension of the above answers follows.

Territorial Changes and Subsequent Militarized Conflict over Land: A Model

The below model proposes a link between a territorial change and future militarized international conflict over land resulting from that change. The above perspectives dealing with territory's value and the process of change represent the bases of the model; yet, by itself, none paints a complete picture of the link. For instance, by relying solely on one perspective, one may not know exactly why future militarized conflict will have been prevented. Using exclusively the territory-as-meaning argument, one may conclude that the land was divided to both countries' satisfaction along these lines. In contrast, considering the peace by empire argument, one may believe that an imposed territorial change is responsible for militarized conflict prevention. To sort through the effects these and other relevant factors may hold, a model that integrates the alternative explanations is necessary. A combined model that is tested empirically in subsequent chapters is able to help determine whether one perspective holds more explanatory power than another, whether all are correct to some extent, or whether no perspective is applicable to the real world.

That is, all of the perspectives are narrow and by integrating them I aim to develop a more complete view of the relationship of interest. The integration of the perspectives allows me to note that there are alternate paths to post-change armed territorial conflict: various aspects of territory's value represent different paths to militarized conflict. Accordingly, for example, militarized territorial conflict is possible because of competition for a strategic piece of land (e.g. the Golan Heights) and/or because of overlapping claims to religious sites (e.g. Jerusalem). Yet, because only integrating the perspectives is insufficient, the model offers extensions as well. For example, one participant's ability to defeat another in the pursuit of valuable lands is considered. Additionally, aftermaths of territorial changes do not occur in a vacuum but in a context of broader relations between the relevant pair of countries. For instance, related research points out that regime type (e.g. Russett 1993) and similarities in countries' foreign policy outlooks (Bueno de Mesquita 1981; Signorino and Ritter 1999) will have an effect on the prospect for future militarized conflict. The roles of these nonterritorial factors are addressed in the research design chapter.

An additional extension to existing research is made by applying the logic linking territorial changes and future militarized conflict over land to the specific types of territorial change. Most of the arguments offered below apply directly to state-to-state territorial transfers, but some adjustments are necessary to make the arguments applicable to secessions and unifications. In addition and where possible, extant literature is consulted to serve as a preliminary support for the hypotheses and as a check of whether the arguments made are consistent with what is already known about the phenomena under study.

For the sake of focusing closely on the questions driving this study, the below model is simplified in the following important ways. First, the model is concerned specifically with militarized, international-level conflict over territory. Admittedly, territorial changes can, in some cases, produce effects that go beyond the issue of territorial control. For instance, a unification of two relatively strong countries could increase the unified country's strength so much that it can now challenge regionally or globally dominant countries—a situation akin to a power transition (Kugler and Organski 1989; Organski and Kugler 1980). Even in this case, however, at least some of the resulting conflicts of transition should be territorial: as Spykman (1944) and Mackinder (1919) argue (see also Morgenthau 1948; Gochman and Leng 1983), control of important territories is an integral part of the struggle for regional or world dominance.

The second major simplification restricts the field of interaction. Except for unifications, interactions with countries not participating in the territorial change are not considered. This is done in large part in order to keep the material under scrutiny manageable. Moreover, the three major works (Goertz and Diehl 1992; Huth 1996; Vasquez 1993) inspiring much of this project similarly consider bilateral territorial relations. This project expands on the existing works by considering the implications of the territorial change to the relationship between the participants and by including secessions and unifications in the analyses. Bringing in parties that are not the original disputants would go even further beyond the scope of those works, but extending the model along these lines is left to future research. In contrast, the situation with unifications is different. Since one of the countries disappears from the international scene through unification, there is no other possibility for militarized international conflict to consider but that between the unified and third countries. Moreover, the number of unifications is relatively low, so the task of expanding the scope of relevant countries in this context is also more manageable.[6]

Let us now turn directly to the development of the model. The model brings together the four answers offered in the previous section dealing with territory's value and territorial change process, by considering the aftermath of territorial change from the perspective of participant countries' opportunistic leaders. I presuppose that in charge of the states gaining and losing land via territorial changes are their respective leaders, who are office holders interested in improving their positions internationally (e.g. greater influence, prestige) and domestically (e.g. extended tenure, promotion of their agenda, a positive place in the country's history). Domestic support is assumed to be important to both democratic and authoritarian leaders. All leaders require the backing of certain domestic groups to remain in office; Bueno de Mesquita and Siverson (1995) refer to these key constituencies as the selectorate. The model ties the leaders' desires for influence and retention of office to the factors related to the change in order to explain the leaders' willingness to engage in militarized conflict in the change's aftermath. These factors are post-change territorial disputes, change process, and non-territorial influences, which are considered separately in Chapter 3. Figure 2.1 depicts visually the main elements of the model. The decision to fight to regain a lost piece of land (from the losing state's perspective) or to extend the newly-acquired territory even further (from the gaining state's perspective) is influenced in part by whether and how much value the land in question possesses. (Re)acquiring the land that can be used to boost the country's relative power or economic clout brings the leader a greater international influence. Domestically, the leader can increase his/her popularity among those portions of the selectorate that are concerned with the country's economic and defensive abilities and its international status. The leader can also reach beyond these narrower constituencies by attempting to (re)take the land the citizens in general consider integral to their national identity.[7] Furthermore, the process by which the territorial change took place presents the leader with potential constraints against and opportunities for using militarized conflict to challenge the change's territorial outcome.

Figure 2.1: Model of the Territorial Change – Subsequent Militarized Territorial Conflict Linkage

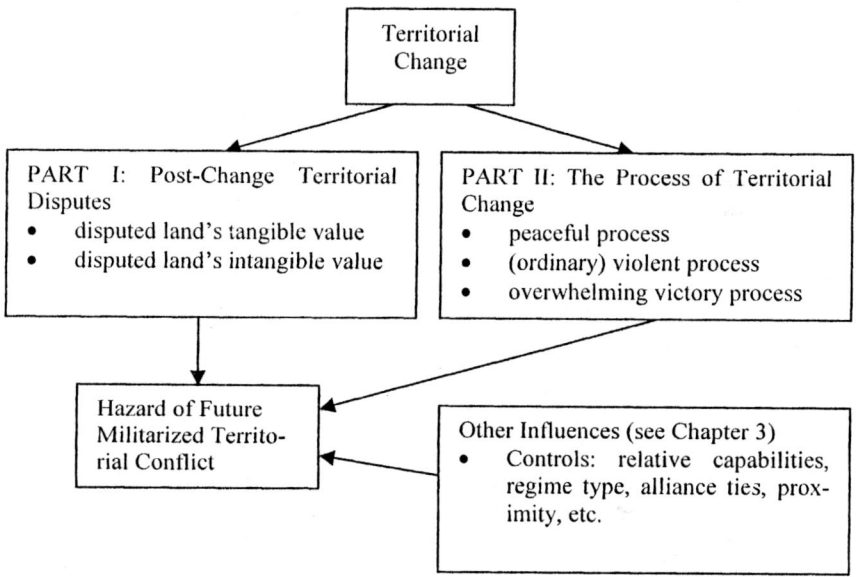

Part I: Post-Change Territorial Disputes

Following a territorial change and from the losing country leader's perspective, the gaining state now possesses land the losing state may value. The potential benefits of retaking the land to the leader, and thus the motivation to rely on militarized conflict, depend on whether the lost territory is actually valuable to the loser. Territory valued little by the loser is not likely to generate notable payoffs to the leader and is hence expected not to provide a sufficient incentive to engage in militarized conflict; the opposite holds true for territory valued by the losing state. Importantly, I also take into account a path to militarized conflict that is rarely given consideration in the literature: the gaining state may not be satisfied with how much land it acquired through the change; that is, the gainer's unsatisfied territorial ambitions can be a motivation for post-change armed conflict. Similarly to the loser, which was assumed for the sake of simplicity to be primarily concerned with re-taking the lost land, the leader of the gaining country has his/her sights set on the lands it finds valuable but which are still controlled by the territorial loser. This means that the gainer acquired control over only a portion of the territory it originally wanted from the loser or that it wants more territory from the loser in a different area. For instance, on the eve of World War II, Germany, by the means of the Munich Conference, acquired Sudetenland from Czechoslovakia. A short time after, it expanded its possessions by occupying the Czech part of Czechoslovakia. Likewise, Israel expanded its borders in a piece-meal process at the expense of its Arab neighbors. In its expansion into the Southeastern Europe in the fifteenth and sixteenth centuries, the Ottoman Empire used a similar process by which it would acquire a portion of a country in an initial territorial change and would then regroup its forces and come back for more. Thus, the first and most basic expectation is that post-change unresolved territorial disputes will motivate the leaders to engage in militarized conflict in order to further redraw the boundary. More formally:

> Hypothesis 1 (H-1): After a territorial change, gaining and losing countries involved in a territorial dispute with one another will be more likely to experience militarized conflict than countries with no territorial dispute.

Next, recall that the above discussion noted that there are different dimensions of territory's value and consequently alternate paths to militarized territorial conflict. Accordingly, the willingness to (re)take the disputed land can differ based on whether the land has tangible (e.g. economic or strategic) or intangible (i.e. ancestral, religious, ethnic kin) value. Even though classical realists favor the militarized conflict over tangibly-valued territory path, several more recent works (e.g. Goertz and Diehl 1992; Diehl 1999; Vasquez 1993; Touval 1972) argue that states are more willing to fight for territory with intangible value. This is so particularly because such land is seen as a non-substitutable part of national identity (Duchacek 1970; Gottman 1973; Sack 1986). Consequently, it is extremely difficult for a group to drop its territorial ambitions toward intangibly-valued territory. In terms of the model, the (re)acquisition of such lands is likely to appeal to a potentially larger portion of the selectorate, broadening the leader's popularity and legitimacy and giving him/her an additional incentive to use military force. Due to the issues of non-substitutability and indivisibility that make compromises difficult, the benefits-driven leader will have an easier time convincing the general population that militarized action is the only alternative offering access to the desired land. Even if the leader is intent on dropping the territorial claim, he/she can be "outbid" by a more extreme politician who claims to represent the nationhood-type interests with a greater degree of zeal than the "sellout" politician. This puts a great deal of pressure on the leader to act on the territorial dispute or to make room for another leader who will do so. In contrast, because it is both comparatively easier to compromise over and share tangibly-valued lands, the leader will have a harder time convincing the broader selectorate that militarized conflict is necessary; a violent approach is therefore expected to be less beneficial for the leader. The inability to control intangibly-valued land is therefore perceived as more serious and is expected to lead to a greater payoff for engaging in militarized conflict. In short, intangibility has an intensifying effect on the chances of militarized conflict.

While the loser's motivation to retake intangibly-valued lost land seems obvious, one could argue that the value of all the intangibly-valued territory the gainer had hoped to acquire from the loser should have decreased due to partial gains made through the change; this in turn decreases the potential payoff to the gaining state's leader. Yet, recall that intangibly valued territory is likely to be perceived as indivisible (Newman 1999; Diehl 1999a). Thus, any partial gains of the indivisible territory are not likely to decrease the value of the remaining disputed territory to a significant extent. In some cases, the desire to acquire additional land may even increase. Acquiring all but one of the important religious sites, for example, can raise the value of the last outstanding site. The leader who conquers the final site may expect even greater domestic payoffs as, beside constituent's admiration, he/she may receive a more favorable place in the nation's history. Thus, intangibility is expected to intensify chances not only for loser- but also for gainer-initiated armed conflict. The following hypothesis captures the distinction based on the type of disputed land.

> H-2: After a territorial change, a territorial dispute between gaining and losing countries that involves intangibly-valued lands will be more likely to be the source of militarized conflict over territory than a territorial dispute involving only tangibly-valued land.

The next tasks are to establish how well the first two hypotheses relate to the findings in the literature and discuss their application to the three types of territorial change. Extant territorial conflict literature offers preliminary support for these expectations. Its findings confirm that the presence of territorial disputes positively impacts the probability of militarized conflict (e.g. Senese and Vasquez 2003; Huth 1996; Hensel 2000; Senese 2005). Moreover, the roles of intangible factors' intensifying influence are supported by Goertz and Diehl (1992), Vasquez (1983), Bremer (1992), Huth (1996), and Huth and Allee (2002). However, apart from Goertz and Diehl, none of these works examine these issues in the context of territorial disputes that result from alterations of international boundaries. That is, the participant countries' motivations to engage in militarized conflict are not necessarily influenced by territorial gains or losses. Only Goertz and Diehl consider this context, but their analysis is limited to the attempts to retake the lost land; that is, the additional territorial ambitions of the state that has already gained land are beyond the scope of their work.[8]

The hypotheses apply to state-to-state territorial *transfers* without modifications. To apply the hypotheses to the context of *secession*, two modifications are necessary. First, the losing state is renamed the rump state, while the gaining state is relabeled the secessionist state. Second, the potentially-contested, secession-created new boundaries may exist not only between rump and secessionist. states, but also—in the cases of multilateral partitioning (e.g. the breakups of Soviet Union and Yugoslavia)—between secessionist states themselves (e.g.

Armenia vs. Azerbaijan, Croatia vs. Bosnia). The model will thus be applied to the interactions between all relevant states emerging from the same pre-partitioned country.

Extant (ethnic) secession literature, unfortunately, does not offer much systematic evidence about the impact of territorial disputes on future militarized conflict. Nevertheless, much of the existing qualitative literature opposing secession in cases of ethnic conflict develops an argument about future armed conflict based on territory's value. Based on illustrative or in-depth case studies of secession failures in cases such as India, Palestine, and former Yugoslavia, a group of authors (e.g. Horowitz 1985; Brown 1993; Posen 1993, Hachey 1972; Fraser 1984; de Silva and May 1991; McGary and O'Leary 1993; Kumar 1997; Kaldor 1996) argues that participant states are likely to push for violent territorial revisions after the secession because territory out of their control includes, in particular, ethnic brethren. That is, they maintain that it is impossible for the secession to create ethnically homogeneous states. The domestic problems associated with the poor treatment of minorities will create tensions between the states, as each seeks to protect its ethnic brethren who have been "left" in the other state. The nationalist leaders will push for the re-drawing of borders by military force, that is for addressing the secession-created ethnically-based territorial disputes. Even the secession's supporters acknowledge these dangers. To assure post-secession peace, Kaufmann (1996, 1998) and Tullberg and Tullberg (1997) advocate (forced) population transfers that would eliminate territorial disputes. (Note, however, that this may simply shift the value of the disputed territory toward another intangible value—that is, ancestral—dimension.) Even if this logic appears compelling, it entails at least two shortcomings. Ethnic territorial disputes are assumed both to exist in every case and to be the sufficient causes of militarized confrontations. In contrast, I allow for the possibility that ethnically-based territorial disputes are not ever-present and that other factors may temper their proneness to escalate into militarized conflict.

Finally, even though this literature as a whole heavily favors the intangible aspects of territory's value as *the cause* of future militarized conflict, the potential importance of the tangible dimension is acknowledged by Schaeffer (1990), Newman (1999), and Vanzo (1999). Based on the case studies of secessions in the Middle East and South Asia, they argue that rump and secessionist states have an interest in obtaining strategically and economically valuable territory. These studies, however, do not address the issue of whether the tangible or intangible dimension of territory's value is more closely associated with militarized conflict.

Because unification subsumes a participant state, the unified country's interaction with third, that is neighboring states, is observed. For example, in the nineteenth century German and Italian unifications, Prussia and Piedmont gained control over other German and Italian states, respectively, in a sequential process. In these cases, the unified countries essentially had outstanding territorial disputes with their neighbors. Following this observation and for the sake of simplicity, I assume that a neighboring country is the likely victim of the unified country's unfulfilled territorial ambitions. Because most territorial disputes exist between neighboring states (Huth 1996; Huth and Allee 2002; see also Vasquez 1995; Senese 2005), if a unified country is to expand beyond its present borders, its immediate neighbors are the most likely victims. Despite a general lack of research on the subject of whether and why unified countries initiate militarized international conflict, there is little reason to think that a unified country wanting another country's territory should not be driven, at least in part, by the value of the disputed land.

The potential sources of territorial disputes include neighbors' lands that either the unification initiator or subsumed state desired prior to the unification—for their tangible or intangible value. In the latter case, the lands may be valued because their acquisition may promote the ideas of uniting ethic kin or different parts of the ancestral homeland. For instance, following the Austrian *Anschluss*, Hitler sought to expand Germany into the lands both Germany and Austria claimed as rightfully theirs based on the presence of German minorities (Gilbert et al. 1971). It is also conceivable that the unified state's appetite for territory has been increased by the unification, so entirely new territorial disputes may emerge as well. Encouraged by the benefits and relative ease of the unification-related territorial acquisition, the leader sets his/her sights on entirely new lands in hope that further acquisitions will help him/her solidify his/her political position even more. For example, the late Medieval Russian expansion in the Baltic and Black Seas regions only increased the Czars' desire to expand Russia into the areas of Caucasus, Central Asia, and Siberia (Gilbert et al. 1971).

A point of partial difference between unifications and other types of territorial change may be that the gains in power made by unifying a country may be greater. Besides the land, local population, and local resources, the unification initiator country acquires the subsumed state's coercive apparatus (e.g. military and police forces, tax extraction system, etc.); the expected gains in military power could be large.[9] For example, China's power would grow substantially were it to unify with Taiwan. Encouraged by these initial gains, the unified state may be after a regional power transition of sorts (Kugler and Organski 1989; Organski and Kugler 1980) and, due to its newly acquired strength, the unified country may now be in a better position to challenge its neighbors for (some of) their territories. In this view, of particular interest are the territories valued along the tangible dimension of value, which could increase the unified state's power even further. This argument is consistent with the power transition theory, which expects that a notable portion of the conflicts associated with transition to be over territory.

In sum, the first part of the model deals with the idea that territorial disputes may continue after the territorial change takes place. The value of the land—be it tangible or intangible—provides the reason for continuing the dispute and the motivation for the leaders to use militarized conflict to redraw the altered boundaries. I turn next to the process of the change, which constitutes the second part of the model. The broader gainer-loser relationship is considered in the following chapter.

Part II: The Process of Territorial Change

In answering the question of whether territorial changes are capable of bringing future peace earlier in the chapter, I noted Vasquez's (1993) argument stating that agreed-upon changes are beneficial. In the model, however, I rely only on the part of the logic that argues that *peaceful,* agreed-upon changes are likely to bring peace. I disagree with the part of the argument stating that post-conflict territorial settlements bring peace. Instead, I maintain that territorial changes preceded by violence create incentives for future militarized confrontations *regardless of whether an agreement has been signed.* The incentives for future militarized conflict are not present, I contend, only in those violent changes that were prompted by overwhelming victories; this is consistent with the arguments found in Aron (1966), Maoz (1984), and Vasquez (1993) and presented earlier in the chapter. I now turn to the impact of the process of territorial change in more detail.

Peaceful Territorial Change
The leaders of both losing and gaining states are for most part constrained against relying on militarized conflict to revisit the outcome of a peaceful change. At the time of the change, the leaders usually sign an agreement indicating that they are satisfied with the new distribution of land (i.e. the change reflects their preferences). A leader who tries to rally the country's people against the foe in the future will hence be hard pressed to find much support and may even be seen as jeopardizing the country's safety and reputation for personal gain. More precisely, there are costs that arise from reneging on the agreement. Damaged international reputation can lead to costs such as greater difficulty in securing cooperation (e.g. trade, alliances) with other countries. In addition, agreements often bring with them side benefits; they may include aid, security guarantees, or even just a decrease in uncertainty over future interactions in the region. These benefits decrease the utility of future armed conflict because some of them may disappear if conflict ensues. The loss of benefits, in turn, deters the leader from initiating militarized confrontations. In short, the leader who uses military force to revisit the outcome of a peaceful territorial change is expected to encounter an array of possible costs.

Yet, a peaceful, agreed-upon territorial change is not a guarantee against future militarized territorial conflict. Preferences over land distribution can change over time—due to the change in the country's leadership or because of the change in the general political climate—and the leader can actually receive increased domestic support by reneging on the agreement that has become unpopular. That is, even though the state is still legally bound by the agreement, the new leader may find it politically beneficial to renege on the agreement. In some cases, the change may have been unpopular from the start because, for example, the leaders signing the associated agreement did not reflect the population's preferences or because non-violent coercion was applied against the leader at the negotiating table. That is, the would-be loser was pressured into giving up land it did not want to give up and/or the would-be gainer was pressured into scaling down its territorial ambitions. In sum, peaceful, agreed-upon changes do not guarantee peaceful outcomes in every case, but still present incentives that should on average associate them with peace.

Ordinary Violent Territorial Change (Short of an Overwhelming Victory)

In contrast to a peaceful change, the countries' leaders are constrained to a lesser degree when trying to take militarized action to revisit the outcome of an ordinary violent change. In the losing state, the leader can rally the people against the gaining state by claiming that the loss of land was unjust and that this injustice needs to be corrected. In some cases, no agreement following the confrontation has been signed. Since no agreement was signed, the country's international reputation is not being hurt,[10] no side-benefits are being lost, and the leader may even receive additional domestic support by claiming that he/she is warding off future territorial conquests against the country by showing that no such action will stand. In cases where a territorial change agreement follows an armed confrontation, the leader of the losing state can claim that the agreement was made under duress and is hence null and void. Given the preceding armed confrontation, he/she is more likely to be believed by the constituents and international observers when making such a claim than a leader of a country that lost land peacefully. The leader is therefore not bound by the imposed agreement to a notable extent.[11]

For the gaining state, it is possible that its victory was incomplete. Its leader desires even more of the losing state's land and sees the opportunity to derive benefits by pushing further. In cease-fire agreement cases, the gaining state can claim that the associated agreement is illegitimate—much like the losing state. The agreement was signed because of the pressure from the battlefield and hence does not reflect the gaining state's preferences about the ensuing territorial distribution. In short, a credible duress claim can be made in this case too.

In addition to the lack of restraints, a violent change may actually encourage the onset of militarized conflict in the future for at least three inter-related reasons. First, violent change involves the mobilization of armed forces on both sides. Demobilization may not be rapid due to the lingering, fighting-related tensions. The presence of mobilized armed forces makes it easier for the leaders to use this instrument in dealing with the other state. Secondly, violent change elevates military leaders to the position of power. Such leaders are, arguably, not only more prone to rely on uses of military force but also to provoke feelings of mistrust and insecurity in the opposing state. This may serve to further increase the stature of military leaders in the other state, creating a spiral of escalating tensions. Finally, the fighting helps construct bilateral relations on the basis of enmity. This creates suspicion on both sides, making future uses of armed force appear more appropriate and justifiable to the selectorate (see Lustick 1993).

Ordinary violent changes therefore provide few notable restraints against the leader's (of either country) pursuit of desirable lands and expected benefits. In contrast, peaceful, agreed-upon changes provide noteworthy constraints—

though no guarantees—against engaging in militarized conflict. The following hypothesis captures the difference in expected outcomes.

> H-3: Ordinary violent territorial changes are more likely to be followed by militarized conflict over territory between the gaining and losing states than are peaceful territorial changes.

The territorial conflict literature offers only mixed support for the hypothesis. Goertz and Diehl (1992) find—somewhat unexpectedly—that peaceful changes are no better in terms of militarized conflict prevention than their violent counterparts; that is, the process makes little difference.[12] In contrast, both Huth (1996) and Kocs (1995) find that legally defined (which by definition means peacefully agreed-upon or, in their language, "settled") borders are rarely fought over. Yet, neither of these two authors presupposes a formal agreement that regulates a change in boundaries, which means that in cases they examine the agreement usually legitimizes the territorial status quo. The participants hence do not undergo territorial gains or losses, so the loser does not have an incentive to re-claim the lost land and the gainer is not encouraged by territorial acquisitions. Thus, there is a fundamental difference between their studies and this one, even though my expectations mirror their findings.

Moving away from the territorial conflict research, the temporal diffusion of militarized conflict literature supports the expectation. The reciprocity argument (e.g. Goldstein and Freeman 1990; Goldstein and Pevehouse 1997; Rajmaira and Ward 1990; Rajmaira 1997; Pevehouse and Goldstein 1999) explains why the losing state would resort to violence—as opposed to peaceful means—in trying to reacquire the lost land. Because the language of violence was used to prompt the change, the use of non-violent techniques may be seen as a sign of weakness or lack of commitment to regain the territory in question and is thus avoided.[13] Unlike the idea of reciprocity, where two states direct similar types of behavior toward one another, the idea of reinforcement (Most and Starr 1980) involves assessing the usefulness of a previously used policy. If the policy was found to be useful in the past, the leader is more likely to rely on the same policy when encountering similar types of problems. Both Starr and Most (1983) and Kirby and Ward (1987) find evidence of reinforcement in African militarized conflict patterns. In the context of territorial changes, if the land was gained through militarized conflict, then use of militarized conflict will seem as a beneficial policy to deal with additional territorial ambitions against the losing state.

The hypothesis is directly applicable to *transfers* and those *secessions* that are bilateral.[14] I argue further that a similar expectation holds for the relationship between two secessionist states following a multilateral secession. The above logic implies that a peaceful departure of secessionist regions indicates that the would-be secessionist states accept the proposed territorial division—both vis-à-vis one another and the rump state. In contrast, violence between the would-be secessionist regions prior to or during the secession and over domestic-level sovereignty issues is an indication of serious problems. The would-be rump state—with its preponderant political and military power—is expected to have prevented the secession-minded regions from fighting one another while they all still belonged to the same country. If the supposedly dominant force was unable to prevent the violence, it is likely that once this factor is removed the post-secession relations will be problematic. A case in point is the Armenia-Azerbaijan conflict, which started prior to the dissolution of the Soviet Union and grew to a full-scale territorial war after the two republics became independent. Linking this observation to the model, the pre-secession violence between two would-be secessionist states lowers the threshold at which the leaders' reliance on militarized conflict is deemed acceptable by their respective constituents. The leaders can argue that the boundary vis-à-vis the other secessionist state has been imposed on the countries against their will. This argument is more believable if the two secessionist groups have fought each other immediately prior to or during the state breakup process. In sum, I expect that in both the rump vs. secessionist and secessionist vs. secessionist states contexts the hypothesis will hold.

Prior research on (ethnic) *secessions* mostly contradicts the proposed hypothesis. Kaufmann (1996, 1998) proposes a diametrically opposed expectation: violent secessions are likely to be followed by peaceful relations. He argues that dividing countries is the only real solution to inter-ethnic civil wars. The conflict produces ethnic "unmixing," a situation in which people flee and seek protection among their own kin. By creating separate countries, secession finalizes and formalizes the homogenization process as well as divides the belligerents and allows them to live on their own and in charge of their own affairs. This will allegedly create few inter-ethnic problems within the rump and secessionist states. Internationally, these states will have little reason to intervene in each other's minority affairs, so the leaders will not be able to benefit from engaging in militarized conflict. Though the author does not explore the converse form of the argument, it would suggest that peaceful secessions do not entail ethnic un-mixing and therefore open up the possibility for the mistreatment of minorities and subsequent international-level military interventions. Sambanis (2000) puts Kaufmann's assertion to an empirical test, but finds that secessions are no better or worse in ending civil wars than other solutions. Though important, this finding does not speak directly to my hypothesis because examining consequences of peaceful secessions is beyond the scope of Sambanis' work. Also contradicting the hypothesis are the secession's opponents, such as Hachey (1972), Fraser (1984), Horowitz (1985), de Silva and May (1991), Etzioni (1992), Brown (1993), McGarry and O'Leary (1993), Posen (1993), and Kumar (1997). By arguing that all secessions will inevitably fail to prevent future violence because new international borders cannot be drawn in a manner that creates ethnically homogeneous states, they implicitly state that the secession process is irrelevant. The cases of Palestine, Ireland, and India are often cited in support, even though each involved pre-secession violence.

Only a small segment of the secession literature supports the hypothesis. Tullberg and Tullberg (1997; see also Gurr 1993; Tir 2002) criticize Kaufmann

(1996) by arguing that people who flee conflict zones will want to return to re-claim their land. (In terms of the model, this means that violent secessions pro-vide incentives for leaders to seize upon the land return issue and use military force against the other country in order to better their political status.) Instead, they maintain that peaceful secessions—preceded by a referendum on whether to keep the country together—are the only way to avert future violence. Finally, Maoz (1989) confirms my expectation even though he analyzes de-colonization and relies on a different conflict-producing reasoning. He argues that new, de-colonizing states that gained statehood through violence are under pressure to establish themselves by showing a willingness to engage in militarized conflict. If they are perceived as weak or reluctant, their re-integration may be attempted. In contrast, states that gained independence peacefully are under no such pres-sure because their statehood is viewed as more legitimate.

In terms of *unifications*, the process of unification refers to the interaction between the unification initiator and subsumed states, while post-unification relations are observed between the unified state and its neighbors. Because the unified and neighboring countries' territorial relations are not governed by the agreement, it is not clear that the above logic of peaceful changes is applicable to unifications. The process expectation is nevertheless applicable if one is will-ing to rely more heavily on the reputational aspect of the argument. If the unifi-cation was violent, the unified country's image is already tarnished. In such cases, the unified country's leader has less to fear in terms of *further* damaging the country's reputation, if he/she were to set out to conquer neighboring lands. In contrast, if the unification was peaceful, the leader contemplating militarized conflict risks *substantial new* damage to the country's international reputation. The leader in this situation can turn the country's image from the one of a re-spectful member of the international community into the one of a rogue state. Thus, similarly to what I have argued above, peaceful unification process places greater constraints on the leader than does violent unification process.

Imposed Territorial Change Following an Overwhelming Victory

As noted in the fourth perspective above, Aron (1966), Maoz (1984), and Vasquez (1993) advance the argument that a certain subset of violent territorial changes may produce peaceful relations between the gainer and loser. These are the changes that result from overwhelming victories, where following a defeat in war the winner/gainer imposes a settlement on the loser that costs it a portion of its territory. In terms of the leader-based model, the people of the losing country have simply grown tired of fighting and want peace following an overwhelming defeat. Accordingly, they are unlikely to reward the leader who advocates mili-tarized conflict as the way of regaining the land lost through the change. Thus, the benefits the leader hopes to gain by taking back the lost land will not materi-alize and the leader may even be replaced by a more moderate politician. From the gainer's perspective, it had the opportunity to take the land it claimed as its own following the victory. A leader wanting to pursue even more of the loser's land by starting another round of militarized conflict is unlikely to find enthusiastic support among his/her people. Thus, the expected benefits are not likely to materialize and the leader is deterred from using military force for this purpose. This reasoning produces the following hypothesis.

> H-4: Future militarized territorial conflict between the gainer and loser is less likely if the territorial change resulted from an overwhelming victory than if it resulted from an ordinary violent confrontation short of an overwhelming victory.

Whether this part of the model is empirically correct is not clear. Aside from Maoz's (1984) confirmatory findings, other works on recurrent conflict (e.g. Hensel 1994; Werner 1999) cast doubt on the idea that imposed, post-conflict settlements bring peace. In addition, the findings on reciprocity—discussed above—challenge the expectation by showing that militarized conflict is more likely to follow such changes than peace.

The hypothesis is mostly applicable to *transfers*. It is clearly not applicable to *unifications*, as the imposed change in this context means that the country opposing unification has been subsumed and consequently ceases to be an international actor. The literature on *secession* does not deal with the overwhelming victory argument. Real-world cases cast further doubt on the applicability of the argument to secessions. It is not clear that any of the secessionists' victories can be considered overwhelming to the point where the secessionist region completely defeated the central government and put the whole country at its mercy. Such decisive defeats usually lead to a regime change favoring the rebel group and not to the country's breakup. In contrast, the battles for independence are commonly confined to the secessionist region and the rump state emerges more-or-less intact (e.g. Eritrea-Ethiopia, Slovenia-Yugoslavia, Croatia-Yugoslavia). Interstate wars, in contrast, have clear examples: overwhelming defeat of Mexico in the Mexican War or Germany in World War II. Given the absence of cases of secession that can be clearly labeled as overwhelming victories and no evidence from the literature that this task is worth pursuing, the hypothesis is not examined empirically in the context of secessions.

In sum, the second part of the model presents potential constraints facing the leaders against reliance on militarized conflict in the changes' aftermath. The constraints depend on the process through which the territorial change occurred. I argue above that peaceful changes entail the most costs for the leader if he/she were to use military force. Similarly, the leaders are constrained against the use of military force following transfers resulting from overwhelming victories. In contrast, ordinary violent changes (short of overwhelming victory) present the leader with the fewest costs against future militarized conflict, and hence generally fail to restrain him/her. Table 2.1 summarizes the expectations from both parts of the model and notes their applicability to the three types of territorial change.

Table 2.1: Summary of the Main Theoretical Expectations

Model Part	Hypothesis	Hypothesis Applies To:		
		Transfers	Secessions	Unifications
	H-1: After a territorial change, gaining and losing countries involved in a territorial dispute with one another will be more likely to experience militarized conflict than countries with no territorial dispute.	Yes	Yes	Yes
Part I	H-2: After a territorial change, a territorial dispute between gaining and losing countries that involves intangibly-valued lands will be more likely to be the source of militarized conflict over territory than a territorial dispute involving only tangibly-valued land.	Yes	Yes	Yes
	H-3: Violent territorial changes are more likely to be followed by militarized conflict over territory between the gaining and losing states than are peaceful territorial changes.	Yes	Yes	Yes
Part II	H-4: Future militarized territorial conflict between the gainer and loser is less likely if the territorial change resulted from an overwhelming victory than if it resulted from an ordinary violent confrontation short of an overwhelming victory.	Yes	No	No

Notes

1. See also Gochman and Leng (1983) who broaden the argument that territorial control is important to a state's power to include much of the classical realist thought.

2. In some cases, such as acquisition of far-away or hard-to-defend land, there may be notable costs associated with defending the newly acquired territory.

3. Note that even intangibly-valued territory can affect a country's power, though in indirect ways. The acquisition of lands valued for their religious or ancestral significance may boost the citizens' morale and sense of self worth, both of which may be useful in future battles. Similarly, acquiring land that contains ethnic kin may lead to a creation of a more coherent, and thus more effective, military force than would be the case if the land contained ethnic strangers.

4. For a general argument showing both theoretically and empirically that disagreements over intangible issues are significantly more likely to escalate to militarized conflict than disagreements over tangible issues, see Vasquez (1983; see also Mansbach and Vasquez 1981; Rosenau 1966, 1967).

5. Consistently with this argument, but also more generally, Weede (1976) maintains that an overwhelming preponderance of power promotes peace. In this context, an overwhelming victory accompanied by a territorial change arguably leaves the loser so weakened that an overwhelming preponderance situation between the territorial gainer and loser results.

6. The model has also been limited by not dealing theoretically with the temporal dynamics of territorial disputes. For example, as the change-determined borders persist, the population may learn to accept them and altering them becomes a less salient issue. This means that there may be a temporally diminishing probability of armed conflict. By relying on an event history technique (see Chapter 3), this problem is kept in check empirically. Moreover, as the time since the change passes, the likelihood that unrelated, intervening events can affect the likelihood of armed conflict between the gainer and loser grows. The design of the study minimizes this impact in two ways: (a) by relying precisely on confrontations over territory, I avoid bringing in non-territorial disputes that may arise in the meantime, and (b) the change is the event that has set the boundary so any future attempts at territorial adjustments are necessarily related to the change regardless of the elapsed time.

7. Note that the leader *hopes* to derive the relevant benefits. Almost certainly, he/she does not have complete control over the outcomes, such as remaining in office, as the outcomes also depend on other factors (e.g. term limits, electoral laws, performance on other issues, existence and strength of opposing candidates, etc.). Thus, the benefits derived from territorial conquest *contribute toward*, but certainly *do not guarantee*, the achievement of the desired goals.

8. This is similar to Huth's (1996; Huth and Allee 2002) theoretical approach, which accommodates only one challenger to the territorial status quo. Here, both the losing and gaining states can challenge the post-change status quo simultaneously.

9. Of course, there are costs associated with governing the newly acquired country, but a net gain in power for the unified state may still be possible.

10. One could argue that any use of military force would hurt a country's international reputation. Yet, the point is that in the violent change scenario the costs would be lower than in the peaceful change scenario, in which the leader suffers reputational costs for both using military force *and* for breaking a peacefully-reached agreement.

11. Similarly to this argument, in the context of the broader militarized conflict research, Werner (1999) finds that war-ending treaties have no effect on the duration of subsequent peace.

12. This finding may be hampered by the problems of dependent variable specification (due to the data limitations at the time, Goertz and Diehl had to include all—not just territorial—militarized conflicts so the link to territorial conflict is not entirely clear) and unintended correlation of the violent change and formal agreement variables. There is a large degree of overlap between the inverse of the violent change (i.e. peaceful territorial change) and formal agreement variables because peaceful changes are accompanied by agreements. This overlap could be responsible for both the insignificance of the prior violence variable and the surprising finding that agreements are associated with a higher likelihood of future militarized conflict.

13. Note, however, that Altfeld (1984) argues that it is difficult to discern empirically whether cooperation begets cooperation because motives behind cooperative behavior are ambiguous. He does, however, agree with the issue more germane to the current argument: violence propagates violence.

14. Even in those cases where the breakup of a country was internally motivated but ultimately enabled by the country's international war defeat (e.g. the breakup of Austria-Hungary following World War I), I argue that the rump and secessionist states will face an incentive structure similar to the one facing countries that emerged from a domestically-induced, violent secession. In either case, the secession is imposed against the rump state's wishes and consequently its leaders are not constrained—as described above—against retaking the lost land. Similarly, the leaders of the secessionist state(s) may be dissatisfied with how much land was put under their control. After all, third parties—and not the secessionists—decided the new borders. Consequently, the secessionist state's leader is also not constrained to a significant extent against pursuing further territorial revisions through militarized means.

Chapter 3

Research Design

The previous two chapters identified and explained the importance of the research question driving this project and, by developing a model, proposed a theoretical link between territorial changes and subsequent militarized conflict over the resulting land redistribution. In this chapter, I discuss the empirical portion of the answer, that is go over the steps necessary to evaluate changes' track record and test the model-associated hypotheses. This is done by covering the following points. I start by operationalizing the three types of territorial change and identifying the relevant cases. Second, the measurement of the outcome or dependent variable is specified. The third portion of the chapter does the same for the independent, or explanatory, variables identified in Chapter 2. Control variables are identified and operationalized in the fourth section; they are necessary to empirical testing in order to make sure that the findings for the hypotheses are not driven by unaccounted-for factors. Finally, the fifth segment deals with the methods for assessing the performance of territorial changes and relationships of interests.

Territorial Changes

Recall that territorial change has been defined as any alteration of internationally recognized borders; the change modifies which country controls what lands. As already pointed out in Chapter 1, I am specifically interested in those cases where the land changing hands is of non-colonial type. That is, I focus on those lands that are considered "homeland" territory (Goertz and Diehl 1992) by both the territorial gainer *and* loser. For example, the 1989 transfer of Taba from Israel to Egypt would qualify as a case of interest; however, the nineteenth and early twentieth century French territorial acquisitions in Africa (at the expense of either the indigenous political units or other European colonial powers) or the case of Angola's independence from Portugal in 1975 would not qualify.[1] Another criterion is that the cases where the land is held only temporarily (i.e. a

45

wartime occupation) are not considered.

Moreover, because I am interested in discovering the general mechanism linking territorial changes with subsequent militarized conflict, there is little reason to restrict the set of cases to particular regions or time periods. Thus, I investigate the aftermath of all (non-colonial) territorial changes regardless of where in the world they took place, making the entire world the spatial domain of this study. Likewise, the temporal domain is also broad, but data availability issues restrict it to the 1900-2000 period. Given the breadth of the cases considered, the findings are unlikely to be driven by unusual and peculiar cases or time periods. To identify the set of cases fitting these parameters, I rely on the list of territorial changes provided by Tir et al. (1998). The list identifies all territorial changes in the above time period, classifies them according to type, and notes whether both parties to the change consider the land in question a part of their homeland territory. Let us now turn to each of the three types.

State-to-State Territorial Transfers

A state-to-state territorial transfer occurs as a consequence of an interstate territorial dispute, when the control of a certain piece of land is transferred between two sovereign countries (e.g. Egypt gaining control over Taba from Israel in 1989). In the period between 1900 and 2000, there are 114 cases of non-colonial transfer (Tir et al. 1998); they are listed in Appendix A. A look at Appendix A reveals that every decade under scrutiny is represented in the set. The decade experiencing the most transfers is the 1940s (nineteen), while the fewest transfers take place in the 1980s (three). Spatially, every region of the world is represented in the data set, except for Australia and Oceania. Europe and Asia (including the Middle East) are particularly well represented, while Africa, in contrast, experiences few transfers. The dearth of African cases reflects the Organization of African Unity's (and later African Union's) setting of a strong norm against border changes. The Americas also experience few border movements, especially in the second half of the twentieth century. This can be expected to some extent, as Goertz and Diehl (1992) find that most borders in the Americas were settled in the nineteenth and the early part of the twentieth centuries.

Secessions

I defined secession in Chapter 1 as an internally-motivated division of a country's homeland (i.e. non-colonial) territory. The breakup results in the creation of at least one *new* independent state (e.g. Eritrea in the 1993 secession of Eritrea from Ethiopia)—with full sovereign rights and legal recognition by the international community—and leaves behind the now territorially smaller rump state (e.g. Ethiopia). Small and Singer's (1982) definition of the state is used to determine whether the secessionist region qualifies as a full-fledged state, while the Tir et al. (1998) list of territorial changes helps one differentiate between secessions—which deal with the division of a state's homeland territory—and cases of colonial independence—a phenomenon not investigated in this study. According to these coding rules, the German and Korean divisions at the end of World War II are excluded because they do not represent cases of internally-motivated state breakup.[2] Yet, two grayer area cases associated with decolonization—the divisions of India and Palestine—are included. Consistently with the definition employed, the Muslim population in India and the Jewish population in Palestine were pursuing states separate from their respective neighbors as the colonial rule was nearing its end, thus indicating an internal motivation for the division. Arguably, these are not so much cases of decolonization but cases of state formation out of the homeland territory of the state the neighboring groups wanted to form after the British departure. This is clearer in the Indian case, while the Palestinian case is more debatable. A portion of Palestine became Israel while the rest was incorporated into Jordan, a state emerging from the neighboring, and likewise British, mandate territory of Transjordan; Jordan is used as a surrogate rump state in the analyses below. These cases are analyzed in just about every prior study of secession's aftermath, so their omissions would render this work less capable of speaking to this literature. In any case, the inclusion of these cases has little effect on the results (see Chapter 5).

A relevant post-secession dyad is composed of a pair of states that belonged to the same unified state prior to the secession (e.g. Ethiopia-Eritrea). This rule is sensible for secessions that produce only one secessionist state. Yet, in some cases (e.g. the dissolution of the Soviet Union), the secession results—in addition to the creation of the rump state (e.g. Russia)—in the creation of several secessionist states (e.g. Estonia, Latvia, Kazakhstan, etc.). Matching all possible pairs produced by such multilateral breakups generates some apparently irrelevant pairings (e.g. Estonia-Kazakhstan). An alternative possibility is to consider only those dyads that are directly contiguous (i.e. include Estonia-Latvia and Estonia-Russia, but not Estonia-Kazakhstan). This solution, however, ignores potential ties the once-dominant rump state may have to the territory of a non-contiguous secessionist state. For instance, Russia may lay claim to parts of Kyrgyzstan based on the presence of a sizable Russian minority. As a compromise, I adopt the politically relevant dyad (PRD) concept (Maoz and Russett 1993) commonly employed in the international relations research as the main approach: for the purposes of this study, politically relevant dyads are all contiguous dyads emerging from the same state plus all rump-non-contiguous-secessionist state pairs. The PRDs resulting from all twentieth century secessions are listed in Appendix B. To ensure that the results are not a function of the dyad selection rule, Chapter 5 analyses are also performed on all and on only contiguous dyads.[3]

In the 1900-2000 period, there are twenty-one cases of state breakup (Tir et al. 1998), which produce sixty-six PRDs. Temporally, the breakups are somewhat scattered. In the 1900s, 1910s, 1920s, 1940s, and 1960s, three breakups take place in each of the decades. In contrast, the 1970s experience only one state dissolution, while the 1930s, 1950s, and 1980s experience none. The apparent dry spell with only four secession in the 1950-89 period is probably a result of the well-entrenched Cold War-era norm against the creation of new countries from the lands of existing states. The grip of the norm lessened after the end of the Cold War and as a consequence we see a relative surge in the number of secessions to five in the 1990s; this is the greatest number in any single decade. The geographic distribution is also somewhat uneven: the greatest number of secessions takes place in Europe (ten), followed by Asia (six) and Africa (four). Only one took place in the Americas, while none occurred in Australia and Oceania.

Unifications

A unification takes place when two or more sovereign countries merge with one another and the subsumed state disappears from the international scene as an independent actor. Operationally, the subsumed state is removed from the list of members of the interstate system (Small and Singer 1982) by becoming a part of another state's homeland territory (Tir et al. 1998). One of the pre-unified states can usually be identified as the initiator of the unification (e.g. Germany in the 1938 German *Anschluss* of Austria). The initiator state seeks to incorporate the subsumed-to-be state's territory and extend its own political institutional arrangements into the newly acquired territory. Some straightforward ways of determining, *ex post facto*, the initiator of the unification are to consider whose political institutions prevail in the unified state and on whose former territory the capital city of the unified state is located.[4]

In the period between 1900 and 2000, there are seven cases of unification (Tir et al. 1998); they are listed in Appendix C. Because one of the participants of the unification is subsumed through the unification, post-unification international-level militarized territorial conflict cannot take place between the unification initiator and subsumed states; they are now one state. Instead, I investigate possible militarized conflicts between the unified state and its neighbors. I assume that a neighboring country is the likely victim of the unified country's territorial ambitions, because if the unified country is to expand beyond its present borders, its neighbors are the most likely targets. See Chapters 1 and 2 for more on this issue. Operationally, I define neighboring states as states that are directly (i.e. non-colonially) contiguous to the unified state according to the Stinnett et al. (2002) criteria. This means that the states either border each other by land or are separated by up to four hundred miles of water. The contiguity by water standard is used to capture possible disputes over off-shore islands and maritime boundaries in general. Chapter 6 analyses also employ more restrictive distance standards to verify the robustness of the hypotheses-related findings.

Appendix C lists the seven twentieth century unifications and ninety-one relevant neighboring states; the pairs formed by the unified state and its neighbors form the universe of cases on which the territorial aftermath of unifications is explored. Spatially, most unifications took place in Europe (three), followed by Asia and Africa (two each). Other continents experienced no unifications. In terms of the temporal distribution, one unification took place in each decade between 1930 and 1979. The 1990s experienced the most unifications (two), while other decades experienced none. After operationalizing the three types of territorial change, I now turn to the dependent variable.

The Dependent Variable and the Unit of Analysis

In this project, I ask to what extent and under what circumstances territorial changes alleviate territorial dispute problems that have prompted the change. As discussed in previous chapters, the main indicator of success or failure is whether the territorial change is followed by militarized conflict with the aim of further altering the change-affected borders. Making the specific outcome of interest more precise, I examine the instance of *the onset of international-level fatal militarized conflict over territory that takes place between territorial gainers and losers*. To operationalize this concept, I consult Ghosn, Palmer, and Bremer (2004), who provide a listing of all Militarized Interstate Disputes (MIDs)[5] through 2001 and note both whether they involved casualties and were fought over territory. Analyzing only fatal MIDs eliminates less serious confrontations and confrontations that are not direct consequences of leaders' attempts to launch territorial conquest attacks, but which are nevertheless listed in the MID data set (e.g. fishing disputes). Moreover, because non-fatal disputes in the Third World often go unreported in the Western press from which the data set draws its information, fatal dispute-only focus reduces the Western bias in the data set. Including both fatal and non-fatal disputes into the analyses does not affect the findings appreciably (see Tir 2001, 2003b). To evaluate hypothesis H-1, I use all fatal MIDs listed because this hypothesis seeks to link post-territorial change territorial disputes with militarized conflict in general. The other hypotheses deal more specifically with the militarized conflict over territorial issues, so I restrict the dependent variable to only those instances in which the fatal MID concerned territorial control for at least one of the disputants.

Per the above theorizing, I rely on the dyadic level of analysis, in which militarized interactions between two countries (i.e. territorial loser and gainer) are observed. For the causal hypothesis testing, the data are arranged on a yearly basis, so that the interaction within each dyad is tracked for every year after the change; dyad-year is therefore the generic unit of analysis. To verify the robustness of the findings, I utilize two more specific versions of the unit: (1) the non-directed design—which tests for whether the dyad members were *involved* in militarized conflict with one another—and (2) the directed design—which tests for whether the territorially dissatisfied party is the actual *initiator* of militarized conflict. The theorizing suggests that the latter design is preferable, but conceptual difficulties surround the actual operationalization of initiation (Hoole and

Zinnes 1976). For example, confusion is introduced by the possible use of pre-emptive strikes (e.g. the 1967 Arab-Israeli war) or by staged events that are meant to portray the victim as the perpetrator;[6] such issues may, to some extent, undermine the reliability of the initiation data. Because neither design is in all its respects clearly superior to the other, both are employed. The fatal territorial MID rates for the aftermath of each territorial change type are reported and discussed in Chapters 4-6.

With the descriptive analyses (see below), I aim to ascertain the portion of territorial change-affected borders that are disputed and challenged through militarized conflict. Therefore, the appropriate unit of analysis in this case is the post-territorial change dyad that contains the border. For each country pairing, the dyad-year data are aggregated in order to make the assessment of the overall experience of a post-change border possible. I turn next to the identification and discussion of the main independent variables.

The Main Independent Variables

The first part of the model identifies the presence of the post-change territorial dispute between the gaining and losing countries (i.e. the land the loser may want back from the gainer or the additional land the gainer wants to acquire from the loser) as the key variable. I rely on Huth and Allee's (2002)[7] data, which note the existence of territorial disputes and report whether or not the disputed land is valued along a set of mutually non-exclusive indicators representing the land's ethnic, economic, and strategic values. Huth (1996, 256-7) defines a disputed piece of land as economically valued if it contains natural resources such as oil, iron ore, uranium, etc., strategically valued if it is in close proximity to major shipping lanes, choke points, military bases, attack routes, etc., and ethnically valued if it contains "a minority [that] speaks the same language and shares the same ethnic background as the largest ethnic group within the challenger" state; see the source for full definitions. Territory's economic and strategic values represent different manifestations of the tangible dimension of land's value. Indicators of intangible value other than the ethnic manifestation are unfortunately not available from this or other data sets at this time. I thus use the ethnic value as the sole indicator of intangible value.

Initially, I attempted to include all three dimensions of value for both the losing and gaining states in the statistical analyses simultaneously, but this created multicollinearity problems because territorial claims are often reciprocated. I thus had to simplify the original design by simply noting the existence of a particular type of territorial dispute within the dyad. This compromise is sensible because previous results suggest that the dyad members' behavior mirrors each other (Tir 2001, 2003a, 2003b) and because the directed-dyad results—in which I track the behavior the challenger directs toward the target—closely resemble the non-directed findings in all of the analyses reported in subsequent chapters. Descriptive statistics for the territorial dispute variable are provided and discussed in the empirical chapters below, as they are important indicators of the extent to which territorial changes resolve underlying territorial disputes.

Part II of the model argues that the process by which land changes owners affects the leader's propensity to rely on militarized conflict in order to challenge the outcome of the territorial change. Violence during the change has been identified above as the key concern, so the main distinction made is whether the change occurred peacefully or not. The main source for the process variable is the Tir et al. (1998) list of territorial changes. The data set codes a territorial change as violent if there was a "[v]iolent conflict between organized forces of *both* sides, within a year of the [change]. . . . Unorganized violence, such as riots, is not so classified" (Tir et al. 1998, 94, italics in the original).

Separating violent from peaceful territorial changes is relatively unproblematic for secessions and unifications, so I start here. For secessions, the violence coding from Tir et al. (1998) shows that thirty-eight (out of sixty-six, about 58 percent) of politically relevant pairs of states parted ways peacefully. Conversely, twenty-eight (about 42 percent) of the pairs parted ways through violent means. For unifications, the percentages are much more lop-sided, because only one unification (between North and South Vietnam) was accomplished by conquest, that is by violent means. Hence, only six out of ninety-one (about 7 percent) of unified-neighboring country dyads receive the violent coding. The remaining eighty-five (about 93 percent) dyads receive the peaceful coding. Note that the rarity of violent unifications in my sample raises questions about the generalizability of the process findings for the unification cases (see Chapter 6).

The coding situation is slightly more complicated for the state-to-state territorial transfers because there are three processes of transfer: peaceful, ordinary violent (short of an overwhelming victory), and overwhelming victory. The latter two processes both include violence, so I first differentiate peaceful from violent transfers. The Tir et al. (1998) list shows that sixty-four transfers (out of 114, about 56 percent) have been performed peacefully.[8] This means that the remaining fifty transfers (about 44 percent) involved some measure of organized violence. The group consisting of fifty violent transfers is further divided according to whether each transfer is associated with an overwhelming victory. Yet, how to operationalize an overwhelming victory is not self-evident. An overwhelming victory is often determined in a *post hoc* fashion: one knows that a victory was overwhelming because it is followed by a long period of peace. Using this definition for my purposes, however, would be tautological. Instead, in an attempt to operationalize this concept, I rely on three criteria: (1) the related militarized conflict between the territorial gainer and loser was a major confrontation; (2) the conflict produced a clear winner; and (3) the outcome was imposed on the loser. Operationally, only militarized conflicts that are wars with a clear winner and an imposed outcome are labeled overwhelming victories. The Militarized Interstate Dispute (MID) data set (Ghosn, Palmer, and Bremer 2004) provides the variables specifying the level of hostility (war or lower-level confrontations), dispute outcome (whether there was a clear victor and, if so, who), and dispute settlement (whether there is a settlement and, if so, whether it is imposed or negotiated). From these codings, I identify eighteen transfers (out of 114, about 16 percent) as arising from overwhelming victories. Ordinary violent transfers short of an overwhelming victory are found in thirty-two cases (about 28 percent). Each process is given its own dichotomous variable in the data set.

Control Variables

In addition to the factors that may contribute to the leader's motivation to engage in militarized conflict considered in the model, several other influences not directly related to the change may temper or exacerbate the chances that the leader actually does so. In this sub-section I consider the roles of variables customarily used in the causes of militarized international conflict research. In this research, the ability to prevail over the foe in a potential confrontation is thought to be one of the most important determinants of the decision to use military force.[9] The significance of relative power distribution is well documented in the international relations research even though there is a disagreement over which relative power configuration is best equipped to preserve peace. Among others, Gulick (1955), Morgenthau (1948), and Waltz (1979) argue that preponderant countries will use military force because they can reasonably expect a victory; when capabilities are more evenly matched (i.e. balanced), the countries will be uncertain about their ability to prevail, so they will avoid militarized confrontations (see also Walt 1987; Conybeare 1992; Niou, Ordeshook, and Rose 1989). Organski (1968), Organski and Kugler (1980), and Gilpin (1981), in contrast, propose that countries with about equal power will fight because one will not want to yield to the other given that its chances for prevailing in a possible confrontation are relatively good; in a preponderant situation, it is clear whose preferences should prevail so there is no need for militarized confrontations to (re)distribute contested resources (see also Kugler and Organski 1989; Kugler and Lemke 1996; Houweling and Siccama 1988; Geller 1993; de Soysa, Oneal, and Park 1997). Although the balance-preponderance debate remains unresolved, the empirical research (e.g. Bremer 1992; Oneal and Russett 2001) generally finds that preponderance favors peace.[10]

While the exact relationship between relative power and armed (territorial) conflict remains in some dispute, I include this important factor into the analyses. To operationalize a country's power, I consult the Correlates of War Material Capabilities data set, as reported by Bennett and Stam (2000). The list provides a yearly composite measure of power for each country, consisting of its military spending, number of military personnel, total population, urban population, energy consumption, and iron and steel (or its equivalents) production. These measures are meant to capture different aspects of a country's power base, and therefore provide a more broad-based measure of military potential—as opposed to relying exclusively on a single measure such as the level of military spending. Following the common practice (e.g. Russett and Oneal 2001), in the non-directed analyses I note the dyad's relative power configuration by taking the natural logarithm of the stronger to weaker state's power ratio. The coefficient sign should be negative if the preponderance logic is correct and positive if the balance argument prevails. Following Huth (1996; Huth and Allee 2002), the power ratio calculation is adjusted slightly in the directed analyses, by measuring the ratio between the initiator's and target's power levels; using the original operationalization produced no appreciable change in the findings.

Second, the anarchical nature of the international environment dictates that being on good terms with countries sharing common security interests is especially important. Acting against such a country brings to the leader international and domestic costs and consequently renders the reliance on militarized conflict to acquire land more detrimental. That is, the leader will have to weigh the expected payoff from territorial acquisition by militarized conflict against the value of the country's security ties. To assess the presence of common security interests, I use the Gibler and Sarkees (2004) alliance data.[11]

Third, extant armed conflict literature has convincingly shown that democratic institutions and/or norms have a pacifying effect when democracies deal with one another (e.g. Russett 1993; Maoz and Russett 1993; Russett and Oneal 2001; for the opposing viewpoint, see Layne 1994). If a leader of a democratic country wants to challenge another democracy over the outcome of a territorial change via militarized conflict, he/she will face normative and/or structural impediments—which provide barriers opposing successful military mobilization against the foe. This means that the citizens and other branches of the government are not likely to support the leader's agenda of territorial conquest against another democracy, making the leader's domestic popularity suffer. Consequently, due to the prospect of reduced benefits of territorial conquest, the democratic leader is less likely to engage in militarized conflict against the democratic foe. To distinguish pairs of "coherent" democracies from mixed or nondemocratic pairs, Polity IV data are used (Jaggers and Marshall 2005).

Fourth, the role of geographic proximity between the members of the dyad is important to consider both because the country's ability to project its force drops over distance (Boulding 1962) and because issues closer to the homeland are perceived as more salient (Vasquez 1995). Yet, the reader should note that this well-documented factor (e.g. Bremer 1992; Senese 2005) may be less influential in the post-territorial change context. Most non-colonial changes take place between states that are not only proximate but that also have a shared history. Dispute salience may hence not drop off as sharply over distance. Furthermore, because states often claim territory over which they exercised influence at some point in the past, they are likely to have an in-depth knowledge of the disputed terrain. This in turn makes it easier for the state to act militarily over distance. In the analyses below, I use the logged form of the Gleditsch and Ward (2001) measure of distance between states. For the secession analyses, I report the findings using the contiguity by land measure (Stinnett et al. 2002) because it acts as a selection mechanism to identify relevant dyads in certain analyses (see below); substantive impact on the findings is negligible regardless of which proximity measure is used. The data for all of the above control variables and the dependent variable are obtained from Bennett and Stam (2000).

The previous control variables are used in all of the subsequent causal analyses, while the ones identified below are used only in particular sets of the analyses, where appropriate. Two such variables—leadership change and the state's side in the territorial change—are thought to have the most impact in the armed conflict initiation context, so they are used only in the directed (i.e. initiation) analyses.[12] Concerning the potential impact of leadership change, a new leader may be more willing to use military force to challenge the change-altered boundary because it was either agreed to by or imposed on someone else.[13] For the general argument linking leadership change to armed conflict, see Chiozza and Goemans (2003). Moreover, a control variable indicating whether the country under scrutiny is on the gaining or losing side of the territorial change is introduced to capture potential differences in the behavior between the two sides. According to the prospect theory (Levy 2000), the leaders will adopt a more risk-acceptant behavior—which includes lowering the threshold for the use of military force—when they operate in the domain of losses. The losing state's leader arguably operates in the domain of losses because it is his/her state that has lost land through the change. The gaining state's leader, in contrast, may be operating in the domain of gains, and adopt a more risk-averse approach in order not to gamble away the state's territorial gains. Operationally, the losing state is identified by Tir et al. (1998). In the context of unifications, the prospect theory logic does not apply because the losing state no longer exists as an independent entity. In the related analyses, the unified state is instead identified, because this is the state I expect to have potential expansionist tendencies against its neighbors.

The final pair of control variables concerns specifically secessions. First, in the non-directed analyses, I distinguish rump-secessionist from secessionist-secessionist state pairs. This is done in order to assure that unanticipated differences in the behavior across the sets do not skew the findings. The secession is likely to create more tension between the rump and secessionist than between two secessionist states. Each new, secessionist state must dismantle its union with the rump state, while the dissolution vis-à-vis other secessionist states is more or less automatic; in fact, some secessionist states may even cooperate with one another to facilitate their departure from the union (e.g. the Baltic republics, Slovenia-Croatia). The rump-secessionist relations are, in contrast, not off to as good of a start. The rump state may harbor resentment over having lost land to the secessionist state, while the secessionist state may be suspicious of the intentions of the rump state—which may include rolling back the secession—and of the rump state's patronizing behavior (e.g. Russia's "we know best" attitude toward the former Soviet republics). In the rump state, the resentment will make it politically less controversial for the leader to engage in militarized conflict to deal with territorial distribution issues that may arise with the secessionist state. Similarly, the secessionist state's leader can argue that the reliance on militarized conflict is appropriate because the state needs to send a signal of determination and strength in dealing with the rump state. These dynamics—which are arguably not present in the interactions between two secessionist states—may lower the threshold for using military force to deal with the territorial outcome of the secession. The operational classification into two sets is done in accordance with the list provided by Tir et al. (1998). Second, a dummy variable identifies dyads resulting from the disintegration of the Soviet Union in 1991. Because this state broke up into fifteen different states, this unique historical event contributes a sizable portion of secession cases and observations to the data set. To assure that the findings for the key theoretically relevant variables are not driven by the Soviet cases alone, I include the dummy variable into the analyses as a statistical control.

Methods of Analysis

In the final section of this chapter, I discuss the statistical methods used to obtain the empirical findings. The first set of analyses is of descriptive nature and it helps determine (1) the extent to which territorial changes resolve the underlying territorial disputes and (2) the danger to international peace the remaining territorial disputes pose. The results not only provide clues to the territorial changes' conflict management potential, but also generate systematic evidence about the consequences of territorial changes, which—aside from the Goertz and Diehl (1992) study—are largely unknown.

In terms of the specific statistical methods used for these descriptive analyses, I rely primarily on simple frequency counts and comparisons of means. That is, I note the portion of territorial change dyads that experience—or fail to experience—post-change territorial disputes. Among such dyads, I investigate what percentage of them avoid or fail to avoid fatal militarized conflict over territorial issues. Though the frequency counts are informative, it is unfortunately difficult to put them into an appropriate perspective and determine statistical significance of resultant trends. At this time, there is no comparable information on the other methods of territorial dispute management (e.g. adjudication, negotiation) to which these figures could be compared. This important task is left to future research, where this study could be used as the first building block for assessing the relative effectiveness of various methods of territorial dispute management. As an imperfect substitute, I compare the frequency count figures to the ones reported by Huth's (1996) study of territorial disputes. The reader should keep in mind that the two studies are not perfectly comparable as they investigate related but not identical phenomena.

The issue of the results' context is less of a problem in the other descriptive analyses. Given that territorial disputes are more likely than any other issue to escalate to (fatal) militarized conflicts (Vasquez 1993; Holsti 1991; Vasquez and Henehan 2001), I also calculate the average yearly frequency of post-change militarized territorial conflict within the dyad. To understand how problematic these dyads really are, I compare these militarized conflict frequencies to what can be considered a "normal" frequency in an average dyad. Accordingly, the average annual number of fatal militarized conflicts fought over land is calculated for all contiguous countries in the twentieth century (mean = .011, s.d. = .105, n = 14,803). Though these analyses are important and informative, they cannot account for intervening factors such as the influence of control variables or the passage of time.

To deal with these and other issues, I also perform a series of causal analyses. The empirical applicability of the model developed in Chapter 2 is determined by testing the associated hypotheses, that is by evaluating the connection between the key dependent and independent variables. In general, I rely on the Cox regression (Cox 1975; Box-Steffensmeier and Jones 2000) with robust standard errors and repeat failures.[14] This method of analysis is appropriate for longitudinal data with a binary dependent variable whose value is almost always zero (Beck 1998). These are precisely the characteristics of the dependent variable. In addition, Cox regression relaxes the assumptions (1) of duration independence, (2) of independence between conflicts, and (3) that the data are not right censored, which are made by other commonly used methods such as logit (Long 1997). Relaxing the former and latter assumptions is particularly important because my dataset is comprised of both older and recent cases of territorial change, which have obviously had unequal opportunities to experience armed conflict.[15] In terms of interpreting the Cox coefficients, one observes the impact of independent variables on the hazard rate (that is, probability of failure, i.e. armed conflict, at a given point in time given survival up to that point) rather than the more familiar, direct impact on the probability of conflict in the logit model. Aside from the technical difference, the *substantive* interpretation of the coefficients is actually similar to logit.[16]

Notes

1. Colonial lands are generally considered to be less important to countries than their homeland territories. Little if any emotional attachment to these lands exists on the part of the colonial power and its population, so they tend to be treated like property. In fact, Goertz and Diehl (1992) report that many nineteenth century colonially-based territorial changes are simple sales and purchases of land. Yet, if one were to assume—as Goertz and Diehl do—that all homeland territories have at least some intangible salience, a potential downside of omitting colonial cases is that the cases with the lowest intangible salience are not considered in the analyses. The universe of cases is instead truncated to those instances ranging from medium intangible salience (i.e. homeland territories with strategic or economic value only) to high intangible salience (i.e. homeland territories with ethnic, ancestral, or religious value).

2. Although Austria-Hungary's breakup was prompted by its defeat in World War I, I include this case because the division of the country had a strong internal impetus: the breakup of the state has been sought by its many ethnic groups for some time.

3. Whether the analyses are restricted to only rump-secessionist state pairs does not change the thrust of the findings; see Tir (2001, 2003b, forthcoming).

4. Recall that even in the case of the 1990 German unification, the original capital city was Bonn and not Berlin.

5. A MID is defined as "a set of interactions between or among states involving threats to use military force, displays of military force, or actual uses of military force. . . . These acts must be explicit, overt, nonaccidental, and government sanctioned" (Gochman and Maoz 1984, 587).

6. An example is the Polish "attack" on Germany on the eve of World War II, in which Germans dressed as Polish soldiers attacked a radio station within Germany.

7. To this list, covering the 1918-1995 period, I add territorial disputes occurring in the early and late parts of the twentieth century using similar coding criteria. The sources for the extension and additional coverage of the data set include Allcock (1992), *The New York Times, Facts on File, World Almanac and the Book of Facts, Keesing's Archives, CIA's World Handbook, Encarta, Encyclopedia Britannica*, etc.

8. This figure should not be confused with the one reported in Goertz and Diehl (1992); that work reports that 75 percent of territorial *changes* have been performed peacefully. The likely reasons for the discrepancy are: (1) the figure reported here refers only to state-to-state territorial transfers, a sub-set of territorial changes, (2) the temporal domains differ (1816-1980 in the Goertz and Diehl study and 1900-2000 in this study), and (3) Goertz and Diehl also include colonial changes, many of which were peaceful sales and purchases of land.

9. Conceivably, constituents could reward their leader for using military force against the foe just for the sake of standing up to the foe and regardless of the outcome of the confrontation. Yet, such actions should entail sharply diminishing returns for the leader. If the constituents start to suspect that the leader's unsuccessful use of militarized conflict is meant to bolster his/her own popularity rather than help the country's well-being, the leader will be curtailed against doing so. In fact, losing a war can cost the leader the office (Bueno de Mesquita and Siverson 1995).

10. Much of the territorial change literature is, however, silent on the topic of potential connections between land distribution, participants' relative power configuration, and propensity to use military force. An exception can be found in the ethnic partition literature. Kaufmann (1996, 1998) and Mearsheimer (1993, 1998; see also Mearsheimer and Van Evera 1995, 1996, 1999) both contend that to prevent future militarized conflicts, the secessionist states should receive military assistance—in form of weapons and skills transfer rather than direct involvement—from major states. The idea is that a strong secessionist state can successfully deter the rump state from attempting to roll back the secession. The authors thus favor the balance of power theory, contending that evenly matched countries will deter one another from attack by making potential armed conflict seem risky. Even if one assumes that policymakers are willing to pursue this advice and that balance of power leads to peace—an assertion with quite weak empirical support—it is not clear that this prescription will be all that effective in the long run. Relative power is in a perhaps sluggish but nevertheless constant flux. Kugler and Organski (1989) point to changing factors such as economic productivity, population size, political capacity of the regime, etc. in the development of their power transition theory. Likewise, Gilpin (1981), Levy (1985), and works on power cycles (Modelski and Thompson 1989; Doran 1989) all argue that the relative power distribution experiences fundamental changes in the long run. Another potential territory-power connection states that because territorial control has been identified as one of the sources of power (e.g. Spykman 1944; Mackinder 1919; Morgenthau 1948; see also Gochman and Leng 1983), territorial changes them-

selves could affect the relative power distribution between states. Yet, besides the cases of unification that place an entire country's apparatus at the disposal of the unified state, most territorial changes involve relatively small pieces of land (Goertz and Diehl 1992). The impact of gaining or losing a piece of land on the country's power base is hence not likely to be substantial. One could even argue that the loss (or gain) of a far away territory may actually increase (decrease) the country's power by reducing (increasing) its over-extension (Snyder 1991; Kennedy 1987).

11. As a check of robustness, I also utilized Bueno de Mesquita's (1981) tau-b score—which compares countries' alliance portfolios—and Signorino and Ritter's (1999) S-score—which combines alliance portfolios with other indicators of the countries' foreign policy similarity, such as voting patterns in the United Nations. Neither of the alternate operationalizations changed the findings (see Tir 2001, 2003a, 2003b).

12. The leadership change variable was not significant in any of the non-directed dyad analyses, so its omission is inconsequential. Note also that the inclusion of this variable lowers the number of available observations because the related data is available only for the post-WW I period.

13. Besides a mechanism that would make future confrontations more likely, the change in leadership could also make them less likely. Suppose that a leader lost land through the change and he/she is concerned that the loss of land will be the legacy by which the leader is remembered. Alternatively, the leader of a gaining country may have failed to acquire all the land he/she promised to the selectorate. Not wanting to be remembered as a (partial) failure, either leader could make desperate attempts to try to take the disputed land. In contrast, a new leader would not have the weight of the history on his/her shoulders and consequently would be less prone to pursue further revisions by the use of military force.

14. Robust standard errors account for the fact that observations from the same dyad are interrelated. The repeat failure setup is used because one confrontation does not exhaust the possibility of future confrontations.

15. More specifically, duration dependence means that as time passes the chances that an event of interest will occur changes. For example, the longer a car is on the road, the more likely it is to experience a mechanical failure. In the realm of international relations, one can argue that the longer a dyad remains at peace, the lower (or greater) are the chances that it will experience armed conflict in the future. Dependence between events (e.g. between militarized conflicts) refers to the probability that event occurrence is influenced by whether the event has occurred in the past. Thus, a previous heart-attack victim is usually thought to be at a greater risk of having another heart attack. In the international relations literature, studies of temporal conflict diffusion (e.g. Goldstein and Freeman 1990; Goldstein and Pevehouse 1997; Rajmaira and Ward 1990; Rajmaira 1997; Pevehouse and Goldstein 1999) show that armed conflicts a pair of countries engages in are related over time, so accounting for conflict dependence is prudent. Finally, (3) right-censoring means that different cases may be under observation for unequal periods of time. For example, in the data set, a territorial change occurring in 1900 has been under observation for ninety-three years by 1992. In contrast, a change taking place in 1990 has been under observation for only three years.

16. Cox regression was chosen over other event history techniques because it is non-parametric, meaning that it relies on fewer and weaker assumptions about the shape of the duration distribution than other techniques. In this project, I am interested in controlling for duration dependence rather than in explaining it; hence, a non-parametric model

is appropriate. The parametric techniques, in contrast, assume a particular duration distribution (e.g. Weibull, log-normal, exponential) even though social science data rarely follow these prescribed patterns. If I were to use a parametric event history technique, I would be buying into the assumptions about the shape of the duration function. Given the choice, Box-Steffensmeier and Jones (2000) recommend that researchers avoid making unnecessary additional assumptions.

Chapter 4

Aftermath of State-to-State Territorial Transfers

This chapter presents empirical evaluation of the aftermath of state-to-state territorial transfers. The first segment of the chapter examines the transfers' ability to resolve the original territorial dispute and the extent to which the still unresolved disputes pose a threat to peace between states gaining and losing land via the transfer. After these descriptive analyses, the chapter assesses the relevance of hypothesized causal links between the remaining territorial disputes and transfer process on the one hand and militarized conflict over the revised boundaries on the other. Per the arguments developed in Chapter 2 that were used to develop the theoretical model, these factors should help explain why some losing and gaining states fight over their adjusted borders while others do not. The final portion summarizes the chapter's empirical findings and discusses their implications. The findings' implications are also related to a currently-relevant case, in order to illustrate how the insights developed in this work may be used to conduct transfers in ways that would minimize the chances for future armed confrontations.

Descriptive Results

Table 4.1 provides assessments of territorial transfers' performance from the territorial dispute and militarized territorial conflict perspectives; a dyad formed by the losing and gaining states is the unit of analysis. The top portion of the table evaluates how often transfers succeed in resolving the territorial dispute that prompted the movement of the boundary. Of the 108 dyads involved in territorial transfers for which territorial dispute data is available, sixty-four (or 59 percent) experience post-transfer territorial disputes. Thus, in a majority of cases the transfer either fails to resolve the original dispute or replaces it with a new one. The percentage of cases with territorial disputes is high in comparison to

Huth's (1996) finding that territorial disputes occur at a general rate of about 33 percent. Yet, on the positive side, the finding means that transfers resolve the initial territorial dispute in about 41 percent of the cases. This percentage is actually fairly encouraging given that much of the territorial conflict research notes the disputes' intractability and longevity (e.g. Huth 1996; Vasquez 1993; Allcock 1992). Moreover, Huth's sample includes many dyads that did not have a territorial dispute in the first place, so his study does not provide information on how frequently territorial disputes are resolved. The current frequency count findings are nevertheless compared to his results in the empirical chapters, as his study represents the best available—but by no means perfect—frame of reference for these findings; see also the related discussion in the final section of Chapter 3.

Table 4.1: Gauging the Effectiveness of Territorial Transfers, 1900-2000

	No	44 (41 percent)
Is transfer followed by a territorial dispute?	Yes	64 (59 percent)
	Total Dyads	108
	No	37 (58 percent)
Given that transfer is followed by a territorial dispute, does the dispute escalate to a fatal territorial MID?	Yes	27 (42 percent)
	Total Dyads	64

Notes: Unit of analysis is a dyad composed of countries losing and gaining land via a transfer. MID = militarized interstate dispute.

Another way of gauging the transfers' effectiveness is to ask to what extent the unresolved post-transfer territorial disputes pose a threat to peace between countries losing and gaining land via the transfer? The bottom part of Table 4.1 reports the conditional probability that these dyads experience at least one fatal militarized interstate dispute (MID) over territory given that they are engaged in a territorial dispute with one another. As the table shows, 42 percent (twenty-seven out of sixty-four) of the dyads embroiled in territorial disputes actually experience fatal militarized conflict over land. That is, escalation from territorial disputes to fatal militarized conflict is far from inevitable and is limited to fewer than one half of the cases. And overall, this means that only one quarter (27/108) of territorial transfers are followed by both territorial disputes and fatal militarized conflict over the transfer-adjusted boundary.

Next, Figure 4.1 illustrates the temporal distribution of transfer failures. It tracks the portion of loser-gainer dyads that have experienced at least one fatal territorial MID over time since the relevant transfer. The figure reveals that most initial confrontations occur in the first few years after the transfer. After this time, comparatively fewer previously peaceful dyads experience their initial fatal territorial conflicts, so one can infer that the situation stabilizes somewhat with the passage of time. Yet, given that new failures occur even after decades of peace, the evidence that transfer-adjusted borders become accepted over time is relatively weak. In more theoretical terms, the finding suggests that the payoff to the leader from challenging boundaries that have become accepted by the population decreases—but certainly does not vanish—with the passage of time.

Figure 4.1: Cumulative Portion of Transfers Followed by Fatal Territorial MIDs, 1900-2000

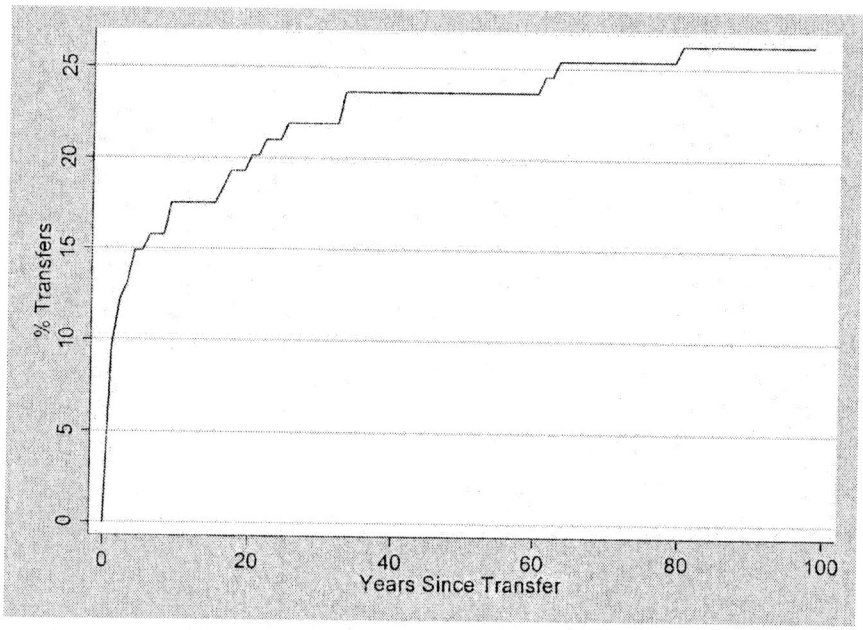

To put these findings into a bit of a perspective and to take into the account the fact that some dyads experience repeated militarized conflict, I investigate how the loser-gainer dyad's proneness to experience fatal territorial MIDs compares with the experience of "normal" states. To do this, I calculate the average annual rate of fatal territorial MID onset for dyads involved in territorial transfers and contrast it with the rate for all countries calculated in the previous chapter (.011). The post-transfer rate (.018, s.d. = .133, n = 3,989) is 64 percent higher and significantly different (p < .00) than the "normal" frequency. The comparison reveals that although transfers are beneficial in the sense that they resolve many underlying territorial disputes, the participant countries continue to fight over territorial issues after the transfer and they do so at well above the "normal" rate. Recall that this fighting is limited to roughly one-quarter of the transfer dyads, so this relatively small portion of the dyads fights at such explosive rates that it increases the average for the entire group to well above the normal frequency.

Yet, despite the higher than normal frequency of militarized confrontations after the transfer, the related figure in fact represents an improvement over the pre-transfer situation. By comparing the pre- vs. post-transfer interactions, Tir (2001, 2003a) reports that the rate of militarized territorial conflict is significantly reduced by 42-50 percent—depending on the time frame examined. The comparison adds further credibility to the idea that transfers are a useful territorial conflict management tool, even if they cannot fully normalize the relations between the disputants.

Next, I revisit some of the above analyses by considering the type of territorial dispute transfers leave behind. In linking territorial disputes with armed conflict, the related research points out that not all pieces of land are equally valuable. This is an important issue to consider because the types of territorial disputes transfers leave behind may impact the likelihood that losing and gaining states fight over their adjusted border; that is, the issue has a bearing on transfers' success. Recall that in Chapter 2 I divided land value into the tangible and intangible dimensions (Newman 1999). In a ceaselessly competitive, zero-sum world of realism, possession of tangibly-valuable lands—which have the ability to affect states' relative power—will not only be desired but also contested militarily. In this view, transfers will generally not be able to resolve such disputes and the ones that leave behind strategically- and/or economically-based territorial disputes will likely be followed by militarized confrontations. In contrast, others argue that while intangibly-based territorial disputes are expected to be common but not necessarily inevitable, the failure to control intangibly-valued land is thought to intensify the willingness to fight more so than the failure to control tangibly-valued land (Goertz and Diehl 1992; Diehl 1999b; Vasquez 1983; Touval 1972; Huth 1996). This is so because the lands valued along this dimension are perceived as personal, indivisible, and un-substitutable (Gottman 1973; Sack 1986). The reader is reminded that territory's ethnic value represents the sole manifestation of land's intangible value that is available from the Huth and Allee (2002) data set at this time. The extent to which transfers leave behind each territorial dispute type and associated dangers of escalation are investigated in Table 4.2.

Table 4.2 reports the results for two analyses. The top analysis breaks down post-transfer territorial disputes by type. Transfers are most likely to leave behind situations in which the participant countries disagree about the location of their border based on cross-border ethnic ties; such disputes are present in 47 percent (51/108) of the cases. Only a slightly smaller proportion of transfers (44 percent, 48/108) leave behind economically-based territorial disputes. In contrast, strategically-based territorial disputes are the most infrequent and occur at the rate of about 24 percent (26/108). Thus, disputes over both intangibly- and tangibly- (i.e. economically-) valued land are about as likely to remain unresolved after the transfer. Yet, that this happens in fewer than half of the cases suggests that both the realist and value-as-meaning arguments tend to underestimate transfers' potential as a conflict management tool. The relative dearth of strategically-based territorial disputes is consistent with the argument that twentieth century technological advancements in weaponry, surveillance techniques, speed of troop and equipment movement, etc. have been undermining the strategic importance of territory (e.g. Keohane and Nye 1977; Rosecrance 1986; Brooks 1999).

Table 4.2: Territorial Transfer Effectiveness by Territorial Dispute Type, 1900-2000

		Strategic Territorial Dispute	Economic Territorial Dispute	Ethnic Territorial Dispute
Is transfer followed by a specific type of territorial dispute?	No	82 (76 percent)	60 (56 percent)	57 (53 percent)
	Yes	26 (24 percent)	48 (44 percent)	51 (47 percent)
	Total Dyads	108	108	108
Given that transfer is followed by a territorial dispute, does the dispute escalate to a fatal territorial MID?	No	12 (46 percent)	28 (58 percent)	30 (59 percent)
	Yes	14 (54 percent)	20 (42 percent)	21 (41 percent)
	Total Dyads	26	48	51

Notes: Unit of analysis is a dyad composed of countries losing and gaining land via a transfer. MID = militarized interstate dispute.

The bottom portion of Table 4.2 reports the conditional probabilities that a particular type of territorial dispute escalates into at least one fatal territorial MID. Although the strategically-based territorial disputes are the least likely to occur after a transfer, they are the most likely to experience escalation: fourteen out of twenty-six (about 54 percent) of relevant cases follow this path. The finding provides some support for the realist viewpoint; yet, also note that the probability of escalation for the ethnic dispute type does not lag all that far behind

(41 percent). Similarly to my results, Huth (1996) reports that military force is the most likely to be used to deal with strategically-based territorial disputes. The rates of escalation themselves are, however, not comparable across the two studies because Huth combines fatal with non-fatal militarized disputes as indicators of escalation; given the lower threshold, he not surprisingly finds escalation rates that are as high as two-thirds. In sum, the escalation analysis suggests no great differences in the proclivity of various types of territorial disputes to escalate to fatal territorial MIDs. Although the strategic (i.e. tangible) territorial disputes are the most prone to escalation, this analysis leaves open the tangibility vs. intangibility debate in the post-transfer context, as the descriptive analyses do not take into account potentially relevant factors identified in Chapters 2 and 3. More sophisticated analyses that tackle this issue follow shortly.

Before presenting the results of the causal analyses, I briefly consider the ability of the three types of transfer process to resolve the underlying territorial dispute. In Chapter 2 I presented arguments maintaining that both peaceful—due to the ability to let the disputants compromise over the location of their boundary—and overwhelming victory—due to the ability of the winner to impose the boundary's location and force the loser to drop its territorial claims—transfers have a greater potential to resolve the underlying territorial dispute than ordinary (i.e. short of overwhelming victory) violent transfers. Do these arguments elicit empirical support? Table 4.3 reveals that—as expected—peaceful transfers have the greatest potential to create borders acceptable to both losing and gaining countries. Their success rate of 50 percent is impressive compared to the other two processes, but it also suggests that a peaceful movement of a boundary is not a foolproof measure for dealing with territorial disputes. This observation is actually consistent with the theorizing presented in Chapter 2, where I argued that non-violent coercive techniques may often be applied in order to redistribute land between countries. That is, countries could be pressured into giving territory they do not want to give up or into scaling down their territorial ambitions even when force is not used against them overtly. Furthermore, changes in the political climate or leadership could lead to the questioning of a peaceful transfer's outcome, much like the Serb/Yugoslav King's decision to cede parts of Slovenia and Croatia was challenged by Tito during and after World War II. Nevertheless, peaceful transfers are still the most effective process for resolving territorial disputes. The rates of success for the overwhelming victory and violent transfers are notably lower, 28 percent and 31 percent, respectively. The observation holds when the post-transfer territorial disputes are broken down by territorial dispute type, though the peaceful transfer's success rate "lead" shrinks to mere 3 percent for strategic and economic territorial disputes; for ethnic territorial disputes, the success rate gap remains rather large, at 20-26 percent.

Somewhat surprising is the overwhelming victory process's poor performance compared to ordinary violent transfers; in three out of the four comparisons reported in Table 4.3, violent transfers actually outperform overwhelming victory transfers in their ability to move the boundary to a mutually-acceptable location. The overwhelming victory logic (Maoz 1984; Vasquez 1993) suggests that the loser dare not question the boundary's new location lest it become involved in yet another devastating conflict against the winner. A potential alternate explanation may be that as the time passes the winner's ability to control the loser diminishes, as even badly defeated countries tend to regain their power (Organski and Kugler 1977). With time, the loser will become more inclined to question the loss of its land—thus erasing any potential difference in territorial dispute resolution vis-à-vis ordinary violent transfers. Indeed, the likelihood with which a territorial dispute within a loser-gainer dyad escalates to a fatal territorial MID following an overwhelming victory as opposed to a violent transfer is about the same (46 percent) for both processes.

Table 4.3: Territorial Transfer Effectiveness by Transfer Process, 1900-2000

Process Type	Territorial Dispute Present?	All Territorial Dispute Types	Territorial Dispute Type		
			Strategic	Economic	Ethnic
Peaceful Transfers	No	29 (50 percent)	47 (81 percent)	34 (59 percent)	37 (64 percent)
	Yes	29 (50 percent)	11 (19 percent)	24 (41 percent)	21 (36 percent)
	Total Dyads	58	58	58	58
Overwhelming Victory Transfers	No	5 (28 percent)	10 (56 percent)	8 (44 percent)	8 (44 percent)
	Yes	13 (72 percent)	8 (44 percent)	10 (56 percent)	10 (56 percent)
	Total Dyads	18	18	18	18
(Ordinary) Violent Transfers	No	10 (31 percent)	25 (78 percent)	18 (56 percent)	12 (38 percent)
	Yes	22 (69 percent)	7 (22 percent)	14 (44 percent)	20 (62 percent)
	Total Dyads	32	32	32	32

Notes: Unit of analysis is a dyad composed of countries losing and gaining land via a transfer. Ordinary violent transfers are violent transfers short of an overwhelming victory.

This brings us to the perhaps more salient issue of whether the three processes also possess differing abilities to affect the leader's decision to engage in militarized conflict in order to revisit the transfer-altered boundary—as argued in the model presented in Chapter 2. For the answer to this question, I turn to the causal analyses results that put the hypotheses from the model to the test. Though insightful and informative, the above-discussed descriptive results regarding the transfer dyad's proclivity to experience a fatal territorial MID may well be skewed because the territorial dispute, process, and control variable factors discussed in Chapters 2 and 3 were not simultaneously taken into account. I now turn these more sophisticated analyses.

Causal Results

Part I: Post-Transfer Territorial Disputes

I begin this section by reporting, in Table 4.4, the results of non-directed analyses that focus on loser-gainer dyad members' proneness to become *involved* in fatal militarized disputes with each other after the transfer. In addition to the observation that all statistical models are highly significant, note that most of the territorial dispute variables that compose the theoretical model (see Chapter 2) are significant—even when controlling for correlates of armed conflict not directly related to transfers (see Chapter 3). Statistical Model 1 presents the results necessary to evaluate hypothesis H-1. According to the theoretical model, leaders of states losing and gaining land via the transfer will be motivated to act on unresolved border issues by the benefits they hope to derive from further territorial revisions. Hence, the related expectation is that those transfers that leave behind territorial disputes will likely be followed by militarized conflict between the dyad's members. As can be seen in Model 1, the territorial dispute coefficient is significant and positive, providing support for hypothesis H-1. The relations between territorial gainers and losers are therefore strongly influenced by the presence of unresolved border issues. The finding that the transfers' inability to resolve territorial dispute issues to the satisfaction of losing and gaining states significantly increases the hazard of fatal MIDs helps extend the territorial dispute research (e.g. Huth 1996; Huth and Allee 2002; Vasquez 1993; Vasquez and Henehan 2001; Senese 2005; Senese and Vasquez 2003) into the post-transfer context.

This finding is consistent with Syrian behavior toward Israel after the loss of Golan Heights in 1967. Syria disagreed with the loss of the land, indicating a post-transfer territorial dispute between the two states. To gain back the land that is strategically (a high ground in an otherwise flat area), economically (fresh water sources), and ethnically (the area was inhabited by Syrians) important, Syria relied on (unsuccessful) uses of military force against Israel in the following years. Moreover, the Turkish attempts to capture the Cypriot capital of Nicosia after the invasion of the northeastern part of the island in 1974 also help illustrate the findings. Nicosia is valuable to the Turks for economic (the center of economic activity on the island), ethnic (a substantial population of the Turkish background lived there) and strategic (a gateway to the western portion of the island) reasons.

Table 4.4: Cox Regression Estimates of Fatal Post-Transfer Militarized Conflict Involvement, 1900-2000

Variable	Model 1: All Fatal MIDs	Model 2: Fatal Terr. MIDs Only	Model 2a: Restricted Model 2	Model 2b: Restricted Model 2
Territorial Dispute	1.974*** (.399)			
Strategic Terr. Dispute		.176 (.415)		.004 (.472)
Economic Terr. Dispute		1.612** (.820)	1.631** (.833)	2.264*** (.592)
Ethnic Terr. Dispute		1.135** (.681)	1.122* (.696)	
Ordinary Violent Transfer	.698** (.305)	1.011** (.455)	1.004** (.451)	1.073** (.469)
Overwhelming Victory Transfer	.178 (.467)	.244 (.608)	.297 (.636)	.294 (.595)
Power Ratio	-.066 (.106)	.171* (.121)	.170* (.126)	.115 (.126)
Allies	-.047 (.266)	.124 (.386)	.124 (.382)	-.102 (.378)
Dyadic Democracy	-.199 (.339)	.058 (.411)	.058 (.410)	.149 (.405)
Distance	-.194* (.126)	-.365*** (.100)	-.351*** (.107)	-.357*** (.097)
χ^2	51.38***	82.97***	80.74***	74.06***
N	3972	3972	3972	3972

Notes: Cell entries report coefficients and robust standard errors (in parentheses). Unit of analysis is a non-directed dyad-year. Each dyad is composed of a losing and a gaining state. MID = militarized interstate dispute. Peaceful transfers are the baseline against which violent and overwhelming victory transfer processes are compared. All significance levels are one-tailed: *** p < .01; ** p < .05; * p < .10.

To determine which aspects of territorial disputes are particularly problematic, I evaluate next the empirical accuracy of hypothesis H-2. Recall that I argued in Chapter 2 that the willingness to rely on militarized conflict to (re)take the land is based on the disputed land's tangible (i.e. economic or strategic) and intangible (i.e. ancestral, religious, ethnic kin) value. According to the reasoning from which hypothesis H-2 is derived, the inability to control intangibly-valued land is perceived to be more serious. The acquisition of intangibly-valued land is thought to appeal to a broader portion of the selectorate than acquisition of tangibly-valued land. This in turn makes the leader more interested in pursuing intangibly- rather than tangibly-valued disputed territories and results in a greater willingness to engage in militarized conflict. This logic is of course disputed by the realist school of thought, which sees little connection between the population's desires and leader's actions. Instead, to bolster the state's power, he/she will be most likely to pursue tangibly-valued disputed territories. Model 2 helps sort through these contradictory expectations. In this model, the dependent variable is a fatal MID fought specifically over territorial issues and the territorial disputes are differentiated according to their underlying characteristics.

The general expectation that both tangibly- and intangibly-valued disputed lands provide motivation to engage in militarized territorial conflict that is likely to result in casualties are supported. Both the economic (i.e. tangible) and ethnic (i.e. intangible) territorial dispute coefficients are significant and positive. Yet despite the initially encouraging results for the ethnic territorial dispute variable, hypothesis H-2 does not receive much support. Although the ethnic value coefficient is positive and significant, its importance is surpassed by that of the economic (i.e. tangible) value coefficient; the economic coefficient has a 42 percent greater marginal effect compared to its ethnic counterpart. The leaders of losing and gaining states hence find more reward in fighting for territories that would increase their countries' economic might than in fighting for lands that would unite lands occupied by ethnic kin.

Examples of such tendencies include the Japanese push to extend its territorial holdings in Manchuria prior to World War II. The region has obvious economic importance, as it possesses large ore deposits. In contrast, the region has little ethnic importance to the Japanese, as few of their countryman inhabited the region prior to the invasion. The Soviet desire to recapture the island of Sakhalin lost to the Japanese in the 1905 Russio-Japanese War further illustrates this tendency. The island was a home to few Russian residents at the time so the Soviets had little desire to control it for this reason. However, the island possesses notable oil reserves, a resource whose importance was growing at the time when the Soviets were seeking to industrialize their country. The Soviets were ultimately successful in recapturing the island during World War II.

Because the logic of hypothesis H-2 receives such strong support in the literature (e.g. Goertz and Diehl 1992; Huth 1996; Huth and Allee 2002; Vasquez 1993) I investigate whether the ethnic coefficient's comparatively smaller impact may be due to the fact that a certain piece of land is often valued for multiple reasons.[1] Statistically speaking, this can create multicollinearity among the territorial dispute type variables, which complicates estimation. While there are no perfect solutions to the problem of multicollinearity, I follow the customary procedure (e.g. Kennedy 1998) and keep the significant territorial dispute coefficients in the model and drop the insignificant territorial dispute variable. The results for this procedure are presented in Model 2a. The impact on the ethnic coefficient is actually the opposite of what has been expected. Both its absolute size and significance level drop. Furthermore, the relative impact gap compared to its economic counterpart expands slightly, to 45 percent. Concerned that the ethnic coefficient's importance may be overstated in Model 2, I now drop it from the analysis and present the results in Model 2b. Importantly, the likelihood ratio test (Long 1997) comparing Models 2 and 2b reveals that Model 2 is superior (p = .002), that is that the ethnic territorial dispute variable is important in accounting for the transfers' aftermath. Therefore, even though I am forced to reject the expectation that ethnically-based territorial disputes are *the* reason states fight after the transfers, one does not have to conclude that they are completely irrelevant. In other words, the ethnic value of the disputed land drives the gainers and losers toward militarized conflict with one another, but not as much as the disputed land's economic value.

Implications of having to reject hypothesis H-2 in the context of transfers provide insights into some well-known historical events. The findings indicate that, on average, territorial losers are the most interested in fighting to regain economically valuable lands. Historically speaking, Alsace-Lorraine changed hands between Germany and France several times. The loss of Alsace-Lorraine hurt the losing country the most due to its economic value—even though the land can be considered ethnically important to both countries. In terms of the gainer's perspective, consider the German expansion into Poland on the eve of World War II. The initial German-Soviet division of Poland did not satisfy Hitler. The results suggest that his desire to acquire the remainder of Poland was motivated more by economic resources—such as industry and ore deposits—than by the Germans living on those lands.

Let us turn briefly to the strategic territorial dispute coefficient, which has not been discussed yet. There is little evidence in the findings that the strategic dimension of territorial disputes is all that relevant. In Model 1, the strategic coefficient has the anticipated sign, but it is insignificant. Marginal effect comparisons reveal that the ethnic and economic coefficients have notably greater impacts on the decision to rely on the use of military force (545 percent and 815 percent, respectively). Moreover, the likelihood ratio test comparing the restricted Model 2a—from which the strategic variable is removed—performs about as well as the unrestricted Model 2 (p = .62); the related coefficient also experiences a substantial drop in absolute value in Model 2b. Cumulatively, the evidence presented here refines the realist arguments by pointing out that both manifestations of the tangible dimension of disputed land's value are not equally important. The suspicion from the previous, descriptive results, section that technological advancements may have substantially reduced the payoff of controlling strategically-valued disputed lands is further solidified.

As an additional check of the findings' robustness, I utilize the directed dyad design discussed in Chapter 3; see the related caveats. This design allows one to go beyond analyzing conflict involvement and observe conflict *initiation*, that is separate armed conflict initiators from targets. Much of the logic presented suggests that the state dissatisfied with the transfer-altered borders will be the one to strike first. Table 4.5 presents Models 3-4b, which follow the setup of the models presented in Table 4.4 and evaluate this portion of the argument. The findings for the first two hypotheses remain applicable in the armed (territorial) conflict initiation context. One change in the results is nonetheless notable. The ethnic territorial dispute coefficient is no longer significant, suggesting that these disputes may provide the leaders with an even lower payoff for militarized conflict than originally thought. Nevertheless, the likelihood ratio test comparing Models 4 and 4b reveals that the ethnic variable contributes significantly to the overall explanation of post-transfer militarized conflict ($p = .03$) and should not be removed from the model. Still, because the economic value coefficient retains its correspondingly strong influence, there is little reason to resurrect hypothesis H-2.

Relating the findings from the first part of the theoretical model to the literature, on the issue of disputed land's value, I followed the territorial conflict literature's (e.g. Vasquez 1993; Huth 1996; Goertz and Diehl 1992; Huth and Allee 2002) lead and divided it into the tangible (i.e. economic and strategic) and intangible (i.e. ethnic) dimensions. Much of the literature consulted in the building of the model (see Chapter 2) argued not only that both dimensions of value are important, but also that intangibly-valued disputed lands are associated with armed conflict onset more so than tangibly-valued disputed lands. Both Huth (1996) and Goertz and Diehl (1992) found evidence supporting these arguments. This is not, however, what the results from this chapter suggest. The only indicator of intangible value available (i.e. ethnic value) fails to convince that it has a stronger impact than the indicator of the disputed land's economic value. A possible cause of discrepancy between the present and Huth's (1996) findings may be the fact that Huth deals with the dynamics of territorial disputes in general, while I deal with territorial disputes through the lens of territorial transfers; the latter scenario introduces the concept of territorial gains and losses, so the leaders do not necessarily face identical circumstances in both situations. The difference between my and Goertz and Diehl's (1992) findings may stem from the issue of colonial lands. In this study, I included only non-colonial, homeland transfers and associated territorial disputes. In contrast, Goertz and Diehl included both colonial and non-colonial lands, but their indicators of intangible—or as they call it, "relational"—value overlap with the colonial vs. non-colonial distinction.[2] Therefore, Goertz and Diehl do not really provide evidence that disputed intangibly-valued *homeland* territories are particularly likely to be fought over; that is, it is not clear that their findings contradict the results from this chapter. These issues notwithstanding, the impact of intangibly-valued disputed land on territorial conflict should not be completely dismissed. Recall both that my results do show that ethnically-valued disputed lands are important

Table 4.5: Cox Regression Estimates of Fatal Post-Transfer Militarized Conflict Initiation, 1900-2000

Variable	Model 3: All Fatal MIDs	Model 4: Fatal Terr. MIDs Only	Model 4a: Restricted Model 4	Model 4b: Restricted Model 4
Territorial Dispute	1.613*** (.304)			
Strategic Terr. Dispute		-.109 (.599)		-.124 (.583)
Economic Terr. Dispute		1.541** (.863)	1.524** (.845)	2.254*** (.511)
Ethnic Terr. Dispute		1.058 (.845)	1.050 (.822)	
Ordinary Violent Transfer	.800** (.357)	.917** (.528)	.921** (.525)	.969** (.537)
Overwhelming Victory Transfer	.896** (.437)	.499 (.641)	.460 (.730)	.492 (.613)
Power Advantage	.043 (.059)	.111 (.114)	.108 (.113)	.101 (.112)
Allies	-.624** (.284)	-.281 (.446)	-.285 (.445)	-.530* (.407)
Dyadic Democracy	.072 (.323)	.532 (.458)	.524 (.459)	.541 (.411)
Distance	-.497*** (.109)	-.283** (.128)	-.291** (.122)	-.312*** (.128)
New Leader	.314 (.270)	.768** (.418)	.764** (.420)	.800** (.418)
Territorial Loser	-.309 (.267)	.057 (.423)	.066 (.418)	.064 (.416)
χ^2	176.61***	114.43***	102.53***	96.15***
N	5331	5331	5331	5331

Notes: Cell entries report coefficients and robust standard errors (in parentheses). Unit of analysis is a directed dyad-year. Each dyad is composed of a losing and a gaining state. MID = militarized interstate dispute. Peaceful transfers are the baseline against which violent and overwhelming victory transfer processes are compared. All significance levels are one-tailed: *** $p < .01$; ** $p < .05$; * $p < .10$.

and that data limitations forced me not to include indicators of intangible value such as religious and ancestral value. A future study coming on the heels of a major data-collecting effort could attempt to correct this omission.

While the particularly strong finding for economically-based territorial disputes compares well with the realist view of territory, it also runs counter not only to the above-discussed value-as-meaning school of thought but also to the arguments made by Brooks (1999). He argues that technological innovations in trade, shipping, resource extraction, ease of foreign direct investments, etc. have overcome the need to conquer economically valuable territories. Yet, he may be overlooking the fact that sovereign control of territory can lead to a more effective extraction of resources than trading could accomplish (Liberman 1996). That is, territorial control is the only policy alternative that grants full access to the land in question. Other policies provide no or at best only a partial control over the valuable land; consequently, preferences and whims of parties controlling the land have to be taken into consideration.[3]

Theoretical arguments aside, the above-presented result is quite robust. In comparing the results to those presented in Tir (2001, 2003a, 2003b), it becomes clear that the finding is not sensitive to dependent variable operationalization (i.e. fatal vs. all MIDs), time frame (i.e. whether the post-Cold War era is included), or theoretical specification (i.e. whether the willingness to fight presented by the disputed land's value and opportunity given by the relative power are treated additively or interactively as jointly necessary conditions).

Part II: Transfer Process

I turn next to the results pertaining to the second part of the model. Recall from Chapter 2 that I focus on three primary processes—peaceful, ordinary violent (short of an overwhelming victory), and overwhelming victory—each of which constrains the leaders of gaining and losing states against relying on militarized conflict to a different degree. The leaders of both states are for most part constrained against using their military forces to revisit the outcome of a peaceful transfer. There are costs that arise from reneging on the associated peaceful transfer agreement, which would damage the country's international reputation, make other countries more reluctant to cooperate on issues such as trade, reduce aid inflows, weaken security guarantees, etc. The prospects of the population backlash and related loss of benefits deter the leader from using military force. Similarly, after a transfer induced by an overwhelming victory, the constituents may be unwilling to support their leaders in the decision to engage in militarized conflict. Through the overwhelming victory, the gaining country was able to take all the land it wanted from the loser. After the transfer, the leader contemplating the reliance on militarized conflict to extend the territorial gains even further is likely to be perceived as acting for his/her own benefit rather than the country's. In the losing country, the constituents have simply grown tired of fighting and want peace. In contrast, the countries' leaders are least constrained when trying to take militarized action to revisit the outcome of a violent (but short of overwhelming victory) transfer. In the losing state, the leader can rally the people against the gaining state by claiming that the loss of land was unjust and that this injustice needs to be corrected. For the gaining state, it is possible that its victory was incomplete. Its leader can capitalize on the selectorate's desire to take even more of the loser's land. Hypotheses H-3 and H-4 formally differentiate between the consequences of peaceful vs. violent and overwhelming victory vs. violent processes, respectively (see Table 2.1).

In terms of the analysis, note that one of the three dichotomous process variables has to be omitted from the statistical models. The omitted process acts as the baseline against which the other two processes are judged. In Tables 4.4 and 4.5, the peaceful transfer variable is omitted, so the violent and overwhelming victory transfers' impacts on subsequent fatal militarized conflict are compared to that of peaceful transfers. A different baseline is presented below.

The results in Tables 4.4 and 4.5 for the process variables are, generally speaking, consistent across the tables. In both tables, the coefficient for the violent transfer is significant and positive. The finding shows that violent transfers significantly increase the probability of post-transfer fatal MIDs, as compared to peaceful transfers. The finding is quite robust as it holds across different operationalizations of the dependent variable (i.e. MID involvement, territorial MID involvement, MID initiation, and territorial MID initiation) and is not sensitive to the inclusion and exclusion of various territorial dispute dimensions. The results thus strongly support hypothesis H-3 and related theorizing, which states that peaceful transfers constrain the leaders against militarized conflict more so than do ordinary violent transfers.

In terms of the substantive impact of the violent process coefficients, in all the Models they are of lower magnitude than their (economic and ethnic) territorial dispute counterparts. For example, according to Model 1, the hazard to peace posed by a territorial dispute is 183 percent greater than the hazard posed by a violent (as opposed to a peaceful) transfer that left no territorial dispute behind; for Model 3, the gap is somewhat smaller but still respectable 102 percent. Turning to specific territorial dispute types, the hazard rates posed by the presence of an economically-based territorial dispute are 59 percent (Model 2) and 68 percent (Model 3) greater. Clearly, the unresolved (economic) territorial dispute has a much more dire impact than does violent vs. peaceful process. That is, while peaceful (vs. violent) transfers are clearly beneficial to dyadic peace, this benefit is undermined by unresolved border issues. In terms of the theoretical model, this means that the payoff to the leader from using military force to acquire (economically) disputed land is greater than the costs he/she will incur for attempting to undo a peacefully- (as opposed to a violently-) performed transfer.

As far as the overwhelming victory transfers are concerned, the coefficient's significance level is below the acceptable range in all of the Models presented in Table 4.4. The related marginal effect is one-quarter to one-third of the size of the violent process coefficient. In terms of the expectations, the insignificance of the overwhelming victory coefficient is actually good news. It means that there is no great difference in the impact of peaceful and overwhelming victory transfers, so both act restrictively against future militarized conflict. This initial result is consistent with Vasquez (1993; see also Maoz 1984) who expects peaceful loser-gainer relations to follow from overwhelming victories that have prompted territorial transfers.

Despite the evidence presented so far, it may be premature to conclude at this point that overwhelming victory transfers are as beneficial as peaceful transfers. Note that the overwhelming victory coefficient—despite being insignificant—is still positive, meaning that peaceful transfers are at least somewhat better. Turning to the directed analyses in Table 4.5 reveals that the impact gap between the overwhelming victory and violent coefficients shrinks in Models 4-4b. This suggests that overwhelming transfers are moving away from peaceful and toward violent transfers in terms of the aftermath they produce. Even more concerning is the result in Model 3, which not only shows a significant difference between overwhelming and peaceful transfers, but also gives the former set a small edge (12 percent) in terms of the impact on the hazard rate in comparison to the violent transfer coefficient. Therefore, though the majority of evidence points toward some benefit of overwhelming victory transfers, we should be careful not to conclude that their consequences are as desirable as those of peaceful transfers.

Moreover, because I found both that peaceful transfers are significantly better than their violent counterparts and because overwhelming victory transfers are a bit—although not significantly—worse than peaceful transfers in seven out of eight tests reported, I also need to check if overwhelming victory transfers are significantly better than ordinary violent transfers. It is possible that overwhelming victory transfers fall in between peaceful and ordinary violent transfers in their impact on future militarized conflict and that they are indistinguishable from both extremes. In other words, hypothesis H-4, which differentiates between overwhelming victory and ordinary violent transfers, needs to be evaluated.

Table 4.6 re-estimates the main models from Tables 4.4 and 4.5 with overwhelming victory transfers as the baseline, to reveal the difference, if any, between the impacts of ordinary violent and overwhelming victory transfers.[4] The statistics for the overall models and for all the territorial dispute and control variables are identical to those reported in Tables 4.4 and 4.5, so, to avoid repetition, they are not discussed here. In three of the four analyses reported, the violent transfer coefficient has a positive sign. Yet, in only one of the tests (Model 2) is there a significant difference between violent and overwhelming victory transfers and even in this case the difference is significant only by the weakest of standards. The majority of the evidence hence suggests that while the relationship expressed in hypothesis H-4 is present, it is not nearly strong enough to meet criteria of statistical significance and robustness. Substantively, overwhelming victory transfer process falls in between its peaceful and violent counterparts and is not clearly distinguishable from either extreme. Maoz's (1984)

Table 4.6: Re-Analysis of Fatal Post-Transfer Militarized Conflict Involvement and Initiation Using Overwhelming Victory Transfers as the Process Baseline, 1900-2000

Variable	Model 1: All Fatal MIDs	Model 2: Fatal Terr. MIDs Only	Model 3: All Fatal MIDs	Model 4: Fatal Terr. MIDs Only
Territorial Dispute	1.974*** (.399)		1.613*** (.304)	
Strategic Terr. Dispute		.176 (.415)		-.109 (.599)
Economic Terr. Dispute		1.612** (.820)		1.541** (.863)
Ethnic Terr. Dispute		1.135** (.681)		1.058 (.845)
Ordinary Violent Transfer	.521 (.431)	.768* (.547)	-.096 (.292)	.419 (.553)
Peaceful Transfer	-.178 (.467)	-.244 (.608)	-.896** (.437)	-.499 (.641)
Relative Power	-.066 (.106)	.171* (.121)	.043 (.059)	.111 (.114)
Allies	-.047 (.266)	.124 (.386)	-.624** (.284)	-.281 (.446)
Dyadic Democracy	-.199 (.339)	.058 (.411)	.072 (.323)	.532 (.458)
Distance	-.194* (.126)	-.365*** (.100)	-.497*** (.109)	-.283** (.128)
New Leader			.314 (.270)	.768** (.418)
Territorial Loser			-.309 (.267)	.057 (.423)
χ^2	51.38***	82.97***	176.61***	114.43***
N	3972	3972	5331	5331

Notes: Cell entries report coefficients and robust standard errors (in parentheses). Unit of analysis is a non-directed dyad year in the armed conflict involvement Models 1 and 2 and a directed dyad-year in the armed conflict initiation Models 3-4. Each dyad is composed of a losing and a gaining state. MID = militarized interstate dispute. All significance levels are one-tailed: *** p < .01; ** p < .05; * p < .10.

and Vasquez's (1993) arguments that post-armed conflict imposed peace is more stable than peace that is arrived through by a compromise between the warring parties finds some weak support in the context of post-transfer relations.

The clear portion of the process finding concerns the relative benefit of peaceful over ordinary violent transfers. This is consistent with cases such as Israel-Egypt vis-à-vis India-Pakistan. The peaceful transfer of Sinai from Israeli to Egyptian control in 1979 has not been followed by major confrontations over that land: Israel has not tried to retake Sinai and Egypt has not used military force to acquire even more land (e.g. the Gaza Strip, which used to be under Egyptian control) from Israel. In contrast to this relatively peaceful outcome, consider the India-Pakistan dispute over Kashmir. The violent movement of the border in Kashmir has only encouraged India and Pakistan to pursue further territorial revisions. Indeed, armed confrontations over the boundary have been a regular occurrence.

The finding that peaceful transfers are better for post-transfer relations than their violent counterparts not only confirms the related theoretical expectation, but also provides an important piece of evidence for the research on this topic in general. No prior work outside this project has shown the empirical existence of this relationship. As a matter of fact, Goertz and Diehl (1992)—contrary to their expectations—found that there was no notable difference in terms of future militarized conflict between violent and peaceful processes. Therefore, we now have evidence supporting a widely-held expectation that peaceful transfers are followed by peaceful gainer-loser relations more so than are violent transfers. Note also that the result is quite robust. In tests that use both fatal and non-fatal MIDs and cover a somewhat different time frame, this finding did not change (see Tir 2001, 2003a, 2003b for comparison).

The success in this study may be due to the fact that, in a significant departure form Goertz and Diehl (1992), I divided violent transfers according to whether they involved overwhelming victories. I did this so based on research suggesting that armed conflicts ending in decisive and imposed outcomes are more conducive to future peace than are conflicts ending in other circumstances (e.g. Vasquez 1993; Maoz 1984). Not finding a clear differences between overwhelming victory, on the one hand, and peaceful and violent processes, on the other, suggests that separating out the overwhelming victory transfers may be helpful in making the difference between the peaceful and ordinary violent transfers discernible. That is, the failure to account for overwhelming victory transfers' "fuzzy borders" may have blurred the difference between peaceful and violent processes for Goertz and Diehl.

More broadly, the overwhelming victory results fall somewhere in between the peace by empire (Aron 1966; Maoz 1984) and temporal diffusion of conflict literatures (e.g. Goldstein and Freeman 1990; Rajmaira and Ward 1990; Starr and Most 1983; Kirby and Ward 1987). Consistently with the former school of thought, I find a somewhat reduced likelihood that foes will fight after transfers prompted by decisive victories. Yet, consistently with the latter school of thought, I also find that overwhelming victory (i.e. forceful) transfers are somewhat more likely to be followed by militarized conflict than are peacefully conducted transfers. I now turn to the discussion of the findings for the control variables.

Control Variables

The controls are added to the two parts of the model to ensure that the findings are not spurious and driven by factors unrelated to territorial changes, but which are commonly associated with armed conflict onset in the literature. Tables 4.4 and 4.5 reveal that as a group the control variables do not perform as well as the key explanatory variables in the post-transfer context. The only consistent exception is the effect of proximity, which shows that that the willingness to fight for disputed land drops with distance. In most of the tests reported in Table 4.5, the leadership variable is positive and significant, revealing that new leaders are indeed less constrained against using military force to challenge the outcome of the transfer that was prompted by, agreed to, or forced onto someone else. In contrast, the relative power, dyadic democracy, and alliance coefficients are at best weakly and occasionally significant. In a sense, these findings resemble the contradictory arguments over whether power balance or preponderance is best equipped to keep peace, over whether allies are more or less likely to fight one another (e.g. Maoz 2000), and Huth and Allee's (2002; see also Hensel 2001) finding that there are limits to the democratic peace in the territorial dispute context. Importantly, these weak and non-robust findings imply that the common conflict management techniques lose much of their effect in the aftermath of territorial transfers. This makes it all the more crucial to conduct transfers "correctly," that is peacefully and with an eye on the potential post-transfer territorial disputes. If these are not handled appropriately, there is little hope that other factors will keep the participant countries from fighting over the altered boundary.

Finally, I investigate whether the prospect theory-based expectation that the states losing land via the transfer will be more likely to initiate militarized conflict to further adjust the boundary. The related argument maintains that—all other things being equal—the leader of the losing state will be more likely to risk engaging in militarized conflict because his/her country is operating in the domain of losses. Yet, Table 4.5 results reveal that the prospect theory-based interpretation finds little support. The reason may be that the gaining state operates in the domain of losses too. It is possible that its constituents and leader see the disputed land still controlled by the loser as rightfully theirs. The inability to control the land is thus interpreted as a loss that took place some time ago. Both states may therefore have a similar psychological perspective toward desired lands controlled by the foe.

An implication of this negative finding for this study is that both parties pursue disputed lands with roughly equal degrees of zeal. This supports the arguments presented in the theoretical model, which treated both the gaining and losing sides as potential perpetrators of post-transfer armed conflict. In contrast, Goertz and Diehl's (1992) primary focus was on the loser and armed conflict over the land that changed owners. Yet, because a transfer does not necessarily give the gainer all of the land it wanted, the loser is not the only party with post-transfer armed conflict on its mind. The finding that the losing countries are no more prone to initiate post-transfer militarized conflict serves as evidence that the gainer's unfulfilled territorial ambitions cannot be dismissed. Further evidence showing statistically that the loser's and gainer's behavior mirrors each other can be found in Tir (2001, 2003a, 2003b).

Conclusions and Implications

This chapter has provided two related sets of findings. The first has been to assess empirically the extent to which transfers are able to resolve territorial disputes that motivated border movement and to determine what kind of danger the remaining disputes pose to the future peace between the states gaining and losing land. The answer to the former query has been that most transfers leave behind territorial disputes. After the transfer, the original territorial dispute is either not resolved or replaced by a new one in about 59 percent of the cases. Still, a success rate of about 41 percent is encouraging, given the reports that territorial disputes are often intractable and difficult—if not impossible—to resolve. Turning to the more encouraging news, the unresolved border problems are unlikely to pose an unusually widespread threat to peace. In fact, only one-quarter of disputed, transfer-adjusted borders are fought over. When these figures are disaggregated into yearly averages, however, we see that those dyads that fight do so at such explosive rates that they vault the entire post-transfer average to well above the "normal" levels.

The second goal of the chapter has dealt with the question of what accounts for why some losing and gaining states fight over their adjusted borders while others do not; that is; why do some transfers end up as successes while others are failures? Following the theoretical model developed in Chapter 2, I have focused on two potential determinants: the presence and nature of post-transfer territorial disputes and transfer process. One of the insights obtained has been that post-transfer relations are to a large extent dominated by the factors associated with transfers and that the standard conflict-reduction approaches (e.g. relative power distribution, security ties, etc.) are not all that helpful. This means that policymakers must pay strict attention to the transfer's circumstances and, if they are interested in promoting future peace, take a more proactive approach.

The following approaches can be used. First, policymakers should recognize not only that transfer-related territorial disputes are dangerous, but also that some of them are more salient than others. Changing the location of the boundary with an eye toward resolving economically- (and to a lesser extent ethnically-) based territorial disputes can help; in contrast, strategically-based disputes are of minor concern. Second, whenever possible, transfers should be performed peacefully. Peaceful, agreed-upon transfers create disincentives against the future reliance on militarized conflict, through reputational and loss-of-side-benefits costs. In contrast, violent transfers make future fighting more likely by promoting suspicion and mistrust and by placing leaders who tend to rely on the uses of military force to deal with problems to positions of power. Given that few states willingly give up land, the central question then becomes how a transfer can occur before the disagreements over land control between two states escalate to the point of armed conflict. Even though answering this question is beyond the scope of this work, some preliminary insights are provided. The key may lie in early and proactive international involvement, as, for example, described in Lund's (1996) approach to preventive diplomacy or Burton's (1990) advocacy of conflict "provention." This can be done by offering mediation efforts, putting pressure on the adversaries to work their problems out peacefully, and, more generally, by trying to deal with root causes of conflict before they produce escalation to violence. Future research should investigate how much pressure international actors can put on the disputants in order to secure a peaceful transfer. If a genuinely peaceful border movement cannot be achieved, does a pressured, but still peaceful border alteration set the stage for peaceful relations in the future?

Policy Application Example: Albania vs. Macedonia

The following illustration does not necessarily advocate the territorial transfer discussed, but rather offers ideas about why and how the countries involved may pursue the transfer and, most importantly, what consequences they are likely to encounter. The discussion, in other words, points out the issues on which peace-making efforts should focus. For the past several years, the country of Macedonia has been teetering on the brink of civil war. The cause of the unrest is the friction between the majority Macedonian and minority Albanian populations within Macedonia. The more moderate Albanians have been asking for a notable degree of autonomy while the more hard-line leaders have been demanding the transfer of Macedonia's northwestern territory to the country of Albania. The land in question is almost solidly populated by Albanians, who constitute about one quarter of Macedonia's population. Even though the official policy of the Albanian government has not supported the hard-line agenda yet, extremist elements within Albania have been repeatedly asking for the land in the past as a part of the Greater Albania program. At the time of this writing, the situation in Macedonia seems to be in somewhat of a limbo. On the positive side, the passage of the decentralization law, which grants a greater degree of self-rule to regional government units, seems to have distanced the country from the brink of civil war and led to a stabilization of the situation for the time being. Though favored by the Albanian minority, the full implementation of the law has been stalled by the ethnic Macedonian resistance—which is worried about the loss of power for Macedonians in what they perceive to be their own country and which resents the related policy that gives amnesty to former Albanian fighters—and by Macedonian and some ethnic Albanian politicians whose positions of power would be reduced or eliminated by the resultant changes. The changes thus remain highly controversial and there is fear that the stalled reforms will test the patience of the former Albanian fighters who have laid down their arms and play into the hands of Albanian hard-liners, who argue that the self-rule laws do not go far enough. From the international standpoint, which is of course the focus of this project, if the situation in Macedonia worsens, there is a real risk that the Macedonian-Albanian relations may worsen too, to the point of armed intervention and war between the two countries. That is, if the Albanian minority in Macedonia comes under threat from majority Macedonians—and regardless of which side would actually initiate the inter-ethnic conflict—the Albanian government will have an incentive to intervene militarily in order to protect its ethnic brethren. This outcome would inevitably be detrimental not only to the two countries but potentially to the entire region.

One of the ways to deal with this problem—a full-fledged territorial dispute in the making—is for Macedonia to give up the northwestern portion of the country to Albania. This move would by and large satisfy the desires of irredentist Albanians and keep the countries of Albania and Macedonia from fighting one another. Therefore, the Albanian side would accomplish its main goal and would have little reason to press Macedonia for future territorial concessions. The territorial loser—Macedonia—could be persuaded to give up the land for the following reasons. One, although Macedonia would become smaller, it would also become more ethnically uniform, a concern important to the hard-line element of the Macedonian population. Two, the idea of the Macedonian country would be more easily protected with the transfer in place. Due to differing rates of population growth, ethnic Macedonians are concerned that their country will be overrun by ethnic Albanians over time. Given the differential population growth rates and no transfer, the percentage of Albanians within Macedonia would continue to rise. As a result, Albanians would be likely to move within Macedonia and settle across the country. With the transfer in place, the Albanian population would more likely stay in the (now greater) Albania proper. The Macedonian government could then act restrictively against immigration requests. Three, the transfer-related stabilization would likely increase Macedonia's prospects for economic prosperity. As a landlocked country, Macedonia needs sea access for its commerce, but disputes over the name Macedonia have strained relations with Greece, its "natural" outlet to the sea. Improved relations with Albania would offer an alternative sea access route. The plans to build highway, rail, and oil pipeline routes connecting the Black and Adriatic Seas that bypass the Istanbul shipping chokepoint could be implemented, providing a real boon to Macedonian economic development. Currently, implementation of these plans remains remote as prospective investors are reluctant to sink their resources into a region with an uncertain future. An accord allowing Macedonia access to the sea via Albania could be made one of the conditions of the land transfer.

I identify next the conditions that would maximize the chances for future peace based on my findings. According to the results, the chances for future peace would increase if the transfer were to take place peacefully, before domestic-level, inter-ethnic Albanian-Macedonian violence spins out of control to the point where the two countries become involved with one another militarily. If the transfer is either imposed on Macedonia after an Albanian victory or agreed to by Macedonia as a part of the war-ending treaty, the chances for post-transfer peace would be reduced. The results also suggest that one should pay attention to territorial disputes the transfer is likely to create or leave behind. From the standpoint of ethnically-based territorial disputes, there are some Albanians scattered throughout Macedonia and likewise there are some Macedonians in the territory that would be transferred; in neither case would the numbers be all that large. Furthermore, the findings suggest that the ethnic minority issue would be of secondary importance in driving Albania and Macedonia toward armed territorial conflicts with one another after the transfer. Forceful territorial revisions are most likely to offer payoffs to opportunistic leaders if they are based on the economic impetus. Yet, fortunately, the potential post-transfer economically-based territorial disputes between the two countries should be nonexistent, from either country's perspective. The land to be transferred is poor, underdeveloped, and thus economically not all that significant; moreover, the Greater Albania program has not expressed any interest in Macedonian lands beyond the northwestern section of the country. In terms of strategically important lands, Albania similarly places no such value on any of the remaining Macedonian territory. From the Macedonian perspective, however, the to-be lost territory has strategic importance, as the transfer would push the Albanian border near the capital city of Skopje. Even though the findings suggest that strategic concerns are unlikely to lead to serious militarized confrontations, it is understandable that they might make Macedonians feel vulnerable. To address this concern—and this is another reason to conduct the transfer peacefully so that Macedonians can bargain for this condition—the transferred territory could be demilitarized; Skopje would thus not have to face imminent military threat.

In sum, though giving up land peacefully and willingly is a difficult and distasteful choice for any country, in this case the promises of future stability, peace, and economic prosperity offer tangible benefits to the territorial loser that may make the tradeoff worth while. Not doing so would of course allow Macedonia to retain the lands it presently controls, but this may come at the expense of peace and prosperity for the state of Macedonia. Over the long run, the retention of the disputed land may cost Macedonia significantly more than giving the land up to Albania.

Notes

1. For instance, economically valuable areas are often centers of human activity. It would therefore make sense that a state controlling such an area would have a portion of

its population living there. If such an area is lost at some point in time, both the economically valued land and some of the ethnic kin would become a part of another state. The loser would hence have both an economic and "ethnic" motivation to re-take such land. Other combinations of value-dimensions are certainly possible and similar scenarios could apply to gaining states as well.

2. As their indicators of intangible value, Goertz and Diehl use the transferred land's non-colonial status and the distance between "homeland" and the land in question—which is zero in just about every case of non-colonial territory. Moreover, colonial lands are more likely to be perceived as simple pieces of property (they matter for their economic value), so no emotional attachment to these lands is likely to exist. Thus, the colonial territorial disputes may be the wrong cases to rely on when testing for the importance of intangibly-valued lands. Yet, see also the note discussing colonial lands at the beginning of Chapter 3.

3. Although one could argue that this study's temporal span is too broad to capture the effect of technological innovations that have taken place only in the past few decades, the reader should note that—because the transfers' aftermath is tracked toward the present time—the proportion of more recent observations is actually relatively high. The median year in the transfers data set is 1968.

4. Reporting the results for the third baseline (i.e. ordinary violent transfers) would be redundant. The other two baselines provide all the necessary information to compare the three processes.

Chapter 5

Aftermath of Secessions

Much like the previous chapter did for state-to-state territorial transfers, this chapter evaluates empirically the territorial aftermath of secessions. I first examine the secessions' ability to resolve the original, domestic-level territorial disputes and the extent to which the remaining disputes pose a threat to peace between rump and secessionist states. In addition to these descriptive analyses, in the second segment of the chapter I assess the relevance of the hypothesized causal links between the remaining territorial disputes and secession process on the one hand and militarized conflict over the new boundaries on the other. Per the arguments developed in Chapter 2 that were used to develop the theoretical model, these factors should help explain why some rump and secessionist states fight over their borders after the secession while the others do not. The final portion of the chapter summarizes the findings for the two sets of empirical analyses and relates their implications to a currently-relevant case; this is done in order to illustrate how the insights developed in this work may be used to prevent future armed conflicts over secession-created boundaries.

Descriptive Results

Table 5.1 provides assessments of secessions' performance from the territorial dispute and militarized territorial conflict perspectives; a dyad formed by the rump and secessionist or two secessionist states is the unit of analysis. The top portion of the table evaluates how often secessions succeed in resolving the domestic-level territorial dispute that prompted the division of the country. Of the sixty-six politically relevant dyads (PRDs) that are produced by secessions, fifty-eight (or 88 percent) experience territorial disputes. Thus, in a great majority of cases, the secession simply transforms the dispute from the domestic to international level. On the positive side, the finding means that secessions resolve the initial, domestic-level territorial dispute in about 12 percent of the cases. Though this percentage is not all that high, secessions can be seen as somewhat helpful given that much of the territorial conflict research notes that territorial disputes tend to be long-lasting and quite difficult to resolve (e.g. Huth 1996; Vasquez 1993; Allcock 1992). Nevertheless, the percentage of cases with territorial disputes is high in comparison to Huth's (1996) finding that territorial disputes occur at a general rate of about 33 percent. Yet, because Huth's sample includes many dyads that did not have a territorial dispute in the first place, his study does not really provide an ideal benchmark against which secessions' territorial dispute managing potential could be measured. In sum, secessions can be seen as able to resolve some—but not the great majority—of the territorial disputes that prompted state breakups.

Table 5.1: Gauging the Effectiveness of Secessions, 1900-2000

Is secession followed by a territorial dispute?	No	8 (12 percent)
	Yes	58 (88 percent)
	Total Dyads	66
Given that secession is followed by a territorial dispute, does the dispute escalate to a fatal territorial MID?	No	44 (76 percent)
	Yes	14 (24 percent)
	Total Dyads	58

Notes: Unit of analysis is a dyad composed of rump and secessionist or two secessionist countries. MID = militarized interstate dispute

Another way of gauging secession's effectiveness is to ask to what extent the unresolved territorial disputes are a threat to dyadic peace? That is, is the leaders' proneness to claim other state's land matched by their resolve to engage in militarized conflict over the disputed territory? The bottom part of Table 5.1 reports the conditional probability that secessionist dyads experience at least one fatal militarized interstate dispute (MID) over territory given that they are engaged in a territorial dispute with one another. As the result shows, only fourteen (24 percent) of the dyads embroiled in territorial disputes actually experience fatal militarized conflict over land. That is, escalation from territorial disputes to militarized conflict is far from inevitable and is limited to fewer than one-quarter of the cases. And overall, this means that just over one-fifth (21 percent, 14/66) of the new boundaries are both disputed and fought over.

Figure 5.1 illustrates the temporal distribution of secession failures. It tracks the portion of secessionist dyads that have experienced at least one fatal territorial MID over time since the relevant secession. The figure reveals that most armed conflicts occur in the first few years. A notably smaller number of secessionist pairs start to fight between this time and the twentieth year. After this time point, the situation stabilizes: no previously peaceful dyads experience fatal territorial conflicts. Substantively, this means that the first few years after the secession are crucial in terms of whether the particular secession-created border will be fought over. Fighting over the previously peaceful border is unusual after the fifth year and highly unlikely after the twentieth year. The implication is that as the time passes the new boundaries tend to become accepted by the population, making it less profitable for the leader to challenge these entrenched boundaries.

Figure 5.1: Cumulative Portion of PRDs that Experience Fatal Territorial MIDs after Secessions, 1900-2000

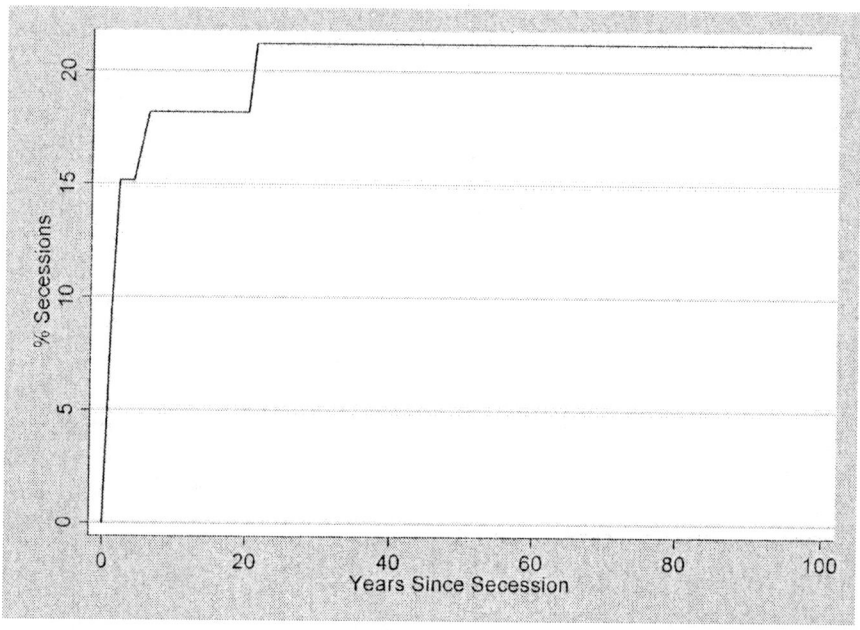

To put the above findings into a bit of a perspective, I investigate how the secessionist dyad's proneness to experience militarized conflict compares with the experience of other states. To do this, I calculate the average yearly rate of fatal territorial MID onset for politically relevant secessionist dyads and compare it to the average for all countries calculated in Chapter 3 (.011); doing this also takes into account the fact that some dyads experience more than one militarized conflict and that some secessionist dyads have existed longer than others.

The post-secession fatal territorial MID rate (.030, s.d. = .170, n = 1,579) is 172 percent higher and significantly different (p < . 00) than the "normal" frequency. The comparison reveals that although more than three-quarters (79 percent) of secessionist dyads do not fight over territorial issues after the secession, the ones that do fight at such explosive rates that they increase the average for the entire group to well above the "normal" frequency. The reader should keep in mind, however, that the "normal" countries did not necessarily have a territorial dispute between them that they were trying to resolve. Moreover, the finding that 79 percent of all secessionist dyads experience no fatal territorial MIDs whatsoever should help dispel the notion that all—or even nearly all—post-secession situations are extremely conflict prone.

In sum, the first set of findings shows that while secessions fail to resolve a great majority of underlying, domestic-level territorial disputes, the unusually grave threat to peace is limited to a relatively small subset of cases. Secession's opponents are thus correct in their argument that secessions are likely to leave behind international-level territorial disputes. Yet, the claim that this creates widespread problems is not supported by the empirical evidence.

Next, I revisit some of the above analyses by considering the type of territorial dispute secessions leave behind. In linking territorial disputes with armed conflict, the related research points out that not all pieces of land are equally valuable. This is an important issue to consider because the types of territorial disputes secessions leave behind may impact the likelihood that rump and secessionist states fight over the new borders; that is, the issue has a bearing on secessions' success. Recall that in Chapter 2 land value was divided into the tangible and intangible dimensions (Newman 1999). In a ceaselessly competitive, zero-sum world of realism, possession of tangibly-valuable lands will not only be desirable but contested militarily. In this view, secessions will generally not be able to resolve such disputes and the ones that leave behind strategically- and/or economically-based territorial disputes will likely be followed by militarized confrontations. In contrast, others argue that the failure to control intangibly-valued land is expected to intensify the willingness to fight more so than the failure to control tangibly-valued land (Goertz and Diehl 1992; Diehl 1999b; Vasquez 1983; Touval 1972; Huth 1996). This is so because the lands valued along the intangible dimension are perceived as personal, indivisible, and unsubstitutable (Gottman 1973; Sack 1986). Weighing in on this debate is the ethnic conflict literature, which by and large takes the anti-realist position. It argues that rump and secessionist states are likely to push for violent border revisions because it is impossible for the secession to create ethnically homogeneous states. Yet, this logic entails at least two shortcomings. The ethnic territorial dispute issue is assumed to both exist in every case and be the sufficient cause of militarized conflict. Are all—or nearly all—secessions indeed likely to create ethnically-based territorial disputes? Are these disputes near guarantees that the rump and secessionist states will fight one another over their newly-created borders? How common are economically- and strategically-based territorial disputes and how much of a danger do they pose? I now turn to answering these questions.

Table 5.2: Secession Effectiveness by Territorial Dispute Type, 1900-2000

		Strategic Territorial Dispute	Economic Territorial Dispute	Ethnic Territorial Dispute
Is secession fol-lowed by a specific type of territorial dispute?	No	43 (65 percent)	51 (48 percent)	13 (20 percent)
	Yes	23 (35 percent)	34 (52 percent)	53 (80 percent)
	Total Dyads	66	66	66
Given that secession is followed by a territorial dispute, does the dispute escalate to a fatal territorial MID?	No	16 (70 percent)	24 (71 percent)	39 (74 percent)
	Yes	7 (30 percent)	10 (29 percent)	14 (26 percent)
	Total Dyads	23	34	53

Notes: Unit of analysis is a dyad composed of rump and secessionist or two secessionist countries. MID = militarized interstate dispute.

Table 5.2 reports the results for two analyses. The top analysis breaks down post-secession territorial disputes by type. Secessions are most likely to create dyads whose members disagree about the location of their border based on cross-border ethnic ties; such disputes are present in fifty-three (or 80 percent) of the dyads. Comparatively smaller subsets of post-secessionist dyads experience territorial disputes along the tangible—thirty-four or 52 percent for economic and twenty-three or 35 percent for strategic—dimension of land value. Therefore, the attempts to resolve domestic-level territorial disputes via secession run into difficulty in dividing the territory along both the tangible and, in particular, intangible dimensions of land value. Yet, note that much like in Chapter 4, strategic territorial disputes are the least common type—which is consistent with the argument that twentieth century technological advancements in weaponry, surveillance techniques, speed of troop and equipment movement, etc. have been undermining the strategic importance of territory (e.g. Keohane and Nye 1977; Rosecrance 1986; Brooks 1999).

In comparison, Huth (1996) observes that ethnically-based territorial disputes between bordering states are the rarest of the three types, occurring at the rate of about 20 percent. The comparison suggests that secessions are abnormal not only in the number but also in the type of territorial disputes they produce. Moreover, the large percentage of dyads with ethnically-based territorial disputes and the fact that these are the most common type of post-secession territorial disputes support the secession opponents' argument that secession-created borders are unlikely to cleanly separate ethnic groups into rump and secessionist states. Nevertheless, the opponents' claim that all—or nearly all—of the cases will be problematic is a bit of an exaggeration, as about 20 percent of secession-created borders are free from ethnically-based territorial disputes.

The bottom portion of Table 5.2 reports the conditional probabilities that a particular type of post-secessionist territorial dispute escalates into at least one fatal territorial MID. A more consistent set of results emerges here: all three territorial dispute types are relatively similar in their escalation likelihood. Although ethnically-based territorial disputes are the most common, their probability of escalation is the lowest (26 percent). The strategically-based territorial disputes, which are by contrast least frequent, have the highest escalation likelihood (31 percent). Notably, these percentages are far below the figure Huth (1996) reports for all bordering countries, but this is not all that surprising as he includes non-fatal MIDs in his study; he also finds that military force is most likely to be used to deal with strategically-based territorial disputes, in about two-thirds of the cases he scrutinizes.

In terms of theoretical implications, the escalation analysis suggests no great differences in the proclivity of various types of territorial disputes to spiral into militarized conflict. That is, this analysis leaves open the tangibility vs. intangibility debate in the post-secession context. Concerning the ethnic conflict literature, the analysis shows that the ethnically-based territorial dispute is far from being a sufficient cause of post-secession armed territorial conflict. In fact, the odds are almost three-quarters that such a dispute will *not* entail fatal militarized conflict. So, again, the fears of secession's opponents—and even of those proponents who advocate population transfers—that secessions automatically lead to future armed conflict via ethnically-based territorial disputes appear to be overstated. These fears seem to be a result of an excessive focus on the cases of secession failure; balancing the cases of failure with successes provides a different, and to some extent a more optimistic, picture about secessions.

Before dealing with the causal analyses, I investigate the ability of the secession process to resolve the original domestic-level territorial dispute. Chapter 2 presented arguments maintaining that peaceful secessions have a greater potential to resolve the underlying territorial disputes than violent secessions. Do these arguments elicit empirical support? Table 5.3 reveals that peaceful secessions have a somewhat greater likelihood of creating borders acceptable to both rump and secessionist countries. The success rate of 18 percent suggests that the peaceful creation of international boundaries is by no means a foolproof measure for dealing with domestic-origin territorial disputes. The reason may be that in cases of peaceful secessions the land is divided between the rump and secessionist countries by utilizing old, internal administrative borders. Wanting to avoid opening the Pandora's box of territorial dispute issues, policymakers by and large avoid trying to devise more acceptable borders; this of course does not make the unresolved territorial issues disappear and the new boundaries are often questioned. Another related dynamic is that rump states generally try to minimize the loss of territory so they offer the secessionist states less land than they would like to receive. The secessionist states are generally willing to accept this compromise because they do not want to risk their main goal—which is statehood; instead, they tend to accept the boundary as a temporary solution, whose location they question once the statehood has been established. Nevertheless, peaceful secessions are still the more effective process for resolving domestic-level territorial disputes. The success rate for the violent process is a dismal 4 percent.

Table 5.3: Secession Effectiveness by Secession Process, 1900-2000

Process Type	Territorial Dispute Present?	All Territorial Dispute Types	Territorial Dispute Type		
			Strategic	Economic	Ethnic
Peaceful Secession	No	7 (18 percent)	26 (68 percent)	23 (61 percent)	8 (21 percent)
	Yes	31 (82 percent)	12 (32 percent)	15 (39 percent)	30 (79 percent)
	Total Dyads	38	38	38	38
Violent Secession	No	1 (4 percent)	17 (61 percent)	9 (32 percent)	5 (18 percent)
	Yes	27 (96 percent)	11 (39 percent)	19 (68 percent)	23 (82 percent)
	Total Dyads	28	28	28	28

Notes: The unit of analysis is a post-secession politically relevant dyad (PRD).

The process performance ranking holds when the post-secession territorial disputes are broken down by territorial dispute type. The peaceful secession's success rate "lead" shrinks, however, to mere 3 percent for ethnic territorial disputes, again revealing that secessions are most likely to be vexed by ethnic territorial distribution issues. For economic territorial disputes, the success rate gap actually increases to about 29 percent.

This brings to the perhaps more salient issue of whether the two processes also possess differing abilities to affect the leader's decision to rely on militarized conflict in order to revisit the secession-created boundary—as argued in the model presented in Chapter 2. For the answer to this question, I turn to the causal analyses results that put the hypotheses from the model to the test. Though insightful and informative, the above-discussed descriptive results regarding the proclivity to engage in militarized conflict may well be skewed because the territorial dispute, process, and control variable factors discussed in Chapters 2 and 3 were not simultaneously taken into account.

Causal Results

Part I: Post-Secession Territorial Disputes

Table 5.4 reports the results of non-directed analyses that focus on secessionist dyad members' proneness to become *involved* in fatal militarized conflict with each other after the breakup of their common state. In addition to the observation that all statistical models are highly significant, note that some of the territorial dispute variables that compose the theoretical model (see Chapter 2) are significant—even when controlling for correlates of armed conflict not directly related to secession (see Chapter 3). Statistical Model 1 presents the results necessary to evaluate hypothesis H-1. According to the theoretical model, the leader's primary motivation to use military force against the dyadic foe comes from territorial disputes secession leaves behind. Through the secession, the rump state has lost some of its territory to the secessionist state and it may want a portion or all of it back. Conversely, the secessionist state may not be satisfied with how much land it has received and may desire even more of the rump (or another secessionist) state's land. As can be seen in Model 1, the territorial dispute coefficient is significant and positive, providing support for hypothesis H-1. The relations between rump and secessionist states are therefore strongly influenced by the presence of unresolved border issues. The finding that the secessions' inability to resolve territorial dispute issues to the satisfaction of rump and secessionist states significantly increases the hazard of fatal MIDs helps extend the territorial dispute research (e.g. Huth 1996; Huth and Allee 2002; Vasquez 1993; Senese 2005; Senese and Vasquez 2003; Vasquez and Henehan 2001) into the post-secession context. The finding is consistent with, for example, the recent Ethiopia-Eritrea war, which was fought over the secession-created boundary separating the two countries.

To determine which aspects of territorial disputes are particularly problematic, the attention is directed to evaluating the empirical accuracy of hypothesis H-2. As the reader will recall, the disputed land may be valuable due to both its tangible (strategic, economic) and intangible (ethnic, religious, ancestral) characteristics. The theoretical model argues that intangibility should provide a greater payoff to the leader for engaging in militarized conflict, a position with which the realist scholars disagree. The initial descriptive tests in the preceding section failed to resolve the debate conclusively, but a clearer result may emerge once other influences are taken into account.

Table 5.4: Cox Regression Estimates of Fatal Post-Secession Militarized Conflict Involvement, 1900-2000

Variable	Model 1: All MIDs	Model 2: Territorial MIDs	Model 2a: All dyads	Model 2b: Contiguous dyads only	Model 2c: No Israel-Jordan
Territorial Dispute	2.973*** (.893)				
Strategic Terr. Dispute		-.784 (.641)	-.763 (.591)	-.643 (.502)	-.911 (.697)
Economic Terr. Dispute		.744* (.461)	.724* (.468)	.927** (.504)	.749* (.504)
Ethnic Terr. Dispute		2.847*** (.851)	2.927*** (.821)	3.569*** (1.333)	2.942*** (.906)
Violent Secession	3.404*** (1.048)	3.592*** (1.125)	3.745*** (1.712)	3.258*** (.941)	3.442*** (1.032)
Relative Power	-.243** (.125)	-.242* (.147)	-.225* (.149)	-.217* (.164)	-.265* (.199)
Allies	.189 (.290)	.411 (.323)	.430* (.328)	.545* (.347)	.362 (.332)
Dyadic Democracy	-.902 (.850)	-.866 (.846)	-.905 (.863)	-.991 (.847)	-1.106* (.835)
Contiguity	.597 (.978)	-.402 (1.000)	-.302 (1.173)		-.212 (1.154)
Secessionist-Only Dyad	-1.106** (.462)	-.850** (.510)	-.936** (.501)	-.924** (.550)	-.792* (.547)
Soviet Union	1.108* (.765)	1.028 (.889)	1.085 (.880)	1.282* (.926)	1.018 (.910)
χ^2	51.40***	74.37***	100.74***	88.57***	71.49***
N	1547	1547	2375	1321	1495

Notes: Cell entries report coefficients and robust standard errors (in parentheses). Unit of analysis is a non-directed dyad-year. Each dyad is composed of two states involved in secessions. MID = militarized interstate dispute. PRD = politically relevant dyad. All significance levels are one-tailed: *** $p < .01$; ** $p < .05$; * $p < .10$.

In Model 2, the ethnic (i.e. intangible) value coefficient is not only positive and significant, but in its influence it also easily surpasses the economic and strategic value coefficients. In fact, the impact of the ethnic value coefficient on the hazard rate is about 3.8 times (or 280 percent) greater than that of the economic value coefficient, which is the only other significant territorial dispute coefficient. This means that rump and secessionist states are substantially more likely to fight for territories that would unite lands occupied by ethnic kin than to fight for lands that would increase their economic or military might. This is understandable given that most twentieth century state breakups are precipitated by domestic-level territorial disputes that question the central government's right to rule ethnic minorities. Secessionist movements therefore often define themselves along ethnic lines and consequently the issue of ethnic territorial unity ranks high on the future political agenda. In addition, intangibly-valued lands are difficult to compromise over because sharing, common access, and division are often seen as unacceptable solutions. The combination of the calls for territorial ethnic unification and inability to compromise makes the use of military force more a attractive—and, some extremist politicians may argue, the only viable—alternative. The states' leaders are thus most likely to benefit by pursuing disputed lands occupied by ethnic kin. In sum, hypothesis H-2 receives strong initial support in the post-secession context.

Before turning to the process findings, I assess the robustness of the territorial dispute results. Recalling the Chapter 3 discussion on the topic of which sets of secessionist dyads to include into the analyses, I re-run Model 2 using all dyads (Model 2a) and only contiguous dyads (Model 2b). In Model 2c, I drop the controversial Israel-Jordan case; similar results (not reported) obtain if the India-Pakistan case is dropped. As can be seen in Table 5.4, the new findings resemble the ones reported for Model 2 closely.

As an additional check of the findings' robustness, I utilize the directed dyad design. This design allows one to go beyond analyzing conflict *involvement* and observe conflict *initiation*; see Chapter 3 and related caveats. Much of the logic presented in the theoretical model (see Chapter 2) suggests that the state dissatisfied with the secession-created borders will be the one to strike first. Table 5.5 presents Models 3-4c, which follow the setup of the Models 1-2c and evaluate this portion of the argument. Importantly, the first two hypotheses remain applicable in the militarized (territorial) conflict initiation context. The only notable change is that the economic territorial dispute coefficients' significance level and magnitude of impact has now increased. This provides stronger evidence that these disputes present the leaders with sufficient potential payoff to use military force. Nevertheless, the earlier finding that the ethnically-based territorial disputes provide the greatest payoff to the leader stands. In Model 4, the latter variable has about a 1.5 times (or 50 percent) greater impact on the hazard of armed conflict initiation than the former.

The territorial dispute findings have an important implication for an earlier query regarding the secession's effectiveness in resolving the original domestic-level territorial dispute. The failure to resolve the ethnic facet of the initial

Table 5.5: Cox Regression Estimates of Fatal Post-Secession Militarized Conflict Initiation, 1900-2000

Variable	Model 3: All MIDs	Model 4: Territorial MIDs	Model 4a: All dyads	Model 4b: Contiguous dyads only	Model 4c: No Israel-Jordan
Territorial Dispute	2.667*** (.622)				
Strategic Terr. Dispute		-.789 (.737)	-.775 (.746)	-.417 (.668)	-.953 (.810)
Economic Terr. Dispute		1.342** (.584)	1.332** (.588)	1.472** (.644)	1.304** (.678)
Ethnic Terr. Dispute		2.018*** (.723)	2.061*** (.714)	2.182*** (.846)	2.068*** (.726)
Violent Secession	3.846** (1.603)	4.254** (1.806)	4.544*** (1.850)	3.873** (1.726)	4.249** (1.753)
Power Advantage	.071 (.068)	.101* (.072)	.103* (.074)	.135* (.082)	.055 (.098)
Allies	.089 (.298)	.347 (.341)	.358 (.342)	.374 (.364)	.352 (.327)
Dyadic Democracy	-.968 (.773)	-1.062* (.780)	-1.062* (.778)	-1.118* (.783)	-1.305* (.799)
Contiguity	.277 (.725)	-.308 (.782)	-.210 (.881)		-.116 (.778)
Rump State	-.604 (.632)	-.660 (.537)	-.643 (.530)	-.742* (.531)	-.402 (.799)
Soviet Union	.364 (1.141)	.966 (1.254)	.964 (1.231)	1.216 (1.347)	.980 (1.193)
New Leader	-.293 (.580)	-.169 (.437)	-.185 (.431)	-.054 (.487)	-.333 (.512)
χ^2	101.48***	78.52***	95.78***	78.69***	61.87***
N	2899	2899	4389	2478	2797

Notes: Cell entries report coefficients and robust standard errors (in parentheses). Unit of analysis is a directed dyad-year. Each dyad is composed of two states involved in secessions. MID = militarized interstate dispute. PRD = politically relevant dyad. All significance levels are one-tailed: *** $p <$ .01; ** $p <$ .05; * $p <$ .10.

territorial dispute has much more serious consequences than the failure to resolve its strategic and, to a lesser extent, economic aspects. Nevertheless, one
should be cautious not to read too much into this finding. Although ethnically-
based territorial disputes clearly present the greatest danger to the post-secession
peace, militarized conflict over ethnically valued disputed territory is not inevitable. Table 5.2 shows that almost three-quarters of the secessionist dyads that
have an ethnically-based territorial dispute do not experience even a single fatal
MID. Thus, though this type of territorial disputes is the most responsible for
secession's failure, its presence still does not guarantee that the secession will
fail.

The behavior analogous to the findings for the first two hypotheses can be
found in the cases of the Serbo-Montenegrin and Croatian interventions in Croatia and Bosnia in the early 1990s. The rump state (Serbia-Montenegro) fought
the secessionist states (Croatia and Bosnia) with the goal of bringing the Serb-
inhabited lands in both countries under its control. Croatia had a similar agenda
of expanding its borders over Croatian-inhabited parts of Bosnia. In fact, the
interventions concentrated on the poorer, less-developed, and relatively remote
regions of Croatia and Bosnia, suggesting only a peripheral interested in acquiring economically or strategically valuable lands. The Serbs concentrated much
of their initial war effort on the eastern portion of Bosnia, while Croatians focused on Herzegovina; both areas are poor in resources and industry—two characteristics for which central Bosnia is actually well-known. Likewise, most of
the Serb war effort in Croatia was focused on the lands inhabited by ethnic
Serbs, and not on economically or strategically important areas. Examples of
secessionist states attacking their rump counterparts can also be easily found. In
both the 1908 Bulgarian secession from the Ottoman Empire and the 1919 Fin-
ish secession from the Soviet Union, the secessionist countries fought later on to
acquire additional territories inhabited by their ethnic brethren; the same lands
held little economic or strategic importance. Finland joined World War II—and
did so on the Axis side despite being the only democracy to do so—exclusively
to fight the Soviet Union and push its boundary eastward. Similarly, Bulgaria
participated in the First (successfully) and Second (unsuccessfully) Balkan Wars
in order to acquire even more of the Ottoman-controlled lands inhabited by Bul-
garians.

The territorial dispute findings are consistent with prior territorial conflict
research while they simultaneously discredit common realist arguments that
power-related (i.e. strategic and economic) territorial disputes are the main foci
of states' territorial interactions. The intensifying role of intangible factors on
the chances for territorial dispute escalation has also been found by Goertz and
Diehl (1992), Vasquez (1983), Bremer (1992), and Huth (1996). Apart from
Goertz and Diehl, however, none of these works examine these issues in the
context of territorial disputes that result from alterations of international boundaries. Furthermore, while Goertz and Diehl consider this context, they do not investigate the consequences of secessions. Therefore, the findings presented here
can be considered important because they extend this literature's coverage to

this rarely explored issue area. In terms of the ethnic conflict literature, the results provide systematic evidence showing that the secession debate appropriately focuses on the most important culprit of post-secession conflict: ethnically-based territorial dispute. Hence, both opponents (e.g. Horowitz 1985; de Silva and May 1991; Posen 1993; McGary and O'Leary 1993; Kumar 1997) and proponents (Mearsheimer 1993, 1998; Mearsheimer and Van Evera 1995, 1996, 1999; Kaufman 1996, 1998) accurately identify this issue as important. Yet, keeping the descriptive results—showing that ethnic territorial disputes do not *guarantee* future armed conflict—in mind, the opponents tend to overstate the gravity of the problem posed by the presence of such disputes.

Part II: Secession Process

Next, I turn to the results for the process variable. I argued above that how the breakup of the state occurred—that is peacefully or violently—may impact the chances that territorial disputes the secession leaves behind escalate to militarized conflict. The leaders of rump and secessionist states are for most part constrained against using violence to revisit the outcome of a peaceful secession. There are costs that arise from reneging on the associated peaceful division agreement, which would damage the country's international reputation, make other countries more reluctant to cooperate on issues such as trade, reduce aid inflows, weaken security guarantees, etc. The prospect of the loss of benefits deters the leader from using military force. In contrast, the countries' leaders are less constrained when trying to take militarized action to revisit the outcome of a violent secession. In the rump state, the leader can rally the people against the secessionist state by claiming that the loss of land was unjust and that this injustice needs to be corrected or to demonstrate to other would-be secessionist groups that even successful secessions will endure high costs. For the secessionist state, it is possible that its victory was incomplete. Its leader can capitalize on the selectorate's desire to take even more of the rump state's land. Furthermore, the leaders of both states will find it easier to and may be even pressured into militarized conflict because their forces have already been mobilized to fight the secessionist conflict. Hypotheses H-3 captures the difference in expectations between the consequences of peaceful vs. violent secessions formally.

Turning to the results, all the Models presented in Tables 5.4 and 5.5 show that the violent secession coefficient is significant and positive. The finding that violent secessions significantly increase the hazard of future militarized conflict is consistent with the expectation of hypothesis H-3. The hazard that a violently created border will be fought over is 760 percent (or 8.6) times greater than if the secession was performed peacefully. The finding corresponds well with the observation that a secessionist dyad whose members parted ways peacefully has experienced future fatal confrontations over land in only about 5 percent of the cases, while for violent secessions this figure skyrockets to 43 percent. Obviously, the stakes relating to how the secession is performed are quite large. In fact, the results presented in Table 5.4 indicate that in terms of substantive impact, the process variable edges out—by the factor of 1.26 in Model 2, for example—the ethnic territorial dispute variable as the most influential in four of the five Models. In the armed conflict initiation context (Table 5.5), the difference is even more discernible. For instance, according to Model 4, the hazard of a fatal territorial MID being initiated is 2.1 times (or 110 percent) greater if the secession was violent than if the potential initiator disputes the target's territorial holdings on the ethnic basis. Sweden-Norway and India-Pakistan separations illustrate that secession process has substantial influence on the quality of future relations. The former, peaceful secession has produced peaceful relations over the past century, while the latter, violent secession has resulted in numerous confrontations, including full-fledged wars.

Though the finding that peaceful secessions lead to peaceful relations may not sound all that surprising, this finding is quite important in the context of territorial conflict research. Despite the expectation that peaceful alterations of borders are beneficial, Goertz and Diehl (1992) fail to show this empirically. In fact, this is the first project to show that peaceful divisions of homeland territories by secession are beneficial; Maoz (1989) has shown this to be the case for states emerging from peaceful decolonization, but his logic is driven by the violently decolonized states' need to demonstrate a general willingness to use force to be taken as legitimate international actors rather than by the logic of territorial conquest. My findings hence extend the territorial conflict literature's arguments contending that peacefully agreed-upon borders are rarely fought over (Kocs 1995; Huth 1996) to the context of secessions. The findings also have bearing on the secession literature. I report evidence contradicting the expectations that all secessions either lead to future confrontations regardless of the secession process (e.g. Horowitz 1985; de Silva and May 1991; Etzioni 1992; Posen 1993; McGary and O'Leary 1993; Kumar 1997) or that violent secessions lead to peaceful relations (Mearsheimer 1993, 1998; Mearsheimer and Van Evera 1995, 1996, 1999; Kaufman 1996, 1998). Instead, I offer first systematic empirical evidence supporting Tullberg and Tullberg's (1997) and Gurr's (1993) arguments.[1]

Note, importantly, that the result pertaining to hypothesis H-3 is quite robust. In addition to the sensitivity tests reported here, the finding is unaffected by using both fatal and not fatal MIDs to operationalize the dependent variable, by relying on a somewhat different temporal domain, or by whether the analyses are restricted to only the interactions between rump and secessionist states; see Tir (2001, 2003b; forthcoming) for comparisons. The beneficial effect of peaceful secessions finding holds even on the domestic level of analysis. That is, peacefully divided countries are significantly less likely to experience armed internal conflict; see Tir (2002, 2005a).

Control Variables

The controls are added to the two parts of the model to ensure that the findings are not spurious and driven by factors that are commonly associated with armed conflict onset in the literature. Tables 5.4 and 5.5 reveal that most of the control variables do not perform as well as the key explanatory variables in the post-secession context. The relative power, dyadic democracy, and alliance coefficients are at best weakly and occasionally significant—with the relative power coefficient exhibiting the most consistency and providing some support for the power preponderance school of thought. In a sense, the alliance findings resemble the contradictory arguments over whether allies are more or less likely to fight one another (e.g. Maoz 2000) while the dyadic democracy result may reflect Huth and Allee's (2002; see also Hensel 2001) finding that there are limits to the democratic peace in the territorial dispute context. Importantly, these weaker than expected results imply that the common conflict management techniques lose much of their effect in the secession's aftermath. This makes it all the more crucial to conduct secessions "correctly," that is peacefully and with an eye on the potential post-secession territorial disputes. The finding is particularly important when one considers the fact that the current conventional wisdom has been to accept the old internal borders as the new international boundaries. This strategy hardly optimizes the chances for territorial dispute resolution and consequently for future peace. Changing the location of the boundary to resolve precisely ethnically- (and to a lesser extent economically-) based territorial disputes can be helpful. If, in contrast, these issues are not handled appropriately, there is little hope that other factors will keep the rump and secessionist countries from fighting over the new boundaries.

Furthermore, I already pointed out in Chapter 3 that the effect of proximity may be muted due to the countries' shared history, and this is what the analyses reveal. The results are similar for the leadership and Soviet Union controls. Change of leadership does not appear to provide an additional impetus to challenge the new border and—despite the momentous and unique nature of the Soviet Union's collapse—the related states do not show much evidence of acting differently than states emerging from the breakups of other countries. The related coefficients achieve only the weakest significance levels and do so in only two of the models presented without altering the thrust of the findings for the key variables. Substantively, the Soviet Union-related cases are not by themselves driving the findings and the theoretically relevant variables can explain both the Soviet and non-Soviet cases.

Finally, in Chapter 3 I suspected that rump-secessionist relations may be more adversarial than relations between two secessionist states, because this is where the main fault line of the state's breakup lies. This would in turn impact the threshold at which the leaders find it profitable to use militarized conflict to challenge the secession-created boundary. The expectation finds at least some support in four out of five models presented in Table 5.4. The result confirms that the main axis of post-secession territorial conflict lies between rump and secessionist states. Yet, is the prospect theory-based explanation for this finding driving the result? The related argument maintains that—all other things being equal—the leaders of rump states will be more likely to risk using military force to alter boundaries because they are operating in the domain of losses. Accordingly, in the directed analyses in Table 5.5 the related variable reflects whether the country initiating a fatal (territorial) MID is the rump state. The incorrect coefficient signs in every model indicate that the prospect theory interpretation finds no support. The reason for the lack of support may be that the secessionist state too operates in the domain of losses. It is possible that the secessionist state's constituents and leader see the disputed, rump state-controlled land as rightfully theirs. The inability to control the land is thus interpreted as a loss that took place during the establishment of the secessionist state. Both states therefore have a similar psychological disposition toward desired lands controlled by the foe. In sum, I find more convincing evidence to support the original explanation arguing that the main axis of conflict lies between rump and secessionist states rather than the prospect theory-based alternative. The broader implication of the finding that both rump and secessionist states pursue disputed lands with roughly equal degrees of zeal supports the theorizing presented in the theoretical model, which treated both the rump and secessionist states sides as potential perpetrators of post-secessionist armed conflict. Expanding upon Goertz and Diehl's (1992) strict focus on the country that lost land therefore presents a fruitful improvement. Further evidence showing statistically that the rump and secessionist states' behavior mirrors each other can be found in Tir (2001, 2003b).[2]

Conclusion and Implications

This chapter has provided two related sets of findings. The first has been to assess empirically the extent to which secessions are able to resolve domestic-level territorial disputes that motivated state breakups and to determine what kind of danger the remaining disputes pose to the future peace between rump and secessionist states. The answer to the former query has been mostly discouraging, as secessions by and large leave behind territorial disputes. After the secession, the original, domestic-level territorial dispute is either transformed into its international counterpart or replaced by a new international-level territorial dispute in about 88 percent of the cases. Still, a success rate of about 12 percent may seem at least somewhat encouraging if one considers the reports that territorial disputes are often intractable and difficult—if not impossible—to resolve. Turning to the more encouraging news, the unresolved border problems are unlikely to pose an unusually widespread threat to peace. In fact, only about one-fifth of secession-created borders are fought over. When these figures are disaggregated into yearly averages, however, we see that those dyads that fight do so at such explosive rates they vault the entire post-secession average well above the "normal" levels. These findings provide much more nuanced insights vis-à-vis the advice given by the vast majority of the ethnic conflict scholars that secessions are dangerous and should thus be avoided at all costs.

The second goal of the chapter has dealt with the question of what accounts for why some rump and secessionist states fight over their new borders while others do not; that is; why do some secessions end up as successes while others are failures? Following the theoretical model developed in Chapter 2, I have focused on two potential determinants: the presence and nature of post-secession territorial disputes and secession process. The results confirm the relevance of these factors. Another insight is that post-secessionist relations are to a large extent dominated by the factors associated with secessions and that the standard militarized conflict-reduction approaches (e.g. Mearsheimer's insistence on creating the balanced power distribution between rump and secessionist states) are not all that helpful. This means that policymakers must pay strict attention to the secession's circumstances and, if they are interested in promoting post-secession peace, take a more proactive approach when secession is being considered as an option.

The following strategies can be used. First, policymakers should recognize not only that secession-created territorial disputes are dangerous, but also that some territorial disputes are more salient than others. The current conventional wisdom has been to accept the old internal borders as the new international boundaries. This strategy hardly optimizes the chances for territorial dispute resolution and consequently for future peace. Changing the location of the boundary to resolve ethnically- (and to a lesser extent economically-) based territorial disputes can help; strategically-based disputes are, in contrast, of minor concern.

Second, whenever possible, secessions should be performed peacefully. Peaceful, agreed-upon secessions create disincentives against the future use of military force, through reputational and loss-of-side-benefits costs. In contrast, violent secessions make future fighting more likely by promoting suspicion and mistrust and by placing leaders who tend to rely on militarized conflict to deal with problems into positions of power. An important cautionary implication of this finding is that secessionist civil wars will be *particularly* difficult to resolve. Walter (2000) finds that civil wars centering around demands for territorial independence are significantly less likely to experience peaceful settlements and that, once achieved, such settlements are significantly less likely to be implemented. Hence, such wars cannot be stopped effectively either within the existing state (Walter 2000) or by dividing it (this chapter). The only effective option that seems to remain is to prevent secessionist demands from escalating into organized violent conflicts in the first place. This means that serious attempts to address secessionist movements' grievances have to take place early on in the process or—closer to the theme of this chapter—that it may be better to let the secessionist region go before the conflict starts to spiral out of control.

Yet, given that few states willingly give up land, the central question then becomes how a secession can occur before the disagreements over land control between the central government and secessionists escalate to the point of organized violence (see Young 1997). Because answering this question is beyond the scope of this work, only a rough outline of a potential approach is discussed. The key may lie in an early and proactive international involvement, as, for example, described in Lund's (1996) approach to preventive diplomacy. This can be done by offering mediation efforts, putting pressure on the adversaries to work their problems out peacefully, and by not waiting until violence occurs (see Burton 1990) under the idea that these are purely domestic issues; as this and other studies demonstrate, secession is clearly a problem with international consequences. It often takes a while before secessionist desires evolve into full-fledged violence, but the international community has been so incapable of facing the prospect and reality of state breakup that it often fails to react in time. For instance, the initial phase of the disintegration of Yugoslavia—between the election of independence-minded leaders in Slovenia and Croatia and the declarations of independence that led to the onset of war—took well over a year (March 1990-June 1991). In general, the lack of timely reaction gives the central government a green light to either ignore the secessionists' frustrations or to repress the group further. Faced with such prospects, the secessionists may feel that they have little choice but to press for a violent secession. This chain of events has ultimately led to secessionist violence, and in some cases to the violent breakup of the state. The international community holds the power of recognition and it can use it as leverage against both the central government that is unwilling to compromise (i.e. threaten recognition) and secessionists who are making unreasonable demands (i.e. withhold recognition). Future research should investigate how much pressure international actors can put on the disputants in order to secure a peaceful secession.[3] If a genuinely peaceful breakup cannot be achieved, does a pressured, but still peaceful breakup set the stage for peaceful post-secession relations?

Policy Application Example: Serbia vs. Montenegro

Serbia and Montenegro are the only two remaining Republics of what once constituted Yugoslavia. For several years now, Montenegrin pro-independence political parties have been working toward establishing statehood. They have controlled the Republic's government and planned on calling a referendum on the issue; the referendum has been postponed under the pressure from the European Union, which has been a firm advocate of preserving the defunct state. Serbia and Montenegro's ties are by now only formal; the latter has, for example, established its own foreign policy and internal economic system—including own currency and monetary policy. Recent opinion polls in Serbia show ambivalence about the issue. The Serbian leadership has expressed little interest in allowing Montenegro to leave the union, even though it also does little more than pay lip service to the idea of a continued union.

By giving Montenegro up, Serbia would be acknowledging the reality of the situation and decreasing the chances that it would become involved in yet another costly secessionist conflict with a (former) Yugoslav Republic. The secessionist drive has been peaceful thus far and my findings suggest that peaceful partitioning would increase the chances for future peace between the rump (i.e. Serbia) and secessionist (i.e. Montenegro) states. Moreover, based on the examples such as Sweden-Norway and Czech Republic-Slovakia, countries that have traditionally been friendly toward one another and who part ways peacefully are likely to be not only at peace but also enjoy good neighborly relations with one another after the secession. The two Republics have had a long history of cooperation; in fact, the two entities have never fought a war against one another, which is quite remarkable in the otherwise conflict-prone Balkan region.

Peaceful secession is hence one of the ways in which the chances of future armed conflict could be reduced. The other concern deals with potential territorial disputes the breakup would leave behind. Starting with disputes over tangibly-valuable land, Montenegro has no economically- or strategically-based territorial pretenses against Serbia. Yet, Serbia does find Montenegro valuable in these terms. Montenegro has traditionally been landlocked Serbia's outlet to the sea; thus, Montenegro is valuable to Serbia in economic terms for its seaports and for the foreign currency-generating tourist industry. Moreover, by letting Montenegro go, Serbia would lose its maritime naval capability, which is of strategic concern. Nevertheless, the results show that strategic concerns do not provide sufficient motivation for future violent confrontations. While economic concerns can be problematic, they are of secondary importance and, more importantly, the results show that the peaceful secession process should be able to provide sufficient future constraints against relying on militarized conflict to deal with these issues. To further reduce the incentive to use military force over territorial questions of the economic nature, the secessionist agreement could stipulate that Montenegro would lease port space so that Serbia could continue to receive goods via Montenegro. This would be economically beneficial to both countries. Given good relations, the Serb tourists would likely continue to vacation on Montenegro's coast, again providing both countries with an incentive to maintain peaceful relations.

In contrast, potential ethnically-based territorial disputes present more of a concern in the post-secession context. Montenegro has no such claims on Serbian land, but there is a notable Serb minority in Montenegro. According to the results, allowing the secession to take place peacefully would provide sufficient costs against using force so that future Serb leaders would not cause armed confrontations between the two countries on this basis. To further reduce Serb incentives to intervene in Montenegro to help ethnic Serbs, Montenegrin policy-makers should concentrate their efforts on making sure that the Serb minority in Montenegro is treated well. That should not be all that difficult to achieve as the two peoples have had historically good relations with one another. In sum, from the perspective of territorial conflict, the union between the two states should be dissolved peacefully. This would optimize the chances for future peace and provide disincentives against using force to deal with the remaining territorial disputes. If, in contrast, peaceful dissolution is not allowed, the history of Yugoslavia's breakup could unfortunately repeat itself yet another time.[4, 5]

Notes

1. The result is also consistent with the findings from the broader international conflict literature. The temporal diffusion of conflict works maintain that a state tends to rely on militarized conflict if it has helped it deal with past problems (i.e. reinforcement; Most and Starr 1980; Kirby and Ward 1987) or if military force was used against it in the past (i.e. reciprocity; Goldstein and Freeman 1990; Rajmaira and Ward 1990). In the secession context, if the secessionists used armed conflict to win independence, then this will encourage both the rump (reciprocity) and secessionist (reinforcement) states to rely on militarized conflict to deal with territorial disputes the secession leaves behind.

2. An additional discussion of empirical findings for the aftermath of secessions can be found in Tir (2005a, 2005b, forthcoming).

3. This is a particularly important point, given Walter's (2003) finding that a state will be reluctant to grant independence to a secessionist region because it may set a precedent that may encourage secessions of other parts of the country. Nevertheless, a peaceful secession still provides the best chance for future stability, especially when compared to the alternative: costly civil wars that may lead to the country's dismemberment and violence-prone relations in the future.

4. Besides the potential rump-secessionist militarized conflict, my research shows that the possibility of conflicts among secessionist states themselves should be taken into account. Were Montenegro to become its own state, it would share borders with Bosnia and Croatia. Montenegro played a relatively minor role in the conflicts surrounding the breakup of Yugoslavia and has enjoyed good relations with the two countries for roughly the past ten years. According to the results, this sets the stage for peaceful (territorial) relations with both of these countries. Potential ethnically-based territorial disputes do exist with these countries: there are Slav Muslims in the Sandžak and Croatians in the Bay of Kotor regions of Montenegro. Yet, the results show that these issues are unlikely to create violent confrontations as long as the breakup between the secessionist states has been peaceful. Concerning the economically- and strategically-based territorial disputes, Montenegro has no such disputes with Bosnia, but a strategically-based territorial dispute exists with Croatia. In addition to the results showing that such a dispute is not likely to lead to militarized conflict, the dispute itself may become resolved by Montenegro's secession. The strategically disputed land is the Prevlaka peninsula, which overlooks the Bay of Kotor—the location of Montenegro's only deep-sea naval base. (The United Nations has had an observer mission on Prevlaka.) This issue should therefore be the focus of efforts to maintain peaceful relations between Croatia and Montenegro. The issue has not been formally resolved yet, but in principle a Croatian-Montenegrin agreement—under which the peninsula would remain under Croatian control but be demilitarized—has been reached. The reason that the issue has not been formally settled yet has been Serbia's reluctance to sign off on it; Serbia, as the senior partner in the Montenegrin-Serbian federation has more of a say over international borders. Thus, once—and if—Montenegro becomes independent, there is a good chance that this dispute will be formally settled.

5. At the time of this writing, Montenegro is scheduled to hold a referendum on independence in May 2006.

Chapter 6

Aftermath of Unifications

Much like the previous two chapters, this chapter investigates the aftermath of another type of territorial change, namely unifications. Yet, unifications are different from transfers and secessions in at least one important respect. Although all three types of territorial change are motivated by territorial disputes, the way unifications manage the dispute causes one of the participant countries to cease being an international actor. That is, the territorial loser is subsumed while the border most directly affected by the unification disappears. This is not, however, necessarily the end of the territorial conflict story because—much like many transfers and secessions that left behind territorial disputes of their own— unification may provide an impetus for the unified country to question the borders it shares with its neighbors. Even though these borders are not new and have not been moved, the unified state and its leader may be encouraged by the territorial success of unification to enlarge the state's territory even further. The settling of the territorial dispute that has led to the unification may therefore enable the leader to focus the attention and resources of the unified country on potential territorial disputes with the neighbors. Concerning the available resources, by merging the military forces and various other resources of the states that have unified, the unified state now arguably commands a greater military force.

Anecdotal evidence suggests that unification may indeed serve as a jumping off point for further territorial expansion. For instance, Prussia's and Piedmont's initial absorption of respective neighboring states was only the beginning of the broader agenda of German and Italian unifications, both of which often proceeded by the use of military force. More recently, upon taking over South Vietnam, Vietnam invaded Cambodia with the hope of not only seizing some of the bordering territories but also of installing a puppet regime in that country. Likewise, the short-lived United Arab Republic, the union between Egypt and Syria, was formed in large part to prevent further Israeli expansion and, ideally, to take over the state of Israel. In sum, unification does not necessarily indicate the end of territorial conflict, so the issue of the stability of the unified state's borders needs to be seriously investigated.

In the discussion below, I move away from the anecdotal evidence and investigate the territorial aftermath of unifications systematically. The format used in the previous two chapters is largely followed. I start the empirical investigation by examining the unification's proclivity to be followed by unresolved territorial disputes between the unified country and its neighbors. That is, I investigate both what portion of unification-related boundaries are disputed and the extent to which the unresolved disputes pose a threat to peace. The second segment of the chapter goes beyond these descriptive analyses in order to assess the relevance of hypothesized causal links between the remaining territorial disputes and unification process on the one hand and militarized conflict over the unified state's boundaries on the other. Per the arguments developed in Chapter 2 that were used to develop the theoretical model, these factors may help explain why some unified and neighboring states fight over their borders after the unification while others do not. The final portion of the chapter summarizes the findings for the two sets of empirical analyses and relates them to relevant research. The findings' implications are also applied to a currently-relevant case, in order to illustrate how the insights developed in this work may be used to prevent future armed conflicts over the unified state's boundaries.

Descriptive Results

Table 6.1 provides assessments of the tendencies for the post-unification borders to be disputed and the frequency with which the disputes escalate into fatal militarized conflict over territory; a dyad formed by the unified state and one of its neighbors is the unit of analysis. Of the ninety-one unified-neighboring state dyads, nineteen (or 21 percent) experience territorial disputes. Thus, in a great majority of cases, the post-unification borders are not questioned by either of the countries. In comparison to Huth's (1996) finding that territorial disputes occur at a general rate of about 33 percent, the post-unification figure is noticeably lower.

As in the previous chapters, I ask next to what extent the unresolved territorial disputes tempt the leaders to rely on militarized conflict and thus pose a threat to dyadic peace? The bottom portion of Table 6.1 reports the conditional probability that a post-unification dyad experiences at least one fatal militarized interstate dispute (MID) over territory given that its members have been engaged in a territorial dispute with one another. As the result shows, only five (26 percent) of the dyads embroiled in a post-unification territorial disputes actually experience fatal militarized conflict over land. That is, escalation from territorial disputes to fatal militarized conflict is far from inevitable and is limited to about one-quarter of the cases. Overall, this means that just over one-twentieth (5.5 percent, 5/91) of the post-unification boundaries are both disputed and fought over. These initial findings show that on average unifications do not pose an unusually grave concern from the territorial dispute perspective.

Figure 6.1 tracks the portion of post-unification dyads that have experienced at least one fatal territorial MID over time since the unification. The figure reveals that most initial militarized conflicts over the unified state's borders occur in the first few years after the unification. After this time, comparatively fewer previously peaceful dyads experience their initial conflicts, so one can say that the situation stabilizes slowly with the passage of time. Given the generally decreasing trend in the rate of new failures, there is some evidence that post-unification borders that are not fought over soon after the unification have a good chance of becoming accepted over time. In more theoretical terms, the finding suggests that the payoff to the leader from challenging boundaries that have become accepted by the population slowly decreases with the passage of time.

Table 6.1: Post-Unification Territorial Issues, 1900-2000

	No	72 (79 percent)
Is unification followed by a territorial dispute?	Yes	19 (21 percent)
	Total Dyads	91
	No	14 (74 percent)
Given that unification is followed by a territorial dispute, does the dispute escalate to a fatal territorial MID?	Yes	5 (26 percent)
	Total Dyads	19

Notes: Unit of analysis is a dyad composed of the unified and neighboring countries. MID = militarized interstate dispute.

To provide some perspective on the above findings, I examine how the unified-neighboring state dyad's proneness to experience fatal territorial MIDs compares with the experience of other states. To do this, I have to adjust the calculation from Chapter 3 that provided the average for all dyads contiguous by land. Unlike in the transfers and secessions analyses—where the territorial losers and gainers generally border each other by land—in the case of unifications I utilize a broader set of countries. This is done to capture more fully the potential for the unified country's expansionist tendencies beyond the most immediate neighbors (see Chapter 3). To make the frequency comparisons valid, I hence have to re-calculate the average for all countries with the similarly relaxed contiguity rules. Accordingly, the average frequency of fatal territorial MIDs for all countries is .0068 (s.d. = .0823; n = 25,105) and .0084 (s.d. = .0915; n = 1,777) for the post-unification dyads. Though the post-unification average is about 24 percent greater, the difference is not statistically significant. The comparison reveals that post-unification borders are not challenged by militarized conflict at a rate that is significantly different from the rate that can be considered "normal." In short, from the militarized territorial conflict perspective, unifications do not create abnormally conflict prone situations.

Figure 6.1: Cumulative Portion of Unified-Neighboring State Pairs that Experience Fatal Territorial MIDs after Unification, 1900-2000

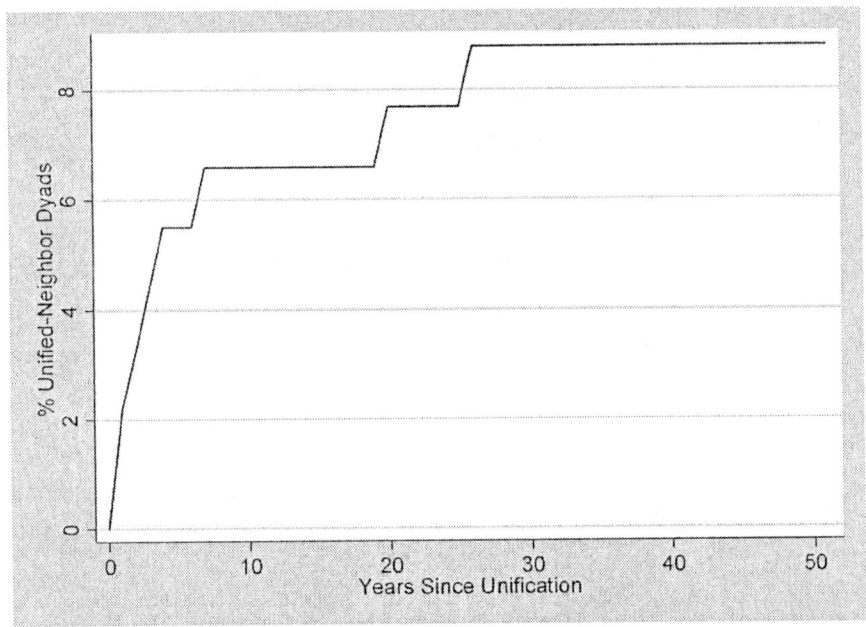

Next, I revisit some of the above issues by considering the type of territorial dispute that follow unifications. In linking territorial disputes with subsequent militarized conflict, the related research points out that not all pieces of land are equally valuable. Recall that in Chapter 2 I divided land value into the tangible and intangible dimensions (Newman 1999). In a ceaselessly competitive, zero-sum world of realism, possession of tangibly-valuable lands will not only be desirable but contested militarily. In this view, strategically- and/or economically-based territorial disputes will likely be followed by militarized confrontations. In contrast, others argue that the failure to control intangibly-valued land is expected to intensify the willingness to fight more so than the failure to control tangibly-valued land (Goertz and Diehl 1992; Diehl 1999b; Vasquez 1983;

Touval 1972; Huth 1996). This is so because the lands valued along this dimension are perceived as personal, indivisible, and un-substitutable (Gottman 1973; Sack 1986). In the context of unifications, disputes based on the presence of ethnic kin may be particularly problematic because unifications often involve bringing together members of a particular nation into the same state (e.g. Germans, Vietnamese, Italians, Yemenis). Capturing territories outside the unified state's control from neighboring states may be particularly beneficial for the leader, since such acquisitions would bring the unified state closer to its goal of providing the home state for all the people of particular ethnic origin. Yet, another purpose behind unification may be a more realist-like quest for power and security (e.g. was the purpose behind the United Arab Republic creation of a pan-Arab state or balancing Israel?), in which case the tangibly-valued disputed territories will be more valuable to the leader. I now turn to answering the questions investigating how common each territorial dispute type is and how much of a danger it poses.

Table 6.2: Post-Unification Territorial Issues by Territorial Dispute Type, 1900-2000

		Strategic Territorial Dispute	Economic Territorial Dispute	Ethnic Territorial Dispute
Is unification followed by a specific type of territorial dispute?	No	83 (91 percent)	75 (82 percent)	78 (86 percent)
	Yes	8 (9 percent)	16 (18 percent)	13 (14 percent)
	Total Dyads	91	91	91
Given that unification is followed by a territorial dispute, does the dispute escalate to a fatal territorial MID?	No	7 (87 percent)	12 (75 percent)	9 (69 percent)
	Yes	1 (13 percent)	4 (25 percent)	4 (31 percent)
	Total Dyads	8	16	13

Notes: Unit of analysis is a dyad composed of the unified and neighboring countries. MID = militarized interstate dispute.

The top analysis in Table 6.2 breaks down post-unification territorial disputes by type. Unifications are most likely to be followed by disagreements about the location of the border based on the economic value of the territory; such disputes are present in sixteen (or 18 percent of the) dyads. A somewhat smaller subset of dyads (14 percent) experiences territorial disputes along the intangible, that is ethnic, dimension of land value. Note that much like in Chapters 4 and 5, I again find that strategic territorial disputes are the least common type (9 percent)—which is consistent with the argument that twentieth century technological advancements in weaponry, surveillance techniques, speed of troop and equipment movement, etc. have been undermining the strategic importance of territory (e.g. Keohane and Nye 1977; Rosecrance 1986; Brooks 1999). The bottom portion of Table 6.2 reports the conditional probabilities that a particular type of post-unification territorial dispute escalates into at least one fatal territorial MID. Here, I find more differentiation based on the escalation proclivity. Although ethnically-based territorial disputes are less common than their economic counterparts, their probability of escalation is the highest (31 percent vs. 25 percent). The strategically-based territorial disputes are not only the most infrequent but also the least likely—by a notable margin—to escalate to fatal militarized conflict (13 percent). In terms of theoretical implications, the escalation analysis suggests some differences in the proclivity of various types of territorial disputes to escalate into fatal militarized conflict. That is, this initial analysis gives the intangibility argument a slight edge in the debate in the post-unification context.

In the previous two chapters, I investigated the ability of the transfer and secession process to resolve the original territorial dispute. A comparable analysis in the post-unification context would reveal little useful information because the border whose alteration lead to the unification no longer exists. Instead, in the next section I investigate whether the peaceful vs. violent unification processes possess differing abilities to affect the leader's decision to rely on militarized conflict in order to challenged the unified state's new boundaries—as argued in the model presented in Chapter 2. For the answer to this question, I turn to the causal analyses results that put the hypotheses from the model to an empirical test. Though insightful and informative, the above-discussed descriptive results regarding the proclivity to engage in militarized conflict may well be skewed because the territorial dispute, process, and control variable factors discussed in Chapters 2 and 3 were not simultaneously taken into account. Let us now turn to these more sophisticated analyses.

Causal Results

Part I: Post-Unification Territorial Disputes

Table 6.3 reports the results of non-directed analyses that focus on the unified and neighboring states' proneness to become *involved* in fatal militarized conflict with each other after the unification. In addition to the observation that all statistical models presented in the table are highly significant, note that some of the territorial dispute variables that compose the theoretical model (see Chapter 2) are significant—even when controlling for correlates of militarized conflict

Table 6.3: Cox Regression Estimates of Post-Unification Militarized Conflict Involvement, 1900-2000

Variable	Model 1: Fatal MIDs	Model 2: Terr. MIDs	Model 2a: 150-mile rule	Model 2b: 12-mile rule
Territorial Dispute	2.252*** (.489)			
Strategic Terr. Dispute		-.171 (.821)	-.030 (.890)	-.043 (.892)
Economic Terr. Dispute		2.270*** (.802)	2.562** (1.085)	2.482** (1.097)
Ethnic Terr. Dispute		.322 (.716)	.289 (.861)	.241 (.866)
Violent Unification	.569 (.627)	.042 (.513)	-.055 (.698)	-.083 (.690)
Relative Power	-.377** (.158)	-.350*** (.128)	-.400** (.187)	-.376** (.191)
Allies	-.782* (.572)	-1.162** (.546)	-1.023** (.575)	-1.056** (.569)
Dyadic Democracy		-36.309*** (.547)		
Distance	-.212 (.373)	-.706*** (.250)	-.815*** (.248)	-.830*** (.262)
χ^2	41.71***	14962.63***	85.48***	79.14***
N	1777	1777	1302	1179

Notes: Cell entries report coefficients and robust standard errors (in parentheses). Unit of analysis is a non-directed dyad-year. Each dyad is composed of unified and neighboring states. MID = militarized interstate dispute. All significance levels are one-tailed: *** $p < .01$; ** $p < .05$; * $p < .10$.

not directly related to the unification (see Chapter 3). Statistical Model 1 presents the results necessary to evaluate hypothesis H-1. According to the theoretical model, the leader's primary motivation to use military force against the dyadic foe comes from the post-unification territorial disputes. The unified state may not be satisfied with how much land it has received via the unification and may set its sights on land controlled by one or more of its neighbors. Though not a focus of the model, the neighboring state may also dispute the unified state's territorial holdings (e.g. Israel in the case of the United Arab Republic); the post-unification timing of the attack may be motivated by the concern that the unified state is seeking expansion at the neighbors' expense. Therefore, the leaders of both countries may be willing to rely on militarized conflict in order to challenge the unified state's borders.

As can be seen in Model 1, the territorial dispute coefficient is significant and positive, providing support for hypothesis H-1. The relations between unified and neighboring states are therefore strongly influenced by the presence of unresolved border issues. This result helps extend the territorial dispute research (e.g. Huth 1996; Huth and Allee 2002; Vasquez 1993; Senese 2005; Vasquez and Henehan 2001; Senese and Vasquez 2003) into the post-unification context, which has not been investigated systematically from this perspective. The finding is consistent with, for example, the Vietnamese invasion of Cambodia. The invasion was precipitated by the Khmer Rouge's fear that united Vietnam would seek to take over portions of Cambodia. As a (failed) preemptive tactic, the Khmer Rouge started incursions into the long-disputed territories Vietnam controlled. Vietnam, however, responded not only by engaging the Khmer Rouge in the border region but also by attempting to occupy the entire country of Cambodia.

To determine which aspects of territorial disputes are particularly problematic, I evaluate the empirical accuracy of hypothesis H-2. As the reader will recall, the disputed land may be valuable due to both its tangible (strategic, economic) and intangible (ethnic, religious, ancestral) characteristics. In the theoretical model, I argue that intangibility should provide a greater payoff to the leader for relying on militarized conflict, a position with which the realist scholars disagree. The initial descriptive tests in the preceding section provided limited evidence in support of the hypothesis, so I now investigate whether this preliminary finding is strengthened or weakened once other influences are taken into account.

Unfortunately, the initial attempts to have Model 2 converge were unsuccessful. The reason is that there is too little variance between some of the independent and dependent (defined as a fatal post-unification MID fought over territory) variables for successful statistical estimation. Specifically, the difficulty is presented by the fact that there is only one strategically-based territorial disputes that escalates to a fatal territorial MID (see Table 6.2). In itself, this is an important finding: it suggests that post-unification militarized conflicts are almost completely unrelated to strategic territorial disputes—as seen from the fatal militarized territorial conflict perspective. In order to assess the hypotheses, I was forced to lower the conflict threshold and in the remainder of the models in Table 6.3 I rely on both fatal and non-fatal MIDs fought over territorial issues. This of course represents a departure from the standards used in the previous chapters, so the territorial dispute type-related causal findings in this chapter should be viewed with a degree of caution.

Turning to the actual territorial dispute type findings, Model 2 shows that only the economic (i.e. tangible) territorial dispute coefficient is significant and positive. That the other tangible, that is strategic, value coefficient is insignificant is not all that surprising given that strategic territorial dispute escalation is rather rare; this rarity of escalation is also responsible for the negative coefficient sign. Furthermore, although the ethnic value coefficient is positive, it is not significant; in its importance it is easily surpassed by the economic value coefficient, which has a 605 percent greater marginal impact. The leaders of unified and neighboring states hence find more reward in contesting militarily those territories that would increase their countries' economic might than those that would bring together lands occupied by ethnic kin.

Table 6.4: Cox Regression Estimates of Post-Unification Militarized Conflict Initiation, 1900-2000

Variable	Model 3: Fatal MIDs	Model 4: Terr. MIDs	Model 4a: 150-mile rule	Model 4b: 12-mile rule
Territorial Dispute	1.824*** (.492)			
Strategic Terr. Dispute		.369 (.727)	.058 (.731)	.019 (.719)
Economic Terr. Dispute		1.645** (.837)	1.779** (.817)	1.720** (.798)
Ethnic Terr. Dispute		.887 (.747)	.688 (.741)	.589 (.732)
Violent Unification	.431 (.610)	.170 (.517)	-.422 (.627)	-.480 (.606)
Power Advantage	.124 (.111)	.137 (.109)	.168* (.130)	.179* (.134)
Allies	-.873* (.536)	-1.246** (.492)	-1.256** (.507)	-1.359*** (.510)
Dyadic Democracy			-44.099*** (.592)	-37.920*** (.604)
Distance	.198 (.362)	-.230 (.408)	-.410 (.457)	-.483 (.422)
Unified State	-.603 (.784)	-.132 (.880)	-.078 (1.015)	-.135 (.977)
New Leader	-.070 (.440)	-.164 (.512)	-.105 (.574)	.062 (.551)
χ^2	67.14***	91.38***	24182.91***	16261.22***
N	3554	3554	2604	2358

Notes: Cell entries report coefficients and robust standard errors (in parentheses). Unit of analysis is a directed dyad-year. Each dyad is composed of unified and neighboring states. MID = militarized interstate dispute. All significance levels are one-tailed: *** p < .01; ** p < .05; * p < .10.

Before turning to the process findings, I assess the robustness of the territorial dispute results. Recalling the Chapter 3 discussion on the topic of which sets of unified-neighboring state dyads to include into the analyses, I re-run Model 2 by restricting the distance between the two states to up to 150 miles of water (Model 2a) and up to twelve miles of water (Model 2b). The new findings for the territorial dispute type resemble the ones reported for Model 2 closely. That is, these results are not a function of the rule by which the domain of neighboring states is determined.

As an additional check of the findings' robustness, I again utilize the directed dyad design. This design allows one to go beyond analyzing militarized conflict *involvement* and observe *initiation*; see Chapter 3 and related caveats. Much of the logic presented in the theoretical model (see Chapter 2) suggests that the state dissatisfied with the post-unification borders will be the one to strike first. Table 6.4 presents Models 3-4b, which follow the setup of the Models 1-2b and evaluate this portion of the argument. Importantly, the conclusions for the first two hypotheses remain applicable in the militarized (territorial) conflict initiation context, with hypothesis H-1 receiving strong support and hypothesis H-2 receiving no support. The only notable change is that the impact gap between the economic and ethnic territorial dispute coefficients has now narrowed somewhat; there have, however, been no changes in the significance or rank order of the relative impact of the two coefficients. Economically-based territorial disputes now provide an 85 to 192 percent greater impetus for the leader to initiate militarized conflicts than do their ethnic counterparts.

Despite the "lessons" of the nineteenth century German and Italian unifications, the idea that unifications will pose the greatest threat to the neighboring countries inhabited by the unified country's ethnic kin is not all that credible—at least not when twentieth century unifications are considered. The findings fit well with Adolph Hitler's behavior following the *Anschluss* of Austria in 1938. Although he did first focus on acquiring German-inhabited portions of neighboring states (e.g. Sudetenland, Memel, Danzig), his territorial conquest agenda was much broader.[1] He continued to invade other countries, even though they did not necessarily contain substantial German minorities. In fact, German-occupied states were often used to provide economic resources and to expand the industrial capacity Hitler needed to further his war efforts.

Relating the findings from the first part of the theoretical model (see Chapter 2) to the extant research, much of the literature consulted in the building of the model argued that intangibly-valued disputed lands are associated with armed conflict onset more so than tangibly-valued disputed lands (e.g. Vasquez 1993; Huth 1996; Goertz and Diehl 1992). Based on the results from this chapter, however, I am unable to support this line of thinking. The only indicator of intangible value available (i.e. ethnic value) fails to convince that it has a stronger impact than the indicator of the disputed land's economic value. A possible cause of discrepancy between the present and Huth's (1996) findings may be the fact that Huth deals with the dynamics of territorial disputes in general, while I deal with territorial disputes through the lens of unifications; the latter scenario introduces the concept of territorial gains and potential further territorial expansion, so the relevant countries' leaders do not necessarily face identical circumstances in both situations. The difference between Goertz and Diehl's (1992) and my findings probably stems from the fact that Goertz and Diehl do not investigate the aftermath of unifications. They focus only on territory that has changed ownership between countries, which in the case of unifications is of little interest because the country formerly controlling this land has become subsumed; in short, consequences of unifications are simply beyond the scope of their work.[2]

While the particularly strong finding for economically-based territorial disputes compares well with the realist view of territory, it also runs counter not only to the above-discussed value-as-meaning school of thought but also to the arguments made by Brooks (1999). He argues that technological innovations in trade, shipping, resource extraction, ease of foreign direct investments, etc. have overcome the need to conquer economically valuable territories. Yet, he may be overlooking the fact that sovereign control of territory can lead to a more effective extraction of resources than trading could accomplish (Liberman 1996). Territorial control is the only policy alternative that grants full access to the land in question. Other policies provide no or at best only a partial control over the valuable land; consequently, preferences and whims of parties controlling the land have to be taken into consideration. Direct control of such lands may be particularly important to unified countries that have a broader agenda of expansions, as economic resources can be used to further their ability to acquire still other territories.[3]

Part II: Unification Process

I now discuss the results for the process part of the model, pertaining to whether unification took place peacefully or not. Recall that I modified the peaceful vs. violent process logic because the border the unification dealt with no longer exists. Instead, I argued that peaceful unifications put the unified country's leader in the position where he/she is held responsible for the condition of the unified country's reputation. In contrast, the leader contemplating the use of military force after a violent unification can cause little *additional* damage to the country's reputation and is hence restrained to a lesser degree. The neighboring state's leader may likewise be less restrained against acting militarily versus a violently unified state because it will be easier to make the argument that—based on the unified state's reliance on violence—such a state poses a threat. Turning to the findings, the results in Tables 6.3 and 6.4 for the unification process variable are consistent across the tables in that the violent unification coefficient is insignificant. The finding means that unification process does not affect the hazard of post-unification militarized conflict to a notable extent. Hypothesis H-3 and related theorizing that the peaceful process places constraints on the leader thus receive no support in the post-unification context. Of course, the reader should note that the process findings are based on a small number of observations. In fact, there is only one case of violent unification (i.e. Vietnam) in my sample. This translates into six (out of ninety-one) of the unified-neighboring state pairs or about 8 percent of the annual observations. Therefore, while the process finding is informative, the reader should keep in mind that it is based on a limited number of cases.

The finding that the process of unification makes little difference in terms of future conflict is consistent with, for example, the cases of Vietnamese and Germany-Austria unifications. The former unification was violent, and a unified Vietnam invaded Cambodia with the agenda of not only defending itself but also of dealing with some long-standing territorial disputes between the two countries. The latter unification was a peaceful one, but it only emboldened Hitler to pursue further territorial acquisition at the expense of Germany's neighbors. Therefore, even though the process differed in these two unifications, the same outcome followed. The process itself thus had little to do with either promoting or detracting from future reliance on militarized conflict to challenge the unified state's boundaries.

The dearth of violent unifications is hardly accidental and we are unlikely to see more violent unifications taking place in the foreseeable future. Via the international sovereignty norm, economic sanctions, and even militarized intervention, the international community has made it difficult to make subjugation of an entire country against its will either legitimate or permanent. For example, the country of Lebanon has been effectively occupied and governed by Syria for over a decade. Yet, neither the international community nor—more narrowly— Syrian allies in the Arab world recognized Syria as the legitimate ruler of Lebanon. In fact, Syria has made a substantial effort to create the appearance that Lebanon is in charge of its own affairs, while the Syrian troops are there only to provide security. Recently, under the mounting international pressure, Syria withdrew its troops from the country. Furthermore, the Vietnamese attempt to occupy and govern Cambodia in the 1980s has not been granted the seal of international legitimacy either. Ironically, the international community chose to recognize the indigenous yet brutal Khmer Rouge regime over the more palatable Vietnamese-installed puppet government as the legitimate representative of the Cambodian people. Finally, the Iraqi and North Korean attempts to annex Kuwait and South Korea, respectively, have not only been widely condemned by the international community but have in fact led to large-scale militarized interventions to reverse the occupations. These examples send a strong deterrent signal that violent unifications will not be accepted—and probably not even tolerated. Hence, the only unifications we are likely to see in the future are the voluntary ones, following the 1990 German or Yemeni formula.

The disappointing finding that peaceful unifications are no better for post-unification relations than their violent counterparts does not unfortunately allow me to extend the insights from the territorial conflict literature (e.g. Vasquez 1993; Huth 1996; Huth and Allee 2002)—that peaceful methods of dealing with territorial problems significantly increase the chances of future peace—into the post-unification context. The process result is also inconsistent with the findings from the broader international conflict literature. The reinforcement argument within the temporal diffusion of conflict school of thought maintains that states tend to chose policies that have been useful for them in the past (e.g. Most and Starr 1980; Kirby and Ward 1987). In the unification context, if the unification initiator state used peaceful means to take over another state, then this should encourage the now unified state to rely on similar policies to deal with additional territorial disputes against neighboring countries. Yet, as the 1938 German and UAR examples illustrate, this is not necessarily the case. Whether the finding challenges either of these literatures is not all that clear due to the near absence of violent unifications in the twentieth century.

Control Variables

The controls are added to the two parts of the model to ensure that the above findings are not spurious and driven by factors the armed conflict literature commonly associated with militarized conflict onset. Table 6.3 reveals that as a group the control variables perform better than in the post-transfer and post-secession scenarios. The relative power (i.e. the preponderance configuration), alliance, distance, and dyadic democracy coefficients are significant in most of the analyses, meaning that they notably impact the leaders' calculations about relying on militarized conflict to challenge unified state's boundaries. In the directed analyses (Table 6.4) the influence of the power and distance variables decreases, while the alliance and regime type variables remain significant. Overall, these findings provide evidence that unified-neighboring countries' interactions are closer to being "normal" inter-country relations than is the case for relations between countries that have undergone transfers or secessions. This also suggests that the common militarized conflict management techniques retain much of their effect in the aftermath of unifications: the negative influence of post-unification territorial disputes can be diminished by relying on non-territorial policy tools.

Most importantly, in both tables the dyadic democracy variable is not only significant but in terms of its relative effect it is the most influential variable in the statistical models. Substantively, this means that the joint democratic regime type can alone negate any detrimental effects of territorial disputes between the unified and neighboring countries. The effect of the variable is in fact so strong that it has to be dropped from some of the analyses in Tables 6.3 and 6.4 to allow the statistical models to converge. The inclusion or the exclusion of the dyadic democracy variable does not, statistically speaking, alter the findings for the key variables, as can be seen by cross-model comparisons.

Finally, I turn to the variables identifying the unified country and new leaders (see Table 6.4). Although both coefficients are insignificant, this is a notable finding for the former variable. Specifically, it indicates that both the unified and neighboring countries pursue disputed lands with roughly equal levels of motivation. This challenges my expectations that the unified state harbors unusually strong expansionist tendencies that bring it on the collision course with its neighbors. The results indicate that unified states are no more inclined to initiate militarized conflict to challenge the unified state's boundary than are its neighbors. This is another piece of evidence in favor of the conclusion that the territorial dispute behavior of unified states is not all that different from states in general.

Conclusions and Implications

This chapter has provided two related sets of findings. The first has been to assess empirically the extent to which a unified country's borders are disputed either by it or one of its neighbors and to determine what kind of danger these disputes pose to the future peace between the states. The answer to the former part of the question has been that unifications are followed by territorial disputes over the unified state's boundaries relatively infrequently, at the rate of about 21 percent. The unresolved border problems are similarly unlikely to pose an unusually grave threat to peace: only about one-quarter of the unified state's borders are fought over. Disaggregating the incidents of armed conflict into yearly averages also shows that the unification-related borders are not significantly more militarized conflict-prone than an "average" interstate boundary. In sum, unlike the post-transfer and post-secession territorial relations, the post-unification territorial relations between the unified and neighboring states can be classified as "normal."

The second goal of the chapter has dealt with the question of what accounts for why some unified and neighboring states fight over their borders while others do not. Following the theoretical model developed in Chapter 2, I have focused on two potential determinants: the presence and nature of post-unification territorial disputes and unification process. Determining the impact of these influences has been somewhat complicated by the relative rarity of strategically-based territorial disputes that escalate into fatal militarized conflict and especially by the near-absence of violent 20th century unifications. These limitations serve to caution the reader to treat some of the causal findings from this chapter as preliminary. These issues notwithstanding, I was able to derive noteworthy information from the empirical assessment of the unifications' aftermath. First, post-unification relations are significantly affected by the territorial disputes surrounding the unified state's boundaries. Second, the type of dispute most associated with escalation to militarized conflict are economically-based territorial disputes. Third, unlike in the case of transfers and secessions, the process by which two countries unify has little bearing on the future proneness to use military force. Fourth, despite the importance of the (economic) territorial disputes in the decision to rely on militarized conflict, the detrimental influence of this factor is tempered by the control variables such as relative power distribution, alliance ties, and distance; in cases where both the unified state and its neighbors are democratic, the detrimental influence is completely negated. And finally, unified states are not particularly dangerous; that is, compared to their neighbors and given comparable circumstances, they are not any more likely to initiate militarized conflict to challenge the new status quo territorial distribution. These pieces of evidence demonstrate that unified states' behavior is not unusually conflict-prone.

From the policymaking standpoint, the overall results indicate that unifications need not be either feared or discouraged. That is, based on the standard of post-unification armed territorial conflict they are unlikely to create either notably peaceful or conflict prone situations. According to the results, policymakers should focus their attention on potential economically-based disputes over the unified state's boundary. One strategy for dealing with this problem would be to use the lessons from the territorial transfer chapter and encourage a peaceful transfer of disputed lands to resolve specifically the economically-based territorial dispute; strategically- and to a lesser extent ethnically-based disputes are of minor concern. An alternative approach would be to manage the escalatory tendencies of unresolved economically-based post-unification territorial dispute. This can be done by promoting democracy in both the unified and neighboring countries or by relying on more realism-oriented techniques such as identifying common security interests in order to forge cooperative security ties. In terms of the unification process, the international community should continue its policy of discouraging violent unifications in favor of voluntary unions. Though there is too little variance to derive strong statistical conclusions about the impact of the process variable, the dearth of violent unifications may well be the factor that can help explain why post-unification situations are notably less conflict prone than the aftermaths of territorial transfers and secessions.

Policy Application Examples: Korean[4] and Chinese Unifications

The issue of potential Korean reunification is one of the most prominent questions on the peninsula. Even though proposals that would allow for the unification under two different systems of governance have been entertained, the unification will likely not be possible until the North Korean Communist Party loses its grip on power. That is, the Korean unification seems poised to follow the German reunification model, where the more advanced South Korean economic and political systems would become the models for the unified state. While the people of Korea would no doubt welcome the opportunity to live in an undivided state, potential concerns from the perspective of this work relate to territorial disputes between Korea and its neighbors.

The unified Korea's boundaries would probably be disputed with both of her immediate neighbors, Japan and China; portions of both boundaries have already contributed to the tensions in the region. The first dispute is with Japan and concerns the Takeshima (or, depending on the transliteration, Tokto, Tokdo, or Dokdo) Islands in the Sea of Japan (or the East Sea). Though the islands are little more than a collection of inhospitable rocks, their control would enable the controlling state to claim the surrounding sea and ocean floor. The sea is rich with fish important to both countries' extensive fishing industries while the bedrock is believed by some to contain oil or natural gas deposits. The strategic and especially ethnic value of the disputed islands is low for both countries. According to the post-unification results presented earlier in the chapter, the fact that the dispute is of the economic type is cause for concern, as it is precisely such disputes that are most likely to escalate to militarized conflict between the unified countries and their neighbors. Nevertheless, the fact that both countries are democratic would provide alternate dispute resolution possibilities, to the point where the dispute is unlikely to escalate to actual militarized conflict. Therefore, from the standpoint of this dispute, much depends on whether South Korean democracy will continue to mature and whether this system of governance can be applied successfully to the northern part of the peninsula.

The fate of the post-unification boundary that may become disputed with China is less certain. One of the complicating factors is that the size of the disputed area north of the Yalu River is somewhat ambiguous. Recent tensions have erupted between China and South Korea over Chinese attempts to revise the region's history by removing any references to the medieval Korean Empire's rule over northeast provinces of contemporary China, including Manchuria; North Korea has not raised notable objections over the Chinese moves, lest it damage friendship with the one remaining ally it has. Even though parts of this vast region are economically—due to raw material deposits and industry—and ethnically—due to a sizable Korean minority inhabiting the portions of the area closer to the Korean border—valuable, it is not likely that the unified Korea would officially demand the return of the former imperial lands. A more plausible territorial dispute between the two countries concerns control over a mountain (along with a small lake and a ski resort) situated just inside the present-day borders of China. This area has some very limited economic value. Yet, according to the findings, this dispute—whether broadly or narrowly conceptualized—is unlikely to escalate. The party dissatisfied with the post-unification border, that is Korea, does not have the military capacity necessary to defeat China and take the disputed lands. Korean capability is actually likely to decline somewhat after the unification because it will need to invest a large amount of its own resources into stabilizing and developing its northern region. This would further handicap Korean leaders' ability to act on the above territorial desires.

While unified Korea is unlikely to attempt to expand its borders by military force due to its inferior military power vis-à-vis China and inter-democratic relations with Japan, potential Chinese unification with Taiwan may pose more of a threat to regional peace from the post-unification territorial dispute perspective. For several decades, one of the main objectives of mainland Chinese foreign policy has been to re-incorporate the island of Taiwan. Assuming that the unification occurs at some point—by either peaceful agreement or Chinese invasion—the results show that Chinese neighbors' borders may come under threat after the unification. According to Huth and Allee (2002), China not only has territorial ambitions toward Russia, Japan, Vietnam, Bhutan, India, Kazakhstan, Kyrgyzstan, and Tajikistan, but the land in question is of economic value in the first three cases on this list.[5]

Unlike in the case of Korea, China's potential interest in questioning these borders by relying on militarized conflict is not tempered by its weak power status or inter-democratic relations because China fits neither of these conditions. The only obvious mollifying force may be cross-border security ties; yet, given the lack of history of security cooperation in East Asia, at this time they remain unsurprisingly rudimentary. Adding to potential post-unification problems is the observation that Taiwan has been a serious distraction in Chinese foreign policy. China has expended tremendous military, diplomatic, and economic (e.g. by granting aid to countries not to recognize Taiwan) effort to keep Taiwan from "getting away." Once this distraction is resolved—and with additional power China would gain from controlling notable Taiwanese resources— China will be even more capable of pressing for (violent) territorial changes. The strategy of the United States and its allies should thus be the one of continual defense of Taiwanese independence in order to prevent a forceful takeover of Taiwan. Yet, if Taiwan and China agree on unifying, then the US will have little choice but to accept the agreed-upon unification. The US strategy should then shift toward peaceful resolution of territorial disputes between China and her neighbors. As the results from Chapter 4 indicate, enacting peaceful territorial changes where appropriate would increase the chances of securing future territorial peace.

Notes

1. Note that even these lands are arguably economically important.

2. Another potential cause of divergent findings is the issue of colonial lands. In this study, I deal only with territorial disputes over non-colonial, homeland territories; see the preceding chapters for the discussion of this issue.

3. Although one could argue that this study's temporal span is too broad to capture the effect of technological innovations that have taken place only in the past few decades, the reader should note that—because the unifications' aftermath is tracked toward the present time—the proportion of more recent observations is actually relatively high. The median year in the unifications data set is 1978.

4. I thank my colleague Professor Han Park for helping me develop a better understanding of potential territorial disputes between unified Korea and its neighbors.

5. Note that there have been attempts to settle some of these dispute since Huth and Allee have released their data set.

Chapter 7

Project Summary, Implications, and Extensions

This final chapter performs several concluding tasks that bring together the key ideas developed in the preceding pages. The first segment of the chapter reviews the project's agenda, approach, and findings. The next portion offers theoretical implications of my research. Although some of my findings are consistent with what is already known about armed territorial conflict, I both offer an application of these findings to a relatively unexplored topic (i.e. territorial change) and provide new insights and refinements. Based on the findings, the third section develops several policy implications that can be used to minimize the chances of confrontations after territorial changes. This is a particularly important task in the light of the fact that even though territorial changes have been used as a means for dealing with territorial disputes for decades, if not centuries, the determinants of their consequences are relatively unknown. In the final section, I offer suggestions for future research.

Project Summary

Agenda

This project set out to enhance our understanding of the link between territorial changes and subsequent militarized conflicts that are connected to the change. Countries often involve themselves in territorial disputes with one another, whereby they seek exclusive control of lands that are not in their possession. From the challenging country's perspective, it wants to acquire the territory in question, while the defender state wants to preserve the territorial status quo. The clash of the viewpoints sometimes produces armed confrontations and in fact prior research (Vasquez 1993; Holsti 1991; Vasquez and Henehan 2001) indicates that militarized conflict is more likely in these kinds of situations than when there is disagreement over issues such as trade or ideology. At times, the challenger is successful in its aim: it acquires the disputed land, or at least a part of it. In such a case, a territorial change—defined as any alteration of international borders—takes place.

This project focuses on the aftermath of territorial change. Extant research almost exclusively investigates the factors leading up to the territorial change (see for example Kacowicz 1994; Huth 1996) while overlooking what happens thereafter. The consequences of territorial changes are not something that can be ignored. As Weede (1973) notes, territorial changes are but a part of the interplay between countries as they seek to define themselves along the territorial dimension. A territorial change is thus not the endpoint of a territorial dispute, at least not in many cases. Instead, the change either leaves the old territorial dispute unresolved or sets the stage for an entirely new territorial dispute. In both cases, the territorially dissatisfied parties seek further territorial revisions, that is additional territorial changes. The territorial loser may want the lost land back while the territorial gainer may not be satisfied with how much land it acquired through the change and, as a result, wants even more of the loser's land. This process of land re-distribution via territorial changes has the potential to go on indefinitely as the cases of repeated confrontations between Germany and France over Alsace-Lorraine or India and Pakistan over Kashmir demonstrate. Because countries seek exclusive control of the same lands, one country's gain is inevitably another country's loss; that is, territory is a zero-sum good. Finding ways to divide the land in ways that would make the relevant countries satisfied to the point where they forgo the reliance on militarized conflict to prompt further territorial changes is therefore a difficult but quite important task.

This project seeks to understand whether the link between territorial changes and future militarized territorial conflict can be broken. Are there some attributes of territorial changes that may make future confrontations over land less likely? Even though Weede (1973) notes that territorial changes are both results of old and causes of new wars, historical experience indicates that some territorial changes indeed represent at least apparent endpoints of territorial disputes. Consider the following examples. The dissolution of the union between Sweden and Norway in 1904, which created the independent state of Norway, has not been followed by major confrontations concerning territorial control between the two countries. A similar outcome arose from the 1979 transfer of the Sinai peninsula from Israeli to Egyptian control; despite several minor skirmishes, the Israeli-Egyptian border has not been seriously challenged. Moreover, the 1990 unification of Germany—despite some initial skepticism—has not produced consequences undesirable from the standpoint of territorial control. Aside from these peaceful, agreed-to territorial changes, some violent changes also produced peaceful outcomes. An example along these lines is the conquest of northern Mexican lands by the US in the Mexican War of the mid-1800s.

In short, while there is ample evidence suggesting that territorial changes lead to future confrontations, other cases suggest the opposite: territorial changes appear to have a conflict-management potential. Puzzled by the variance in the consequences of territorial changes, I seek to answer questions about the extent to which territorial changes resolve the underlying territorial disputes and about the factors that help determine why some territorial changes are followed by militarized confrontations while others lead to peace. The elaboration of these questions can be found in Chapter 1.

Approach

To pursue the answers to the two main questions, I first acknowledge that not all alterations of international borders are alike. Some of these alterations take place between two sovereign countries, through a process by which they transfer ownership of a certain piece of land between them. I call the related movement of the boundary a state-to-state territorial transfer, in which one country's territorial holdings increases (gainer) while the other's holdings decrease (loser). In contrast, a secession creates a new international border, which divides an existing country into multiple states. One of the states—labeled the rump state—carries on the institutions of the former, whole state; this state is the territorial loser in this scenario, because it has lost control over a portion of the land it once controlled. Secession also creates one or more new, secessionist states, which have not existed prior to that point. These states are the territorial gainers, because they now have sovereign control over land that they did not control before the secession. Finally, through a unification, the initiator state subsumes another country by erasing the boundary between them. As a result, the subsumed state ceases to exist as an independent entity. The unified state is the territorial gainer, while the territorial loser country ceases to exist. In these cases, I evaluate the aftermath of the unification by examining the interactions between the unified country and its neighbors (see Chapters 1, 2, and 6).

I propose that there is a similar though not necessarily the same logic that can help explain why some territorial gainers and losers engage in post-territorial change militarized territorial conflicts with one another while others do not. I argue that the motivation for militarized conflict given by the disputed land out of the state's control is largely the same across the three types of territorial change. For instance, the loser in a transfer may want to retake the land lost to the gainer. In the post-secession scenario, a similar motivation holds for the rump state wanting to reacquire some or all of the land lost to the secessionist country. Moreover, the unified state may want to acquire a portion of its neighbor's land—a motivation that is comparable to territorial gainers and secessionist states that have not received as much land in the transfer or secession, respectively, as they have hoped. Therefore, the basic land-control oriented motivation is the same regardless of the type of change.

This logic link is developed in Chapter 2, where a theoretical model connecting territorial changes with future confrontations over land is presented. The model consist of two main parts. In the first part of the model, I argue that the leaders of countries involved in territorial changes are likely to rely on militarized conflict to seek future territorial revisions when they can expect notable domestic and international payoffs from such actions. The potential payoffs, and therefore the leaders' decisions, are influenced by the value of the sought-after land. Furthermore, I postulate that land can be valued for its tangible (e.g. economic, strategic) or intangible (e.g. ethnic, religious, ancestral) characteristics and argue that militarized conflict is more likely when the latter aspect of value is involved, ceteris paribus. The intangibly-valued land is likely to be perceived as indivisible and non-substitutable, and it is therefore harder to compromise or peacefully reach mutually-acceptable divisions over such lands. Moreover, control of intangibly-valued land is important to a larger segment of the selectorate, which in turn makes the acquisition of these lands more profitable for the leader. The second part of the model proposes that the process of territorial change affects the leaders' motivation to fight for the disputed land. The territorial change process alters the costs of the use of militarized conflict for the purpose of land conquest. The costs are the most pronounced when the prior territorial change has been performed peacefully or, somewhat less so, when it is a result of an overwhelming victory. Ordinary violent changes, in contrast, produce few costs for the leaders and may in fact even make the reliance on militarized conflict easier or more desirable. See Chapter 2 for more details regarding the model.

I argue that the two parts of the model apply to all three types of territorial change. That is, the basic logic of the model drives the leaders toward (or away from) militarized conflict regardless of whether they are the leaders of gaining, losing, rump, secessionist, or unified countries. I maintain that the model is sufficiently abstract to cover all three types of territorial change, even though I do not necessarily expect that every detail of the model will be equally applicable in all three contexts of territorial change. The model is applied to the three types of territorial change separately in Chapters 4-6. I take such an approach in order (1) to account for variations among the three types (e.g. unifications do not produce a territorial loser, while secessions and transfers do) and (2) to test the premise that a single, general model can explain post-change militarized territorial conflict in all three instances.

Evaluation

Descriptive Analyses
   The three empirical chapters provide information about the extent to which a particular territorial change type is followed by unresolved original or entirely new territorial disputes and about the degree to which the remaining territorial disputes are a threat to peace between losing and gaining states. These analyses allow one to investigate how problematic the aftermath of territorial change is

and provide clues about the change's conflict management potential. The answers obtained from the first set of tests are relatively discouraging (see Tables 4.1, 5.1, and 6.1). Territorial changes are often followed by disputes over the affected border. The exact post-change rates at which the affected borders are disputed range from 21 percent for unifications, to 59 percent for transfers, and to 88 percent for secessions. Escalations to fatal militarized interstate disputes (MIDs) fought over land are, however, far less common. The portion of territorial disputes that escalate to militarized conflict ranges between about 25 percent, for secessions and unifications, and 42 percent, for transfers. This means that in every type of territorial change, the participant (i.e. gainer-loser, rump-secessionist, and unified-neighbor) pairs of states (or "dyads") *completely* avoid future fatal militarized conflict over territory in a great majority of the cases. The actual portions of these peaceful dyads range from 75 percent for transfers, to 79 percent for secessions, and to 94 percent for unifications. After a territorial change, the participant countries are notably more likely not to fight than to fight. Consequently, these findings provides evidence that territorial change-future militarized conflict link can and indeed is routinely broken: territorial changes can be used as conflict management tools.

Returning to the more pessimistic aspect of the descriptive analyses, Figures 4.1-6.1 provide only limited evidence that post-change boundaries stabilize—that is become accepted—over time. Though the rate at which the post-change boundaries are initially fought over drops markedly as the time since the change passes, a span of at least one generation is required before the rate drops to zero. Change-affected boundaries are therefore not safe from initial militarized challenges until long after the change. In terms of the model, the leaders' payoff from challenging a border that is becoming more established by the passage of time decreases but does not disappear. Moreover, the evaluation of the post-change militarized conflict frequencies reveals that although the great majority of the post-change dyads do not fight, the remaining portion of them fight quite a bit. In fact, these conflict-prone dyads fight so much that they bring the overall frequency of post-change militarized conflict to a level that is greater than "normal." Specifically, post-transfer and post-secession dyads experience significantly higher militarized conflict frequencies (+64 percent and +172 percent, respectively, compared to the "normal" frequency); yet, recall that the pre- vs. post-transfer comparisons of militarized territorial conflict rates performed by Tir (2001, 2003a) show that the post-transfer rate is significantly *lower*, by 42-50 percent. Post-unification dyads' frequency of militarized conflict is 24 percent greater but not significantly higher than "normal."

Combining the results from these descriptive analyses suggests the following. Territorial changes definitely have a conflict management potential, but in the cases where they fail to prevent future militarized conflict, the consequences are disastrous. This means that if territorial changes are to be used as conflict-management tools, there is a lot at stake: we either enter a peaceful world devoid of militarized territorial conflict or a highly conflictual world. The question of how to go down the former path begs the explanation of what influences which path is taken. This is precisely the focus of the second research question and related causal analyses, to which I turn shortly.

Yet before reviewing the results of the causal analyses, note that another set of the descriptive analyses partly addresses this concern. This is done by examining the ability of the process of territorial change to prevent post-change territorial disputes in the first place. These analyses differentiate between peaceful and violent processes for transfers and secessions.[1] For both of these territorial change types, the results (see Tables 4.3 and 5.3) clearly indicate that the peaceful process is *notably* more capable of resolving the territorial dispute that prompted the change than is the violent process. Nevertheless, the peaceful process by no means guarantees that the affected border will not be disputed. The success rate—measured by the lack of territorial disputes between the participant countries—for peaceful transfers is 50 percent while for peaceful secessions it is 18 percent. For the violent process(es), the success rate drops to 28-31 percent for ordinary violent and overwhelming victory transfers and to mere 4 percent for secessions. These results indicate that how transfers and secessions are performed matters a great deal from the territorial dispute management perspective and that performing them peacefully increases the chances that the affected border will not be disputed. In turn, this has a bearing on the likelihood that the conflict management efforts via territorial changes will be successful. Even though this finding may not sound all that surprising, recall that no prior work on territorial changes has demonstrated this systematically. I now turn to the results of causal analyses, to further refine our understanding of why some post-change dyads succumb to militarized conflict to challenge the new territorial distribution while others do not.

Causal Analyses

The results of the causal analyses provide insights into what factors determine whether the change is likely to be followed by militarized or peaceful outcomes. More formally, the analyses evaluate the empirical accuracy of the four hypotheses developed in Chapter 2 and presented in Table 2.1. Overall, the results confirm the argument that the same, abstract model can explain the onset of post-territorial change militarized conflict across the three types of change. Hence, a similar logic indeed drives the leaders of countries participating in territorial changes toward (as well as away from) future armed territorial conflict, regardless of whether the countries participated in a transfer, secession, or unification. Yet—as expected—the results also reveal some differences among the findings for the three types.

In terms of the first part of the model, the results confirm the expectation that the leaders' use of military force decisions are driven, to a significant extent, by the territorial disputes the change leaves behind. This finding holds across the three types of territorial change and provides strong, robust support for hypothesis H-1. The related territorial dispute coefficients are positive, significant, and responsible for sizable marginal effects; importantly, the finding holds in both the militarized conflict onset and initiation contexts (see Models 1 and 3 in Tables 4.4-4.6, 5.4-5.5, and 6.3-6.4). Substantively, one of the key predictors of the chances for post-change peace is whether the territorial changes left behind lands in disputed ownership.

Though the results for generic territorial disputes are consistent across the territorial change types, a differentiation with respect to the results pertaining to the three types of change is necessary when one considers specific attributes of the disputed land's value. I noted an important difference between tangibly- and intangibly-valued lands and hypothesized that—all other things being equal—the latter dimension of value will appeal to a broader section of the selectorate and therefore provide the leader with a greater payoff for using militarized conflict to conquer the land disputed on this basis. Yet, hypothesis H-2 holds up only in the aftermath of secessions. Given that the only intangible value data available is the ethnic value of the disputed land, it is not completely surprising that the hypothesis holds precisely in the context of secession. Most 20th century secessions were motivated by the desire for ethnic self-determination, so it is to be expected that future militarized confrontations over land distribution would focus precisely on the land valued for ethnic reasons. The finding in favor of H-2 for secessions is robust with respect to both militarized conflict onset and initiation contexts as well with respect to how the appropriate set of post-secessionist dyads is determined (see Tables 5.4-5.5). Finally, note that even though ethnically-based territorial disputes do not dominate states' territorial relations in the aftermath of transfers, the results reported in Tables 4.4-4.6 and associated discussion show that these disputes should not be ignored. That is, ethnically-based territorial disputes do affect the leaders' decision to engage in militarized conflict to some extent.

In terms of the aftermaths of transfers and unifications, tangibly- and especially economically-based territorial disputes are the disputes that have the most impact on the leader's decision to rely on militarized confrontations (see Tables 4.4-4.6 and 6.3-6.4). These results undermine hypothesis H-2, but, at the same time, they support the realist arguments that disputed lands that could be used to bolster countries' relative power will provide the leader with the greatest potential payoff for conquering them. Yet, importantly, I also find that the argument in favor of the tangible dimension is not supported in its entirety. The strategically-based territorial disputes provide little impetus for the leader to engage in militarized conflict. Furthermore, recall that these disputes were also less frequent than the other two types. I suspect that these findings are reflective of the argument that technological developments in weaponry have caused a decline in the strategic importance of land (see Brooks 1999).

In sum, the available evidence shows that the economic—rather than strategic—manifestation of disputed territory's tangible value is more beneficial to the leaders of countries involved in territorial changes. An explanation for this intra-tangible value difference consistent with the theoretical model can be offered. In addition to bolstering the country's power, economically valuable land can provide greater employment and wealth improvement opportunities to a broader segment of the selectorate than can strategically valuable lands. In some cases, strategically-important territories are little more than inhospitable terrains such as mountain peaks, swamps, deserts, remote and barren islands, etc. Furthermore, and also consistently with underlying logic of the model, economically-valued lands are of only secondary importance precisely in the secession context, which—due to its agenda of ethnic self-determination—offers the leaders an issue with which they can appeal to an even broader segment of the selectorate: ethnic unity. This explanation points out a difference in the behavior of newly established (i.e. the secession context) versus older (i.e. the transfer and unification contexts) states and the incentives for militarized conflict that they provide to their leaders. Newly established states focus more on issues that directly affect their reason for statehood, which is the state as the expression and "container" of the nation; in a sense, the rump states are also "new" and subject to this agenda, as they seek to redefine and reinvent themselves in the face of substantial territorial loss and decreased ethnic diversity. These goals can be met by acquiring disputed lands populated by ethnic kin. In contrast, the older states—whose statehood does not need further legitimizing—focus more on the satisfaction of population's material demands. One of the ways of meeting this goal is by the acquisition of economically-valuable disputed territories.

The post-change territorial dispute findings show that the postulation that there are multiple paths to armed post-change territorial conflict is correct. The conceptual breadth of the model incorporates the differing paths, while allowing for the possibility that not every path is equally important to each type of territorial change. In short, the first part of the model successfully explains the motivation behind why participants of territorial changes become involved in future militarized conflicts over change-related land division with one another. A summary matching the theoretical expectations with empirical findings is provided in Table 7.1. I now discuss the findings relating to the second part of the model and dealing with the process of territorial change.

The causal analyses of the role the process of territorial change plays in general confirm my expectations. As argued in the model, peaceful changes create disincentives against militarized conflict, which constrain the leaders' actions in the aftermaths of transfers and secessions (see Tables 4.4-4.5, and 5.4-5.5). Conversely, this is not the case when ordinary violent transfers (short of overwhelming victory) and violent secessions are at stake: in both cases, these processes provide no notable restrictions against future militarized conflict and, in fact, they may even serve to enable it. After secessions, the influence of the process variable is actually so strong that it overwhelms the importance of the (ethnic) territorial disputes; the decisions to rely on militarized conflict by the leaders of rump and secessionist states are therefore influenced more by the process than by territorial dispute considerations. These findings provide strong and robust—with respect to influencing both militarized conflict onset and initiation—support for hypothesis H-3 in the context of transfers and secessions.

Table 7.1: Summary of the Main Findings

Model Part	Hypothesis	Hypothesis Supported in the Aftermath of:		
		Transfers	Secessions	Unifications
Part I	H-1: After a territorial change, gaining and losing countries involved in a territorial dispute with one another will be more likely to experience militarized conflict than countries with no territorial dispute.	Yes	Yes	Yes
	H-2: After a territorial change, a territorial dispute between gaining and losing countries that involves intangibly-valued lands will be more likely to be the source of militarized conflict over territory than a territorial dispute involving only tangibly-valued land.	No	Yes	No
Part II	H-3: Violent territorial changes are more likely to be followed by militarized conflict over territory between the gaining and losing states than are peaceful territorial changes.	Yes	Yes	No
	H-4: Future militarized territorial conflict between the gainer and loser is less likely if the territorial change resulted from an overwhelming victory than if it resulted from an ordinary violent confrontation short of an overwhelming victory.	Weak support only	N.A	N.A

The results for overwhelming victories are somewhat supportive of hypothesis H-4, but not to point of statistical significance. Turning to unifications, the process variable makes little difference in terms of preventing or promoting subsequent militarized conflict between the unified and neighboring countries. The related analyses (see Tables 6.3-6.4) are, however, handicapped by the dearth of violent unifications. Moreover, recall that the theoretical link is weaker in these cases as well, because neighboring counties had little to do with how the unification proceeded. Table 7.1 summarizes these findings as well. Overall, the preferred method of conducting territorial changes is by peaceful means. If the changes are performed peacefully, one can expect reduced chances for militarized conflicts after both transfers and secessions. In the cases of unification, while unifying peacefully is not expected to help diminish the chances of future unified-neighboring country confrontations, it is also not likely to make the subsequent situation any worse off either.

Besides the territorial dispute and change process variables, the causal analyses include variables commonly used in statistical research on militarized conflict in order to make sure that the key findings are not driven by unaccounted-for factors. Except in the aftermath of unifications (see Tables 6.3-6.4), these control variables did not perform as well as expected (see Tables 4.4-4.6 and 5.4-5.5). The decisions to use military force to revisit the transfer- and secession-altered boundaries are therefore driven more by the factors associated with these changes rather than by issues such as the relative power distribution, security ties, and (democratic) regime similarity. Probably the most crucial implication of this finding is that policymakers cannot rely on these secondary measures to assure peace after the transfers and secessions. Instead, altering borders peacefully and in ways that minimize future territorial disputes is critical. Another important finding that emerges with respect to the control variables is that the behavior of territorial gainers and loser is not all that different from each other. This is particularly noteworthy because one of the key improvements provided by this project vis-à-vis prior territorial change work performed by Goertz and Diehl (1992) has been to take into account the gainer's motivation to push for further territorial gains. The finding indicates that the losers are not the only countries one has to be concerned about in the aftermath of territorial change. The next task is to contrast these findings to the extant literature on territorial conflict.

Research Implications

In this section, I compare my approach and findings to three relevant literatures: territorial conflict, ethnic conflict, and temporal conflict diffusion. This is done by explaining the theoretical improvements made in this project, discussing the implications the advancements have produced, and comparing the empirical findings with what the prior literature has shown. With respect to the extant territorial conflict literature, in the model I make several advancements that help push this research vein further. The first improvement is that I investigate the aftermath of territorial change. Works focusing on territorial disputes commonly consider the process leading up to a territorial change (e.g. Kacowicz 1994; Huth 1996). They assume—probably for the sake of analytic convenience—that the dispute is over once territorial change takes place (for an exception, see Goertz and Diehl 1992). In this work I show that this assumption does not hold up. The descriptive analyses reveal that many changes are followed by territorial disputes over the new land distribution and that some of the change-affected borders are the loci of frequent militarized confrontations. Hence, in the pursuit of greater understanding of the phenomenon of territorial dispute, it is crucial to broaden the scope of the research to include the aftermath of territorial changes.

Second, in the explanation of the post-territorial change militarized conflict, I include both the gainer's and loser's motivations for militarized conflict. Goertz and Diehl's (1992) primary focus was on the loser and militarized conflict over the land that changed owners. Expanding on this view, I also add the gainer's motivation for post-change armed conflict. Because a territorial change often fails to give the gainer all of the land it originally wanted, it is clear that the loser is not necessarily the only party that can benefit from pushing for future territorial revisions.[2] Accordingly, I include both parties' perspectives. That the variable indicating whether the party was on the losing or gaining side of the territorial change is insignificant in all the reported analyses reveals that there are no great differences in their behaviors and that omitting the gainer's perspective would undermine the credibility of the findings.

The third advancement with respect to the territorial conflict literature concerns the issue of process. Works such as Kacowicz (1994) focus only on peaceful territorial changes, while Goertz and Diehl (1992) divide the process of change into two basic categories: peaceful and violent. In a significant departure form Goertz and Diehl (1992), I divide violent territorial changes according to whether they involved overwhelming victories. I do so based on research suggesting that militarized conflicts ending in decisive and imposed outcomes are more conducive to future peace than are the ones ending in other circumstances (e.g. Aron 1966; Vasquez 1993; Maoz 1984). I test this expectation in the context of transfers. In their impact on post-transfer militarized conflict, I find some but not a significant difference between overwhelming victory, on the one hand, and ordinary violent and peaceful transfers, on the other hand. The overwhelming victory transfers fall in between the two processes, so their effects are not clearly distinguishable from either extreme. Though this finer-grained differentiation among the different processes of change does not produce as clear-cut of findings as hoped for, it helps confirm one widely expected but so far empirically unsupported finding. The finding that peaceful transfers are better for post-transfer relations than their ordinary violent counterparts not only confirms the related theoretical expectation, but also provides an important piece of evidence for the research on this topic in general. No prior work has shown the empirical existence of this relationship in the context of international boundary alterations. As a matter of fact, Goertz and Diehl (1992)—contrary to their expectations— found that there was no notable difference in terms of post-change militarized conflict between violent and peaceful territorial changes.[3] Therefore, we now have evidence supporting a widely-held expectation that peaceful transfers are followed by peaceful gainer-loser relations more so than are ordinary violent transfers. Moreover, this peaceful vs. violent process finding carries over into the realm of secessions; see below for how this finding compares to the ethnic conflict literature on secessions. The process findings do not, however, apply to uni-fications, as only one of the unifications in the sample has been performed vio-lently.

Besides the above theoretical advancements, I follow the territorial conflict literature's lead on the issue of tangibly- vs. intangibly-valued lands, but derive somewhat divergent findings. I divide the concept of land's value into two dif-ferent dimensions: tangible (i.e. economic and strategic) and intangible (i.e. eth-nic). Much of the literature consulted in the building of the model (see Chapter 2) argued that both dimensions of value are important and, more critically, that intangibly-valued disputed lands are associated with militarized conflict onset more so than tangibly-valued disputed lands. Both Huth (1996; see also Huth and Allee 2002) and Goertz and Diehl (1992) found evidence supporting these arguments. Yet, the results from the transfer and unifications chapters do not lend support to this expectation. The only indicator of intangible value for which the data are available (i.e. ethnic value) fails to show that the intangible dimen-sion of disputed land's value is more important in provoking militarized confron-tations than its tangible dimension. Even though I find the expected direction of impact, I do not find the anticipated levels of significance or magnitude of im-pact.

Possible causes for discrepancy between the present and earlier findings may be the following. Huth's (1996) study does not deal with territorial disputes in the context of territorial changes, so his challengers to the territorial status quo are not necessarily motivated by losing or gaining land nor are they constrained by the change process. A possible cause for the discrepancy with Goertz and Diehl's (1992) work may stem from the issue of colonial lands. In this study, I included only non-colonial changes and associated territorial disputes. In con-trast, Goertz and Diehl included both colonial and non-colonial lands, but their indicators of intangible—or as they call it, "relational"—value identify precisely and only homeland territories.[4, 5] Therefore, by assuming that all homeland terri-tories are intangibly valued, Goertz and Diehl do not really provide evidence for intangibly-valued *homeland* territories that contradict the current findings.

Furthermore, the greater importance of economically-valued disputed lands is not entirely inconsistent with the logic presented in the theoretical model. In addition to bolstering the country's power, economically valuable land can pro-vide greater employment and wealth generation opportunities to a population. This may be particularly important in established states where the statehood is taken for granted and the population may be more interested in the material qual-ity of life issues. In contrast, in states that have only recently been established or reconstructed via ethnic secessions, the (new) statehood may still seem in the need of legitimatization and maturing. For the secessionist states, the acquisition of ethnically-valued land speaks directly to these issues, given that the state was formed on the idea of ethnic self-determination and that complete ethnic unity of the nation has still not been achieved. The rump states, meanwhile, may be ex-periencing the flip side of the same coin. After the departure of ethnic minorities and related reduction in the rump state's ethnic heterogeneity, its statehood is now also driven more by the idea of being an ethnic state. Consequently, acquiring lands inhabited by the brethren will be important in order to justify their statehood in the confines of a now territorially smaller state. The findings in Chapter 5 on secessions are consistent not only with this refined argument but also with the literature's expectations about intangibility as a militarized-conflict intensifying condition. In the aftermath of secessions, I find that intangibly-valued lands are associated with subsequent militarized conflict onset significantly more than tangibly-valued lands. The overall findings for territorial changes thus show that the literature is not necessarily incorrect in stating the importance of intangibly-valued lands, but rather that this line of reasoning may not hold across as broad of a spectrum of cases as previously thought.

In addition to the implications for territorial conflict research, this study produces implications relevant to the portion of the ethnic conflict literature dealing with ethnic secessions.[6] A major improvement this study makes vis-à-vis this literature is a systematic evaluation of post-secession militarized conflict patterns. Rather than arguing the benefits and drawbacks of partition based on a handful of usually dubiously selected cases, I evaluate the territorial aftermath of all 20th century secessions. The descriptive analyses show that while most secession-created borders are not challenged militarily by either the rump or secessionist states, the dyads that do experience militarized conflict do so at explosive rates. Yet, many anti-partition authors, including Horowitz (1985), presume that almost all secessions will be plagued by such problems. The analyses show that nearly four-fifths of the borders created by secessions do not experience fatal militarized confrontations. In short, while the anti-secession authors are correct in pointing out that secessions can lead to undesirable consequences, they overstate the scope of the problem by a wide margin.

Furthermore, the causal results show that the debate over desirability of secession correctly focuses on an important culprit of post-secession militarized interstate conflict involving rump and secessionist states: ethnically-based territorial disputes. Hence, both secession opponents (e.g. Horowitz 1985; Brown 1993; Posen 1993, Hachey 1972; Fraser 1984; de Silva and May 1991; McGary and O'Leary 1993; Kumar 1997; Kaldor 1996) and proponents (Kaufmann 1996, 1998; Mearsheimer 1993, 1998; Mearsheimer and Van Evera 1995, 1996, 1999) accurately identify this issue as important. Yet, they largely fail to note that relatively few (i.e. 26 percent) ethnically-based territorial disputes ever escalate to fatal militarized conflict and that the peaceful secession process can negate the detrimental effects of ethnically-based territorial disputes.

Concerning the issue of process, very few of the secession scholars take it seriously. Secession's opponents generally dismiss the process factor as unimportant, by stating that all secessions are undesirable. The proponents argue that secessions emerging from violent conflict bring peace. I find important and robust evidence contradicting both of these expectations. The secession process matters, and peaceful secessions are significantly more beneficial than violent ones. The finding thus supports Tullberg and Tullberg (1997) and Gurr (1993, 1995), who argue that secessions should be conducted before violence breaks out and before ethnic battle lines are drawn. Besides showing that process matters, I am able to make another contribution to the secession debate by comparing the relative importance of the factors from the two parts of the model. Prior, case-study works are not able to do this, because comparing the relative effects of key variables is beyond the scope of qualitative methods. The results show that peaceful secessions are able to keep ethnically-based territorial grievances from turning violent. That is, such grievances are unlikely to provide the leaders with payoffs that can outweigh the costs of challenging the peacefully-created borders.

Finally, this project also relates to the temporal diffusion of conflict literature; the variables most relevant to this research involve the process of territorial change. The results generally confirm this literature's expectations, though there are some exceptions. In terms of transfers and secessions, the results for the process variable are consistent with both the reciprocity (e.g. Goldstein and Freeman 1990; Goldstein and Pevehouse 1997; Rajmaira and Ward 1990; Rajmaira 1997; Pevehouse and Goldstein 1999) and reinforcement (Most and Starr 1980; Starr and Most 1983; Kirby and Ward 1987) schools of thought. (Ordinary) violent transfers and secessions create incentives for the leaders of losing and rump states to pursue the lost lands by relying on militarized conflict; this pattern is consistent with the idea of reciprocity. Moreover, (ordinary) violent transfers and secessions also create incentives for the leaders of gaining and secessionist states to pursue further territorial revisions by engaging in militarized conflict; this finding is consistent with the idea of reinforcement. The inability to distinguish clearly between the consequences of overwhelming victory and violent transfers also provides some support to the reinforcement and reciprocity schools of thought. Overwhelming victories provide insufficient disincentives against future militarized conflict, which is, broadly speaking, consistent with the temporal diffusion of militarized conflict dynamics. In contrast, the results for the process of unification variable do not support the reinforcement school of thought (Most and Starr 1980; Starr and Most 1983; Kirby and Ward 1987), but this finding may well be driven by insufficient variance on the unification process variable. After relating my approach and findings to the extant works, I turn to policy implications.

Policy Implications

In this section, I offer several general policy guidelines that arise from the findings. Examples of specific applications to cases of current interest can be found in the empirical chapters. The findings from this project suggest that territorial changes can indeed be used as tools for dealing with the most contentious issue in international politics, that is territorial control. The results imply that altering international boundaries commonly leads to an absence of future militarized territorial conflict between the participants. This is true for at least three-quarters of the participant-country dyads in all three types of territorial change. Yet, it is also true that the remaining dyads experience post-change militarized conflict and that they do so at explosive rates. In fact, they experience so much militarized conflict that they push the average post-change frequency figure for both conflictual and peaceful dyads to well above the "normal" rates. The combination of the two results means that policymakers must pay strict attention to the conditions that determine toward which outcome the dyad involved in a territorial change is being driven.

The model and related results point out that post-change territorial disputes are important motivators of future militarized conflict. Hence, re-drawing the boundaries is an important task. Simply using old or previously internal boundaries without paying much attention to the potential territorial disputes such moves create will not optimize the chances for peace. This message is especially important in the light of recent, post-Cold War secessions that have divided countries such as Yugoslavia and the Soviet Union. In both instances, previously internal borders were simply externalized. The policy-makers wanted to avoid opening the Pandora's box of negotiating the boundaries, so they simply recognized the old administrative boundaries as new international borders. The findings suggest that such strategies may be short-sighted. The decision-makers may be so caught up in the fact that countries are gaining independence to overlook the longer-term consequences of the exact location of the boundary.

Four different strategies can be used to minimize the prospects of future confrontations. The first approach is the most obvious but also probably the most impractical. When territorial changes are conducted, the border should be (re)drawn in ways that eliminate the border disputes between the participants. To do this, one needs to know each party's potential land claims in the area. In some cases, such (re)drawing is possible as the claims may not be overlapping.[7] In most cases, however, claims toward the same land by both participants are likely to exist, so resolving the dispute may be problematic.

In these cases, the second strategy could be used. It involves recognizing that some territorial disputes are more salient than others. In the case of an (ethnic) secession, the policymakers should recognize that ethnically-based territorial disputes are the most likely cause of future problems. Accordingly, in these cases the ethnically-based territorial disputes could be resolved by creating "ethnically-correct" boundaries at the expense—if necessary—of creating strategically- or, to a lesser extent, economically-based territorial disputes. With varying success, this strategy has been used in the past, to determine the boundary between India and Pakistan and post-World War II boundary between Italy and Yugoslavia/Slovenia. The strategy asks that states give up some lands they are claiming, which is no small feat. To encourage such concessions, third-party carrot and stick methods could be used (e.g. aid, membership in coveted international institutions, security guarantees, etc.). The countries may also be motivated by the idea that settling the boundary at this time positions them for peaceful and potentially even prosperous future relations. By removing the most explosive issue—the ethnic territorial question—other disputes are not likely to produce as much impetus for fighting. According to Gurr (1993, 1995), the democratic institutions and fair treatment of "leftover" minorities in both countries will go a long way toward stabilizing the situation between the countries vis-à-vis the minority question; hence, such goals could be encouraged by interested international players. Although I certainly do not claim that creating ethnically-correct borders is actually possible in every case, the results do point out that this is where the focus of conflict management efforts should lie.

The opposite recommendation is given to the countries involved in transfers, where ethnically-based territorial disputes are less of a culprit in post-transfer militarized confrontations. By changing the location of the boundary, economically-based disputes should be resolved at the expense—if necessary—of resolving strategically- and, to a lesser extent, ethnically-based territorial disputes. According to the literature, economically-based territorial disputes should be easier to resolve, because the associated resources can be divided or shared. The failure to successfully resolve the trickier issue of dividing the ethnically-valued lands should not be as detrimental in this context.

Note that the advice about how to distribute the land between the partici-pants of the territorial change is not applicable to unifications because the merger has little to do with the unified country's neighbors. Since the unified-neighboring country boundary is not being altered through the change, the insight about how to re-draw the border simply does not apply. The advice given in this case pertains more to the early warning rather than conflict resolution approach. I found evidence suggesting that unified and neighboring countries are most likely to pursue disputed lands valued for economic reasons. Thus, letting potential post-unification economically-based territorial disputes simmer would likely represent missed conflict management opportunities.

The third conflict-management strategy involves recognizing that, whenever possible, transfers and secessions should be performed peacefully. This is important for two reasons. One, pursuing the above-identified territorial-dispute resolving strategies will be simpler and more productive if the disputants can negotiate their boundaries. Unilaterally-imposed, violent solutions are unlikely to take into consideration the losing side's perspective (Vasquez 1993). In some cases, they may not even give the winning side all it wants, because the boundary may be simply a cease-fire frontier. Two, peaceful, agreed-upon changes also create incentives against the future reliance on militarized conflict, through reputational and loss-of-side-benefits costs and make it harder for the participants to mobilize their military forces (see Chapter 2). For both reasons—and also for the reason of avoiding the loss of human life in combat—altering borders peacefully is more beneficial than doing so violently.[8]

In addition to the third-party pressure that can be applied toward the territorial disputants to encourage them to execute the change peacefully, both gainers and losers possess certain incentives to follow the peaceful course of action. The would-be losing side can try to avert losing lands that it deems the most important and give up only lands to which it is less attached. Furthermore, combat may create the boundary that gives the gainer additional—but unimportant—lands while the loser may have lost key lands and still be in possession of lands that it cares little about. A peaceful land change could avert such scenarios. By averting such scenarios, the incentives for future confrontations are in turn decreased, as the participants are less motivated to pursue further border adjustments. Finally, peaceful and stable inter-country relations are valuable and their value should be considered when weighing it against the costs of future instabilities and confrontations. Yet, although peaceful territorial changes are beneficial, policymakers should not be overly optimistic about their benefits. A peaceful change decreases the risk of post-change territorial disputes turning violent, but it does not eliminate it. In other words, post-change territorial disputes cannot be ignored—especially in the case of transfers—just because the change is performed peacefully.[9]

Fourth and finally, recall that except in the aftermath of unifications, the control variables did not perform as well as hoped for in the statistical analyses. More precisely, in the aftermath of transfers and secessions, the relative power distribution, joint democracy, and security ties did not exhibit the expected strong and consistent dampening effects on the chances of militarized territorial conflict. These weaker than expected findings have important policymaking implications. They indicate that the common conflict management techniques lose much of their effect in these contexts. This makes it all the more crucial to conduct transfers and secessions "correctly," that is peacefully and with an eye on the potential post-change territorial disputes. If these are not handled appropriately, there is little hope that the secondary factors will keep the participant countries from fighting over the altered or new boundary. In the aftermath of unifications, I have found that factors such as joint democracy and common security interests can serve as powerful disincentives against future militarized conflict over the unified country's boundary. This is especially fortuitous in this context, because this is precisely the scenario in which the outside policymakers have the least amount of say over whether the change is to take place or not. These secondary factors give the policymakers some potential leverage in assuring that post-unification borders remain peaceful.

Suggestions for Future Research

In this final section of the book I offer several suggestions for future research, that is ideas on how the research in this topic area could build on the current work. First, the question of how to achieve peaceful territorial changes should be pursued in future scholarly research. Some preliminary work on this basis has already been conducted by Kacowicz (1994) and Young (1997), who study the phenomena of peaceful transfers and secessions, respectively. An implicit assumption made by both works is that the phenomena of peaceful transfers and secessions are important because they are expected to create future peace. Yet, this is not something either author investigates and in fact it is this study—and not theirs—that demonstrate that this assumption is on the right track. Furthermore, their inductive method and problematic research design (i.e. investigating *only* the cases of peaceful transfer and secession) prevents the authors from being able to derive conclusions that are not potentially skewed by the dependent variable selection bias (see Most and Starr 1989; King, Keohane, and Verba 1993). That is, a theory of why some transfer and secession attempts succeed while other do not come to fruition needs to be developed. The following step would be to test systematically this newly-developed theory using the cases of both peaceful *and* violent transfers and secessions. These are the necessary steps researchers need to pursue if one is to develop an understanding of both the causes and consequences of territorial changes.

The second proposed extension is also related to the issue of process. The process of territorial change should be further divided into several categories beyond the basic peaceful-violent dichotomy. This has already been done to some extent in this work by dividing violent transfers according to whether they are a consequence of overwhelming victories. Peaceful changes could be divided into specific methods by which they were implemented: negotiation, mediation, arbitration, court ruling, threat of third party involvement, etc. Similarly, violent changes could be further divided according to whether they involved third-party military intervention, resulted from a bilateral or multi-lateral confrontations, etc. In each of these processes the degree to which the participants of the territorial change agree to the change and its details and the degree to which they are satisfied with the ensuing territorial distribution potentially varies. As the extent of satisfaction changes, arguably so do the chances that the leaders will try to alter the borders in the future. One could start by considering the cases of unification, because it is in this type of territorial change that we encountered only one example of violent unification. Perhaps dividing the concept of process into voluntary vs. forced would provide a stronger explanatory leverage. Pursuing this suggestion would involve identifying involuntary unifications, a potentially complicated task. Consider for instance the 1938 Germany-Austria case. The Austrian government agreed to the unification and welcomed the German troops even though the popular sentiment in Austria was against the unification. Accordingly, one would have to conceptually define what voluntary and involuntary means and then operationalize the concept. Unfortunately, the extent of consensus is not as observable as is the presence of organized violence.

The third refinement involves methodological, or more specifically data, improvements. I was able to support the hypothesis that intangibly-valued lands are more likely to be fought over than tangibly-valued lands only partially. Part of the reason for a less-than-expected degree of support may be that—due to data limitations—I had but one indicator of land's intangible value: the presence of ethnic kin. Assuming an extensive data-collecting effort, a future study could include indicators such as religious and ancestral value. The data collecting effort could start out by consulting historical works, maps, and national myths and legends identifying areas once (or still) inhabited by various groups. In these areas, one could look for traces of the group's identity—gravesites, structures of religious importance, names of places or geographical features, and the like. Once these characteristics are identified, they could be coded according to which indicator of intangible value they represent (i.e. ancestral homeland and/or religious site). Once the data is in place, testing the associated hypothesis from the model would be relatively straightforward.

A different type of a research extension would consider some of the overlooked consequences of territorial changes, such as the domestic repercussions. Although armed domestic conflict is generally not of primary concern in the territorial conflict literature, its occurrence is important particularly in the contexts of secessions and unifications. When a new country is formed through an ethnically-motivated secession, the goal of ethnic separation may not be achieved in its entirety—leaving the rump and secessionist states ethnically heterogeneous. Ethnic minorities that have been "left behind" may fight to protect their privileges or to join their brethren in the other country. For instance, the secession of Bosnia from Yugoslavia meant that the Serbs (the largest group in the former Yugoslavia) would be relegated to a minority status in Bosnia. The Serbs did not want to give up the privileges that came along with the status of the largest ethnic group and moreover they did not want to be separated from their brethren in Serbia. These goals were diametrically opposed to the goals of other ethnic groups in Bosnia; out of a disagreement over these issues, a bloody conflict ensued. See Tir (2002, 2005a) for more on the domestic consequences of secessions.

Furthermore, secessions may create a demonstration effect (Walter 2003) for other ethnic groups not involved in the original secession decision and living in the now rump and secessionist countries. As an ethnic group leaves the rump state by forming its own country, other ethnic groups may want to pursue the same goal. In effect, a new domestic-level territorial dispute over who has the right to sovereign control of the disputed land and its inhabitants is created. If an agreement for a further division of the rump or new division of the secessionist state cannot be struck, violence is possible. To illustrate, consider the disintegration of the Soviet Union. After Ukraine, Belarus, Turkmenistan, etc. left Soviet Union, the rump state (i.e. Russia) was pressed by various other ethnic groups to grant them independence as well. The case in point is the unsuccessful secession of Chechnya, which resulted in two recent wars. In addition, the secessionist states themselves may become targets of secessionist movements for similar reasons. An example of a recent, violent secessionist movement taking place in a secessionist state is the attempted secession of Abkhazia from Georgia.

Unifications may also be followed by armed internal conflicts. In one scenario, a unification could internalize previously external conflict. Two countries may be fighting over unification, where the unification initiator state is pushing for unification while the targeted state is trying to resist it. If the initiator is successful in getting its way, the people of the targeted state may continue their struggle against the now unified state, that is push for independence via secession. In a hypothetical example, a hostile conquest of Taiwan could result in something akin to a secessionist conflict where Taiwanese people, organized on an ideological or ethnic basis, would fight to re-establish their independence. In another scenario, even a peaceful unification may leave some independence-minded Taiwanese groups fighting for independence and against the Chinese government that is trying to neutralize them.

Even transfers may result in armed domestic conflicts. In one scenario, a hostile minority is brought against its will into the gaining country and it resists the central government. In Romania, for example, the relations between the country's government and its Hungarian minority—which Romania acquired along with substantial territory after the dissolution of the Austro-Hungarian empire—have often been tense. In another scenario, a minority group may be more than willing to depart the losing country by the means of a territorial transfer, but the transfer is only partial and consequently only a segment of the group joins the gaining country. The remaining people fight an irredentist conflict against the loser's central government, in an effort to join the gaining country. One could hypothesize that if Kosovo were to become a part of Albania, ethnic Albanians living in southern Serbia's Preševo Valley would intensify their current efforts to join their ethnic brethren. As the above discussion illustrates, post-change armed domestic conflict deserves attention in future research.

Keeping with the theme of additional consequences of territorial changes, another extension would study territorial change's impact on the participants' relations with third parties. In particular, territorial gainers may be encouraged by the success of acquiring the land to pursue territories held by other countries. The impetus could be (1) purely psychological where the initial success motivates the country to pursue other lands, but more "rational" motivations are conceivable as well. After acquiring the land, (2) the underlying territorial dispute with the loser has been settled in the gainer's eyes so it can now focus its attention and resources solely on potential territorial disputes with third countries. The land acquisition could also (3) bolster the country's power and with those extra resources at hand, the gainer may be more encouraged to fight another country for its land. Although historical example of this type of behavior are not that common, they are important in terms of global history: the ancient Roman expansion from a city-state to the rulers of the Apennine peninsula and then the entire Mediterranean basin and beyond; the late 1930s/early 1940s German expansion into Austria, Sudetenland, Czechoslovakia, Poland, France, the Benelux countries, Denmark, Soviet Union; American westward expansion that put it at odds with the United Kingdom, France, Spain, Mexico, and even Russia; the Ottoman conquest of the Byzantine Empire, Levant, North Africa, and the Balkans; and the historical expansion of Russia toward central Europe, into the Baltic region, Caucasus, and the Far East. The strategy used to deal with unifications—that is identifying neighbors as the most likely targets of further expansions—could be used here, with some modifications to the model presented. The three proposed motivations could be further developed theoretically and then tested to assess their relative levels of contribution to the explanation of post-territorial change expansions.

Another extension to the study of territorial change's repercussions advocates investigating the consequences of territorial changes more broadly. One way to do this is to consider that future territorial changes may follow. I noted at the outset of this project that territorial changes occur because dissatisfied states want to acquire disputed territories. I argued that fighting may ensue or continue after the change because the participants are not content with the resulting land distribution. That is, when engaging in militarized conflict, the participants are hoping to prompt another territorial change that would re-distribute the land in a way that more closely reflects their preferences. Therefore, territorial changes may not result only in militarized territorial conflicts but also in further territorial changes. For the sake of analytic convenience, I narrowed the scope of this project to the former possibility. Yet, the latter possibility—the territorial change-territorial change link—is also worthy of investigation. Example of this link can be found in cases such as the German and French confrontations over Alsace-Lorraine, Russian/Soviet dispute over the Sakhalin Island with Japan, and Indo-Pakistani dispute over Kashmir. A study of the connection could start out by identifying empirical patterns (e.g. how often are territorial changes followed by other territorial changes) and attempting to explain them. The current model could be used as the basis of the explanation.

The final extension proposes an analysis of the link between democracy and post-change territorial conflicts. The expected pacifying effect of joint democracy is exhibited in the interactions between unified and neighboring states. The effect is more or less muted, however, in the aftermaths of transfers or secessions. This is somewhat surprising given that the effect of democracy on militarized international conflict has been well documented. The basic research question that should be pursued asks how democracies deal with post-change territorial disputes. The question pits two opposing forces when it comes to militarized international conflict. On the one side, we have the best know pacifying force (i.e. democracy) and on the other side we have the most contentious issue in international politics (i.e. territorial control). Huth and Allee (2002) provide insights into how democracies deal with territorial disputes differently from autocracies and in doing so expose some limits of the democratic peace (see also Hensel 2001). Their insights could be applied to the aftermath of territorial change to incorporate the dynamics that are unique to territorial changes vis-à-vis territorial disputes (e.g. land gains or losses, process). For example, to what extent are the usual conflict-preventing mechanisms found in democracies not at work when it comes to the aftermath of territorial redistribution? Are democracies less willing to compromise with one another after territorial changes and why? Are political institutions and citizenry more easily mobilized against another democracy if territorial integrity of the country has been affected by suffering a land loss? Answers to these questions would not only shed more light onto the democracy-militarized conflict relationship in the post-territorial change context but would also provide greater prominence to the issue-based study of international politics.

Notes

1. Unifications are not examined from this perspective because the border affected by the unification ceases to exist.

2. Tir (2001) reports that territorial gainers place additional territorial demands on territorial losers in roughly 40 percent of the available annual observations.

3. See also Hensel (2001), who finds that previously successful attempts to settle territorial disputes peacefully actually increase the likelihood of future militarized conflict.

4. As their indicators of intangible value, Goertz and Diehl use the transferred land's non-colonial status and the distance between "homeland" and the land in question—which is zero in just about every case of non-colonial territory.

5. Unlike toward homeland territories, people seldom develop an emotional attachment toward colonial lands they control. Colonial lands are thus more likely to be treated as pieces of property, while homeland territories become a part of national identity because groups of people often associate themselves with certain pieces of land (Duchacek 1970; Gottman 1973; Sack 1986). In terms of state behavior this means that acquiring and losing colonial lands is a simple business transaction, while controlling homeland territories is of essential importance. Accordingly, states will be more likely to fight for latter lands. Consistently with this expectation, Goertz and Diehl (1992) find that many of the 19th century territorial changes are simple—and *peaceful*—sales and purchases of colonial lands between European powers.

6. One concern of ethnic secession opponents I do not deal with in this project centers around the idea that secessions produce a demonstration effect (see Walter 2003 and the below discussion of research extensions).

7. Yet, even in the cases where the current territorial dispute can be resolved by the territorial change, new territorial disputes may be generated in the future. To be mindful of this possibility, one would also need to rely on theories of why and how territorial disputes are created—a subject beyond the scope of the present work (see Huth 1996).

8. See work by Lund (1996) and Burton (1990) regarding strategies for conflict prevention.

9. For unifications, the situation is a bit different because there are too few cases of violent unifications to derive strong conclusions about the role of the process. As the results show, the hazard of post-unification territorial disputes turning violent is not decreased regardless of the process through which the unification was accomplished. Yet even though this is the case, combat and casualties could at least be avoided during the unification itself if it is a peaceful one.

Appendix A

List of State-to-State Territorial Transfers, 1900-2000

Transfer Year	Territorial Gainer	Territorial Loser
1900	Russia	China
1902	Chile	Argentina
1903	Brazil	Bolivia
1904	Brazil	Ecuador
1905	China	Russia
1905	Japan	Russia
1907	Brazil	Bolivia
1907	Brazil	Colombia
1909	Peru	Bolivia
1913	Bulgaria	Turkey
1913	Greece	Bulgaria
1913	Greece	Turkey
1913	Romania	Bulgaria
1913	Saudi Arabia	Turkey
1913	Yugoslavia	Bulgaria
1913	Yugoslavia	Turkey
1914	Albania	Greece
1914	Italy	Albania
1919	Belgium	Germany
1919	France	Germany
1919	Greece	Bulgaria
1919	Italy	Austria
1919	Luxembourg	Germany
1919	Poland	Austria
1919	Poland	Germany
1919	Yugoslavia	Austria
1919	Yugoslavia	Bulgaria
1920	Czechoslovakia	Hungary
1920	Denmark	Germany

1920	Italy	Yugoslavia
1920	Poland	Czechoslovakia
1920	Poland	Lithuania
1920	Romania	Hungary
1920	Romania	Soviet Union
1920	Yugoslavia	Hungary
1921	Costa Rica	Panama
1921	Finland	Sweden
1921	Hungary	Austria
1921	Poland	Soviet Union
1921	Soviet Union	Turkey
1922	China	Japan
1922	Colombia	Venezuela
1922	Germany	Poland
1924	Italy	Yugoslavia
1929	Peru	Chile
1932	Japan	China
1934	Colombia	Peru
1934	Saudi Arabia	Yemen, A.R.
1935	Paraguay	Bolivia
1937	Japan	China
1938	Germany	Czechoslovakia
1938	Hungary	Czechoslovakia
1938	Poland	Czechoslovakia
1939	Germany	Lithuania
1940	Bulgaria	Romania
1942	Peru	Ecuador
1945	China	Japan
1945	Czechoslovakia	Hungary
1945	Poland	Germany
1945	Soviet Union	Czechoslovakia
1945	Soviet Union	Germany
1945	Soviet Union	Japan
1945	Soviet Union	Poland
1947	Albania	Italy
1947	France	Italy
1947	Greece	Italy
1947	Soviet Union	Finland
1947	Soviet Union	Romania
1947	Yugoslavia	Italy
1949	Bhutan	India
1949	Egypt	Israel
1949	India	Pakistan
1949	Jordan	Israel
1951	Poland	Soviet Union
1955	China	Taiwan
1956	Japan	Soviet Union
1956	W. Germany	Belgium
1958	Pakistan	India
1960	Honduras	Nicaragua

1961	China	Burma
1961	Nepal	China
1963	Mexico	U.S.A.
1963	Pakistan	China
1963	W. Germany	Netherlands
1965	Jordan	Saudi Arabia
1967	Israel	Egypt
1967	Israel	Jordan
1967	Israel	Syria
1968	Pakistan	India
1969	Saudi Arabia	Kuwait
1971	India	Pakistan
1971	Iran	U.A.E.
1972	Yemen, A.R.	Yemen, P.R.
1973	Israel	Syria
1973	Libya	Chad
1974	Sri Lanka	India
1974	Turkey	Cyprus
1975	Egypt	Israel
1975	Saudi Arabia	Iraq
1976	Syria	Israel
1979	Egypt	Israel
1980	Morocco	Mauritania
1986	Mali	Burkina Faso
1989	Egypt	Israel
1992	Yemen	Oman
1992	Bangladesh	India
1993	Kuwait	Iraq
1994	Namibia	S. Africa
1995	Jordan	Israel
1996	China	Russia
1997	Slovakia	Czech Republic
1998	China	Kazakhstan
1998	Moldova	Ukraine
1999	Estonia	Russia

Appendix B

List of PRDs Produced by Partitions/Secessions, 1900-2000

Secession Year	Dyad Members	
1903	Colombia	Panama
1905	Sweden	Norway
1908	Turkey	Bulgaria
1913	Turkey	Albania
1919	Austria	Czechoslovakia
1919	Austria	Hungary
1919	Estonia	Latvia
1919	Germany	Poland
1919	Hungary	Czechoslovakia
1919	Latvia	Lithuania
1919	Poland	Latvia
1919	Poland	Lithuania
1919	Soviet Union	Estonia
1919	Soviet Union	Finland
1919	Soviet Union	Latvia
1919	Soviet Union	Lithuania
1919	Soviet Union	Poland
1921	China	Mongolia
1921	Turkey	Yemen
1922	Great Britain	Ireland
1947	India	Pakistan
1948	Jordan	Israel
1949	China	Taiwan
1960	Mali	Senegal
1961	Egypt	Syria
1965	Malaysia	Singapore
1971	Pakistan	Bangladesh
1990	South Africa	Namibia
1991	Armenia	Azerbaijan
1991	Armenia	Georgia

1991	Croatia	Slovenia
1991	Estonia	Latvia
1991	Georgia	Azerbaijan
1991	Kyrgyzstan	Kazakhstan
1991	Kyrgyzstan	Uzbekistan
1991	Latvia	Belarus
1991	Latvia	Lithuania
1991	Lithuania	Belarus
1991	Moldova	Ukraine
1991	Russia	Armenia
1991	Russia	Azerbaijan
1991	Russia	Belarus
1991	Russia	Estonia
1991	Russia	Georgia
1991	Russia	Kazakhstan
1991	Russia	Kyrgyzstan
1991	Russia	Latvia
1991	Russia	Lithuania
1991	Russia	Moldova
1991	Russia	Tajikistan
1991	Russia	Turkmenistan
1991	Russia	Ukraine
1991	Russia	Uzbekistan
1991	Tajikistan	Kyrgyzstan
1991	Tajikistan	Uzbekistan
1991	Turkmenistan	Kazakhstan
1991	Turkmenistan	Uzbekistan
1991	Ukraine	Belarus
1991	Uzbekistan	Kazakhstan
1991	Yugoslavia	Croatia
1991	Yugoslavia	Slovenia
1992	Croatia	Bosnia
1992	Yugoslavia	Bosnia
1993	Czech Republic	Slovakia
1993	Ethiopia	Eritrea
1993	Yugoslavia	Macedonia

Note: PRD = politically relevant dyad.

Appendix C

List of Unifications, 1900-2000

Unif. Year	Unified State (Initiator + Subsumed)	Neighboring States
1938	Germany (Germany + Austria)	Belgium, Czechoslovakia, Denmark, Estonia, Finland, France, Hungary, Italy, Latvia, Lithuania, Luxembourg, Netherlands, Norway, Poland, Soviet Union, Sweden, Switzerland, United Kingdom, Yugoslavia
1940	Soviet Union (Soviet Union + Estonia, Latvia, and Lithuania)	Afghanistan, Bulgaria, China, Czechoslovakia, Denmark, E. Germany, Finland, Germany, Hungary, Iran, Japan, Mongolia, N. Korea, Norway, Poland, Romania, S. Korea, Sweden, Turkey, United States, W. Germany
1958	United Arab Republic (Egypt + Syria)	Cyprus, Greece, Iraq, Israel, Jordan, Lebanon, Libya, Saudi Arabia, Sudan, Turkey
1964	Tanzania (Tanganyika + Zanzibar)	Burundi, Comoros, D.R. Congo, Kenya, Malawi, Mozambique, Rwanda, Seychelles, Somalia, Uganda, Zambia
1975	Vietnam (N. + S. Vietnam)	Cambodia, China, Indonesia, Laos, Malaysia, Thailand
1990	Yemen (A.R. + P. R. of Yemen)	Djibouti, Eritrea, Ethiopia, Saudi Arabia, Somalia, Sudan, Oman
1990	Germany (W. + E. Germany)	Austria, Belgium, Czech Republic, Czechoslovakia, Denmark, Estonia, France, Latvia, Lithuania, Luxembourg, Netherlands, Norway, Poland, Russia, Sweden, Switzerland, United Kingdom

Notes: The initiator state is the state that initiates the unification and whose institutions dominate in the new, unified state. The subsumed state is the state absorbed through the unification. The unified state may not be proximate to each of the states listed at the same time due to border changes.

Bibliography

Akenhurst, Michael. 1987. *A modern introduction to international law*. New York: Harper Collins.

Allcock, John B. 1992. *Border and territorial disputes*. Detroit: Longman Group.

Altfeld, Michael. 1984. Measuring issue-distance and polarity in the international system: A preliminary comparison of an alliance and an action flow indicator. *Political Methodology* 10:29-66.

Anderson, Ewan W. 1999. Geopolitics: International boundaries as fighting places. *The Journal of Strategic Studies* 22:125-36.

Aron, Raymond. 1966. *Peace and war: A theory of international relations*. Garden City: Doubleday.

Azar, Edward E. 1980. The code book of the Conflict and Peace Data Bank (COPDAB). Chapel Hill: University of North Carolina Press.

Banks, Arthur S. 1979. Cross-national time-series data archive: User's manual. Binghamton: State University of New York at Binghamton.

Beck, N., J. N. Katz, and R. Tucker. 1998. Beyond ordinary logit: Taking time seriously in binary-time-series-cross-section models. *American Journal of Political Science* 42:1260-88.

Beck, Nathaniel. 1998. Modelling space and time: The event history approach. In *Research strategies in the social sciences*, edited by E. Scarbrough and E. Tanenbaum. London: Oxford University Press.

Bennett, D. Scott, and Allan C. Stam. 2000. EUGene: A conceptual manual. *International Interactions*, 26:179-204.

Boulding, Kenneth. 1962. *Conflict and defense: A general theory*. New York: Harper.

Box-Steffensmeier, Janet M., and Bradford S. Jones. 1997. Time is of the essence: Event history models in political science. *American Journal of Political Science* 41:1414-61.

———. 2000. *Timing and political change: Event history modeling in political science*. Ann Arbor: University of Michigan Press.

Box-Steffensmeier, Janet M., and Christopher Zorn. 1999. Modeling heterogeneity in duration models. Paper presented at the Summer Meeting of the Political Methodology Society. Texas A&M University.

Brams, Steven, and Jeffrey Togman. 1996. Camp David: Was the agreement fair? *Conflict Management and Peace Science* 15:99-112.

Braumoeller, Bear F. 1997. Deadly doves: Liberal nationalism and the democratic peace in the Soviet successor states. *International Studies Quarterly* 41:375-402.

———. 1999. Small-n logic and large-n research: Statistical tests of multiple causal path theories. Paper presented at the Annual Meeting of the American Political Science Association. Atlanta, GA.

Bremer, Stuart. 1992. Dangerous dyads: Conditions affecting the likelihood of war. *Journal of Conflict Resolution* 36:309-38.

Brooks, Stephen G. 1999. The globalization of production and the changing benefits of conquest. *Journal of Conflict Resolution* 43:646-70.

Brown, Michael E., ed. 1993. *Ethnic conflict and international security.* Princeton: Princeton University Press.

———. 1993. Causes and implications of ethnic conflict. In *Ethnic conflict and international security,* edited by M. E. Brown. Princeton: Princeton University Press.

Bueno de Mesquita, Bruce. 1981. *The war trap.* New Haven: Yale University Press.

———. 1989. The contribution of the expected-utility theory to the study of international conflict. In *Handbook of war studies,* edited by M. Midlarsky. Boston: Unwin Hyman.

Bueno de Mesquita, Bruce, and Randolph M. Siverson. 1995. War and the survival of political leaders: A comparative study of regime types and political accountability. *American Political Science Review* 89:841-55.

Bueno de Mesquita, B., R. M. Siverson, and G. Woller. 1992. War and the fate of regimes: A comparative analysis. *American Political Science Review* 86:638-46.

Bueno de Mesquita, Bruce, and Randolph M. Siverson. 1995. War and the survival of political leaders: A comparative study of regime types and political accountability. *American Political Science Review* 89:841-55.

Burton, John. 1990. *Conflict: Resolution and provention.* London: Macmillan Press.

Carment, David, and Patrick James, eds. 1997. *Wars in the midst of peace: The international politics of ethnic conflict.* Pittsburgh: University of Pittsburgh Press.

Carment, David. 1993. The international dimensions of ethnic conflict: Concepts, indicators, and theory. *Journal of Peace Research* 30:137-50.

———. 1997. Modeling ethnic conflict: Problems and pitfalls. *Politics and the Life Sciences* 16:249-51.

Cashman, Greg. 1993. *What causes war? An introduction to theories of international conflict.* New York: Lexington Books.

Chan, Steve. 1984. Mirror, mirror on the wall . . . Are the freer countries more pacific? *Journal of Conflict Resolution* 28:617-48.

———. 1993. Democracy and war: Some thoughts on future research agenda. *International Interactions* 18:205-13.

Chiozza, Giacomo, and Henk E. Goemans. 2003. Peace through insecurity: Tenure and international conflict. *Journal of Conflict Resolution* 47:443-67.

Conybeare, John. 1992. A portfolio diversification model of alliances. *Journal of Conflict Resolution* 36:53-85.

Cooper, R. 1997. *International Herald Tribune,* 18 September.

Cox, David R. 1975. Partial likelihood. *Biometrika* 62:269-76.

Davis, David R., and Will H. Moore. 1997. Ethnicity matters: Transnational ethnic alliances and foreign policy behavior. *International Studies Quarterly* 41:171-84.

Day, Alan J. 1982. *Border and territorial disputes.* Detroit: Longman Group.

———. 1987. *Border and territorial disputes.* Detroit: Longman Group.

de Silva, K. M. and R. J. May, eds. 1991. *Internationalization of ethnic conflict.* New York: St. Martin's Press.

de Soysa, Indra, John R. Oneal, and Yong-Hee Park. 1997. Testing power-transition theory using alternative measures of national capabilities. *Journal of Conflict Resolution* 41:509-28.

Deutsch, Karl, and J. David Singer. 1964. Multipolar power systems and international stability. *World Politics* 16:390-406.

Diehl, Paul F. 1999a. Territorial disputes. In *Encyclopedia of violence, peace, and conflict volume 1*, edited by L. Kurz. San Diego: Academic Press.
———. 1999b. Territory and international conflict: An overview. In *Road map to war: Territorial dimensions of international conflict*, edited by P. F. Diehl. Nashville: Vanderbilt University Press.
Diehl, Paul F., and Gary Goertz. 2000. *War and peace in international rivalry*. Ann Arbor: University of Michigan Press.
Doran, Charles. 2000. Power cycle theory of system structure and stability: Commonalties and complementarities. In *Handbook of war studies*, edited by M. Midlarsky. Boston: Unwin Hyman.
Doyle, Michael. 1983a. Kant, liberal legacies and foreign affairs. Part I. *Philosophy and Public Affairs* 12:205-35.
———. 1983b. Kant, liberal legacies and foreign affairs. Part II. *Philosophy and Public Affairs* 12:323-53.
Duchacek, Ivo D. 1970. *Comparative federalism: The territorial dimension of politics*. New York: Reinhart and Winston.
Esman, Milton J. 1997. *One size cannot fit all*: The case for flexibility in managing ethnic conflicts. *Politics and the Life Sciences* 16:251-2.
Etzioni, A. 1992. The evils of self-determination. *Foreign Policy* 89:21-35.
Fearon, James D. 1995. Rationalist explanations for war. *International Organization* 49:379-414.
Feith, Herb, and Alan Smith. 1995. Self-determination in the 1990s: Equipping the UN to resolve ethno-nationalist conflicts. In *Conflict transformation*, edited by K. Rupesinghe. London: St Martin's Press.
Fraser, Thomas G. 1984. *Partition in Ireland, India, and Palestine: Theory and practice*. New York: St. Martin's Press.
Geller, Daniel. 1993. Power differentials and war in rival dyads. *International Studies Quarterly* 37:173-93.
Gibler, Douglas M., and Meredith R. Sarkees. 2004. Measuring alliances: The correlates of war formal interstate alliance dataset, 1816–2000. *Journal of Peace Research* 41:211-22.
Germany's imminent unification revives old myths, stirs new concerns and demands clarity on which is which. 1990. *Time Magazine*, 26 March.
Ghosn, F., G. Palmer, and S. Bremer. 2004. The MID3 data set, 1993–2001: Procedures, coding rules, and description. *Conflict Management and Peace Science* 21:133-54.
Gibler, Douglas. 1996. Alliances that never balance: The territorial settlement treaty. *Conflict Management and Peace Science* 15:75-98.
———. 1999. Alliances that never balance: The territorial settlement treaty. In *A road map to war: Territorial dimensions of international conflict*, edited by P. F. Diehl. Nashville: Vanderbilt University Press.
Gilbert, F., E. F. Rice, Jr., R. S. Dunn, L. Krieger, C. Breunig, and N. Rich. 1971. *The Norton history of Modern Europe*. New York: W.W. Norton & Co.
Gilpin, Robert. 1981. *War and change in world politics*. New York: Cambridge University Press.
Gleditsch, Kristian S., and Michael D. Ward. 2001. Measuring space: A minimum-distance database and applications to international studies. *Journal of Peace Research* 38:739-59.
Gochman, Charles S., and Russell J. Leng. 1983. Realpolitik and the road to war. *International Studies Quarterly* 27:97-120.
Gochman, Charles S., and Zeev Maoz. 1984. Militarized interstate disputes, 1816-1976:

Procedures, patterns, and insights. *Journal of Conflict Resolution* 28:585-616.

Goertz, Gary, and Paul F. Diehl. 1992. *Territorial changes and international conflict.* London: Routledge.

———. 1996. Taking enduring out of enduring rivalries. *International Interactions* 21:291-308.

———. 1998. (Enduring) Rivalries. In *Handbook of war studies*, edited by M. Midlarsky. Ann Arbor: University of Michigan Press.

Goldstein, Joshua S. and John R. Freeman. 1990. *Three-way street: Strategic reciprocity in world politics*. Chicago: University of Chicago Press.

Goldstein, Joshua S., and Jon C. Pevehouse. 1997. Reciprocity, bullying, and international cooperation: Time series analysis of the Bosnia conflict. *American Political Science Review* 91:515-29.

Gottman, Jean. 1973. *The significance of territory*. Charlottesville: University Press of Virginia.

Greene, William. 1993. *Econometric analysis*. New York: Macmillan Publishing Company.

Gulick, Edward V. 1955. *Europe's classical balance of power*. New York: W.W. Norton.

Gurr, Ted R. 1993. *Minorities at risk: A global view of ethnopolitical conflicts*. Washington, D.C.: United States Institute of Peace Press.

———. 1995. Transforming ethno-political conflicts: Exit, autonomy or access. In *Conflict transformation*, edited by K. Rupesinghe. London: St Martin's Press.

Hachey, Thomas E. 1972. *The problem of partition: Peril to world peace*. Chicago: Rand McNally.

Halliday, Fred. 1995. The third inter-Yemeni war and its consequences. *Asian Affairs* 26:131-40.

Hayes, Carlton J.H. 1968. *The historical evolution of modern nationalism*. New York: Russell & Russell.

Henderson, Errol A. 1997. Culture or contiguity: Ethnic conflict, the similarity of states, and the onset of war, 1820-1989. *Journal of Conflict Resolution* 41:649-68.

Henderson, Gregory, and Richard N. Lebow. 1974. Conclusions. In *Divided nations in a divided world*, edited by G. Henderson, R. N. Lebow, and J. G. Stoessinger. New York: D. McKay Co.

Henderson, G., R. N. Lebow, and J. G. Stoessinger, eds. 1974. *Divided nations in a divided world*. New York: D. McKay Co.

Hensel, Paul. 1994. One thing leads to another: Recurrent militarized disputes in Latin America, 1816-1986. *Journal of Peace Research* 31:281-97.

———. 1996. Charting a course to conflict: Territorial issues and interstate conflict, 1816-1992. *Conflict Management and Peace Science* 15:43-74.

———. 1999a. Charting a course to conflict: Territorial issues and interstate conflict, 1816-1992. In *A road map to war: Territorial dimensions of international conflict*, edited by P. F. Diehl. Nashville: Vanderbilt University Press.

———. 1999b. Issue Correlates of War (ICOW) Project, <www.icow.org>.

———. 2001. *Contentious issues and world politics*: The management of territorial claims in the Americas, 1816-1992, *International Studies Quarterly* 45:81-109.

Holsti, Kalevi J. 1991. *Peace and war: Armed conflicts and international order 1648-1989*. New York: Cambridge University Press.

Hoole, Francis W., and Dina A. Zinnes, eds. 1976. *Quantitative international politics: An appraisal*. New York: Praeger.

Horowitz, Donald L. 1985. *Ethnic groups in conflict*. Berkeley: University of California Press.

Houweling, Henk, and Jan Siccama. 1988. Power transitions as a cause of war. *Journal of Conflict Resolution* 32:87-102.

Huth, Paul. 1996. *Standing your ground: Territorial disputes and international conflict.* Ann Arbor: University of Michigan Press.

Huth, Paul, and Todd L. Allee. 2002. *The democratic peace and territorial conflict in the twentieth century.* Cambridge: Cambridge University Press.

Jaggers, Keith, and Ted R. Gurr. 1995. Tracking democracy's third wave with the Polity III data. *Journal of Peace Research* 32:469-81.

Jaggers, Keith, and Monty G. Marshall. 2005. Polity IV Project, <http://www.cidcm.umd.edu/inscr/polity/>.

James, Carolyn C., and Patrick James. 1997. Solomon, sovereignty, and ethnic conflict. *Politics and the Life Sciences* 16:252-4.

Johnson, Gary R. 1997. The architecture of ethnic identity. *Politics and the Life Sciences* 16:257-62.

Jones, D. M., S. A. Bremer, and J. D. Singer. 1996. Militarized interstate disputes, 1816-1992: Rationale, coding rules, and empirical patterns. *Conflict Management and Peace Science* 15:163-213.

Kacowicz, Arie. 1994. *Peaceful territorial change.* Columbia: University of South Carolina Press.

Kaldor, Mary. 1996. Balkan carve-up. *New Statesman & Society* 9:24-5.

Kant, Immanuel. 1957. *Perpetual peace.* Edited and translated by L.W. Beck. Indianapolis: Bobbs-Merrill.

Kaufmann, Chaim. 1996. Possible and impossible solutions to ethnic civil wars. *International Security* 20:136-75.

———. 1998. When all else fails: Ethnic population transfers and partitions in the twentieth century. *International Security* 23:120-56.

Kennedy, Paul. 1987. *The rise and fall of the Great Powers: Economic change and military conflict from 1500 to 2000.* New York: Random House.

Kennedy, Peter. 1998. *A guide to econometrics.* Cambridge: MIT Press.

Keohane, Robert O., and Joseph S. Nye. 1977. *Power and interdependence: World politics in transition.* Boston: Little, Brown.

King, G., R. Keohane, and S. Verba. 1994. *Designing social inquiry: Scientific inference in qualitative research.* Princeton: Princeton University Press.

Kirby, Andrew M., and Michael D. Ward. 1987. The spatial analysis of peace and war. *Comparative Political Studies* 20:293-313.

Kocs, Stephen. 1995. Territorial disputes and interstate war, 1945-1987. *Journal of Politics* 57:59-175.

Kohn, Hans. 1955. *Nationalism, its meaning and history.* Princeton: Van Nostrand.

Krain, Matthew. 1997. Democracy and civil war: A note on the democratic peace proposition. *International Interactions* 23:109-18.

Kugler, Jacek, and A. F. K. Organski. 1989. The power transition: A retrospective and prospective evaluation. In *Handbook of war studies*, edited by M. Midlarsky. Boston: Unwin Hyman.

Kugler, Jacek, and D. Lemke. 1996. *Parity and war: Evaluations and extensions of the war ledger.* Ann Arbor: University of Michigan Press.

Kumar, Radha. 1997. The troubled history of partition. *Foreign Affairs* 76:22-34.

Layne, Christopher. 1994. Kant or cant: The myth of the democratic peace. *International Security* 19:5-49.

Levy, Jack S. 1985. Theories of general war. *World Politics* 37:344-74.

———. 1992. An introduction to prospect theory. *Political Psychology* 13:171-86.

————. 1997. Prospect theory, rational choice, and international relations. *International Studies Quarterly* 41:87-112.

————. 2000. Loss aversion, framing effects, and international conflict: Perspectives from prospect theory. In *Handbook of war studies II*, edited by M. I. Midlarski. Ann Arbor: University of Michigan Press.

Lewis, Flora. 1995. Reassembling Yugoslavia. *Foreign Policy* 98:132-44.

Liberman, Peter. 1996. *Does conquest pay? The exploitation of occupied industrial societies*. Princeton: Princeton University Press.

Lind, Michael. 1994. In defense of liberal nationalism. *Foreign Affairs* 73:87-99.

Long, J. Scott. 1997. *Regression models for categorical and limited dependent variables*. Thousand Oaks: Sage.

Lund, Michael. 1996. *Preventing violent conflicts: A strategy for preventative diplomacy*. Washington: United States Institute of Peace Press.

Lustick, Ian S. 1993. *Unsettled states, disputed lands*. Ithaca: Cornell University Press.

MacKenzie, David. 1994. Serbia as Piedmont and the Yugoslav idea, 1804-1914. *East European Quarterly* 28:153-82.

Mackinder, Halford. 1919. *Democratic ideals and reality*. New York: H. Holt and Company.

Mandel, Robert. 1980. Roots of modern interstate border disputes. *Journal of Conflict Resolution* 24:427-54.

Mansbach, Richard W., and John A. Vasquez. 1981. *In search of theory: A new paradigm for global politics*. New York: Columbia University Press.

Mansfield, Edward and Jack Snyder. 1995. Democratization and the danger of war. *International Security* 20:5-38.

Maoz, Zeev, and Bruce Russett. 1993. Normative and structural causes of democratic peace. *American Political Science Review* 87:624-37.

Maoz, Zeev. 1984. Peace by empire? Conflict outcomes and international stability, 1816-1976. *Journal of Peace Research* 21:227-41.

————. 1989. Joining the club of nations: Political development and international conflict, 1816-1976. *International Studies Quarterly* 33: 199-231.

————. 1999. Dyadic Militarized Interstate Disputes (DYMID1.0) dataset – Version 1.0, <http://spirit.tau.ac.il/~zeevmaoz/>.

McGarry, J. and B. O'Leary, eds. 1993. *The politics of ethnic conflict regulation: Case studies of protracted ethnic conflicts*. New York: Routledge.

McGarry, John, and Brendan O'Learry. 1993. Introduction: The macro-political regulation of ethnic conflict. In *The politics of ethnic conflict regulation: case studies of protracted ethnic conflicts*, edited by J. McGarry and B. O'Leary. New York: Routledge.

Mearsheimer, John J. 1993. Shrink Bosnia to save it. *The New York Times*, 31 March, final edition.

Mearsheimer, John J. 1998. A peace agreement that's bound to fail." *The New York Times*, 19 October, final edition.

Mearsheimer, John J., and Stephen V. Evera. 1995. The partition that dare not speak its name: When peace means war. *The New Republic*, 5 December.

————. 1996. Partition is the inevitable solution for Bosnia. *International Herald Tribune*, 25 September, final edition.

————. 1999. Redraw the map, stop the killing. *The New York Times*, 19 April, final edition.

Modelski, George, and William R. Thompson. 1989. Long cycles and global war. In *Handbook of war studies*, edited by M. Midlarsky. Boston: Unwin Hyman.

Montville, Joseph V., ed. 1990. *Conflict and peacemaking in multiethnic societies.* Lexington: Lexington Books.

Moravcsik, Andrew. 1997. Taking preferences seriously: A liberal theory of international politics. *International Organization* 51:513-53.

Morgan, T. Clifton, and Sally H. Campbell. 1991. Domestic structure, decisional constraints, and war. *Journal of Conflict Resolution* 35:187-211.

Morgenthau, Hans J. 1948. *Politics among nations.* New York: Knopf.

Most, Benjamin, and Harvey Starr. 1980. Diffusion, reinforcement, geo-politics, and the spread of war. *American Journal of Political Science* 74:932-46.

———. 1989. *Inquiry, logic, and international politics.* Columbia: University of South Carolina Press.

Navaratna-Bandara, Abeysinghe M. 1995. *The management of ethnic secessionist conflict: The big neighbour syndrome.* Aldershot: Dartmouth.

Nelan, Bruce W. 1994. Confidence in old King Kohl. *Time Magazine,* 31 October, 42.

Newman, David. 1999. Real spaces, symbolic spaces: Interrelated notions of territory in the Arab-Israeli conflict." In *A road map to war: Territorial dimensions of international conflict,* edited by P. F. Diehl. Nashville: Vanderbilt University Press.

Nincic, Miroslav. 1992. *Democracy and foreign policy: The fallacy of political realism.* New York: Columbia University Press.

Niou, E., P. Ordeshook, and G. Rose. 1989. *The balance of power.* New York: Cambridge University Press.

Organski, A.F.K. 1968. *World politics.* New York: Knopf.

Organski, A.F.K., and J. Kugler. 1977. The costs of major wars: The Phoenix factor. *American Political Science Review* 71:1347-66.

Organski, A.F.K., and Jacek Kugler. 1980. *The war ledger.* Chicago: University of Chicago Press.

Pevehouse, Jon C., and Joshua S. Goldstein. 1999. Serbian compliance or defiance in Kosovo? Statistical analysis and real-time predictions. *Journal of Conflict Resolution* 43:538-46.

Posen, Barry R. 1993. The security dilemma and ethnic conflict. In *Ethnic conflict and international security,* edited by M. E. Brown. Princeton: Princeton University Press.

Ra'anan, Uri. 1990. The nation-state fallacy. In *Conflict and peacemaking in multiethnic societies,* edited by J. V. Montville. Lexington: Center for the Study of Foreign Affairs.

Rajmaira, Sheen, and Michael D. Ward. 1990. Evolving foreign policy norms: Reciprocity in the superpower triad. *International Studies Quarterly* 34:457-75.

Rajmaira, Sheen. 1997. *Indo-Pakistani relations*: Reciprocity in long-term perspective. *International Studies Quarterly* 41:547-60.

Ray, James L. 1990. Friend as foes: International conflict and wars between formal allies. In *Prisoners of war? Nation-states in the Modern Era,* edited by C. Gochman and A. Sabrosky. Lexington: Lexington Books.

Reiss, Hans, ed. 1991. *Kant: Political writings.* Cambridge: Cambridge University Press.

Rosecrance, Richard. 1986. *The rise of the trading state.* New York: Basic Books.

Rosenau, James. 1966. Pre-theories and theories of foreign policy. In *Scientific study of foreign policy,* edited by J. Rosenau. New York: Free Press.

———. 1967. Foreign policy as an issue area. In *Domestic sources of foreign policy,* edited by J. Rosenau. New York: Free Press.

Rothchild, Donald. 1997. Secession is a last resort. *Politics and the Life Sciences* 16:270-72.

Rousseau, D. L., C. Gelpi, D. Reiter, and P. K. Huth. 1996. Assessing the dyadic nature of the democratic peace, 1918-88. *American Political Science Review* 90:512-33.

Roy, A. Bikash. 1997. Intervention across bisecting borders. *Journal of Peace Research* 34:303-14.

Rummel, Rudolph J. 1985. Libertarian propositions on violence within and between nations. *Journal of Conflict Resolution* 27:419-55.

Rupesinghe, Kumar, ed. 1995. *Conflict transformation.* London: St Martin's Press.

Russett, Bruce, and John Oneal. 2001. *Triangulating peace: Democracy, interdependence, and international organizations.* New York: Norton.

Russett, Bruce. 1993. *Grasping the democratic peace.* Princeton: Princeton University Press.

Sack, Robert. 1986. *Territoriality: Its theory and history.* Cambridge: Cambridge University Press.

Sambanis, Nicholas. 2000. Partition as a solution to ethnic war: An empirical critique of the theoretical literature. *World Politics* 52:437-83.

Sandholtz, Wayne. 1993. Choosing union: Monetary politics and Maastricht. *International Organization* 47:1-39.

Senese, Paul D. 2005. Territory, contiguity, and international conflict: Assessing a new joint explanation, *American Journal of Political Science* 49:769-79.

Scarbrough, Elinor, and Eric Tanenbaum, eds. 1998. *Research strategies in the social sciences.* Oxford: Oxford University Press.

Schaeffer, Robert K. 1990. *Warpaths: The politics of partition.* New York: Hill and Wang.

Senese, Paul, and John A. Vasquez. 2003. A unified explanation of territorial conflict: Testing the impact of sampling bias 1919-1992. *International Studies Quarterly* 47:275-98.

Senese, Paul. 1999. Geographical proximity and issue salience: Their effects on the escalation of militarized interstate conflict. In *A road map to war: Territorial dimensions of international conflict,* edited by P. F. Diehl. Nashville: Vanderbilt University Press.

Signorino, Curtis, and Jeffrey Ritter. 1999. Tau-b or not tau-b: Measuring the similarity of foreign policy positions. *International Studies Quarterly* 43:115-44.

Simmons, Beth. 1999. See you in court: The appeal to quasi-judicial legal processes in the settlement of territorial disputes. In *A road map to war: Territorial dimensions of international conflict,* edited by P. F. Diehl. Nashville: Vanderbilt University Press.

Singer, J. David. 1994. Early warning indicators for cultural groups in danger. *Journal of Ethno-Development* 4:105-10.

———. 1995. *Alliances, 1816-1984.* Ann Arbor: University of Michigan, Correlates of War Project.

Small, Melvin and J. David Singer. 1982. *Resort to arms: International and civil wars, 1816-1980.* Beverly Hills: Sage Publications.

Snyder, Jack L. 1991. *Myths of empire: Domestic politics and international ambition.* Ithaca: Cornell University Press.

Spykman, Nicholas. 1944. *The geography of peace.* New York: Harcourt Brace.

Starr, Harvey, and Benjamin A. Most. 1983. Contagion and border effects on contemporary african conflict. *Comparative Political Studies* 16:92-117.

Stinnett, D., J. Tir, P. Shafer, P. F. Diehl, and C. Gochman. 2002. The Correlates of War Project Contiguity Data. *Conflict Management and Peace Science* 19:59-68.

Taylor, Peter, and John House, eds. 1984. *Political geography: Recent advances and future directions.* London: Croom Helm.

Thucydides. 1993. The Melian dialogue. In *Realism, pluralism, and globalism*, edited by P. Viotti and M. Kauppi. New York: Macmillan.

Tir, Jaroslav. 2001. Never-ending conflicts? Transfers, partitions, and unifications as potential solutions for territorial disputes. Ph.D. diss., University of Illinois, Urbana-Champaign.

———. 2002. Letting secessionists have their way: Can partitions help end and prevent ethnic conflicts? *International Interactions* 28:261-92.

———. 2003a. Averting armed international conflicts through state-to-state territorial transfers. *Journal of Politics* 65:1235-57.

———. 2003b. Never-ending conflicts? Territorial changes as potential solutions for territorial disputes. *Conflict Management and Peace Science* 20:59-84.

———. 2005a. Dividing countries to promote peace: Prospects for long-term success of partitions. *Journal of Peace Research* 42:545-62.

———. 2005b. Domestic-level territorial disputes: Conflict management via secessions. *Conflict Management and Peace Science* 49:713-41.

Tir, Jaroslav, Phil Schafer, Paul F. Diehl, and Gary Goertz. 1998. *Territorial changes, 1816-1996*: Procedures and data. *Conflict Management and Peace Science* 16:89-97.

Touval, Saadia. 1972. *The boundary politics of independent Africa*. Cambridge: Harvard University Press.

Tullberg, Jan, and Brigitta S. Tullberg. 1997. Separation or unity? A model for solving ethnic conflicts. *Politics and the Life Sciences* 16:237-48.

UNHCR (United Nations High Commission for Refugees). 1992. Working document for the humanitarian issues working group of the International Conference on the Former Yugoslavia. New York: United Nations.

Van Evera, Stephen. 1994. Hypotheses on nationalism and war. *International Security* 18:5-39.

Vanzo, John. 1999. Border configuration and conflict: Geographical compactness as a territorial ambition of states. In *A road map to war: Territorial dimensions of international conflict*, edited by P. F. Diehl. Nashville: Vanderbilt University Press.

Vasquez, John A. 1983. The tangibility of issues and global conflict: A test of Rosenau's issue area typology. *Journal of Peace Research* 20:179-92.

———. 1993. *The war puzzle*. Cambridge: Cambridge University Press.

———. 1995. Why do neighbors fight? Proximity, interaction, or territoriality. *Journal of Peace Research* 32:277-93.

Vasquez, John A., and Marie T. Henehan. 2001. Territorial disputes and the probability of war, 1816-1992. *Journal of Peace Research* 38:123-38.

Walt, Stephen M. 1987. *The origins of alliances*. Ithaca: Cornell University Press.

Walter, Barbara F. 2002. *Committing to peace*. Princeton: Princeton University Press.

———. 2003. Explaining the intractability of territorial conflict. *International Studies Review* 5:137-53.

Waltz, Kenneth. 1979. *Theory of international politics*. Reading: Addison-Wesley.

Waterman, Stanley. 1984. Partition – a problem in political geography. In *Political geography: Recent advances and future directions*, edited by P. Taylor and J. House. London: Croom Helm.

———. 1989. Partition and modern nationalism. In *Community conflict, partition, and nationalism*, edited by C. H. Williams and E. Kofman. New York: Routledge.

Weede, Erich. 1973. Nation-environment relations as determinants of hostilities among nations. *Peace Science Society (International) Papers* 20:67-90.

———. 1976. Overwhelming preponderance as a pacifying condition among contiguous Asian dyads, 1950-1969. *Journal of Conflict Resolution* 20:395-414.

Werner, Suzanne. 1999. The precarious nature of peace: Resolving the issues, enforcing the settlement, and renegotiating the terms. *American Journal of Political Science* 43:912-34.

Williams, Colin H., and E. Kofman, eds. 1989. *Community conflict, partition, and nationalism.* New York: Routledge.

Young, Robert A. 1997. How do peaceful secessions happen? In *Wars in the midst of peace: The international politics of ethnic conflict,* edited by D. Carment and P. James. Pittsburgh: University of Pittsburgh Press.

"Yugoslav Parliament Votes to Join Russia-Belarus Union," CNN, 12 April 1999, <http://www.cnn.com/WORLD/europe/9904/12/nato.attack.07/#1> (12 April 1999).

Index

About the Author

JAROSLAV TIR (b. 1972 in Makarska, Croatia) received his PhD in Political Science from the University of Illinois at Urbana-Champaign in 2001. He is currently an Associate Professor in the Department of International Affairs at the University of Georgia, Athens, GA, USA. His research interests include territorial and ethnic conflict management, diversionary theory of war, and politics of international resource scarcity. His work has been published by the *Journal of Politics, International Studies Quarterly, Journal of Conflict Resolution, Journal of Peace Research, Political Geography, International Interactions*, and *Conflict Management and Peace Science*.